AF644405

MODI
Energising a Green Future

MODI
ENERGISING A GREEN FUTURE

Editors:
R.K. Pachnanda
Bibek Debroy
Anirban Ganguly
Uttam Kumar Sinha

PENTAGON PRESS LLP

Copyright © Dr. Syama Prasad Mookerjee Research Foundation, New Delhi, 2023

All rights reserved. No part of this publication may be reproduced, stored in a retrieval system, or transmitted in any form or by any means, electronic, mechanical, photocopying, recording or otherwise, without the prior written permission of the Publisher.

First published in 2023 by

PENTAGON PRESS LLP
206, Peacock Lane, Shahpur Jat
New Delhi-110049, India
Contact: 011-64706243

Typeset in AGaramond, 11 Point
Printed by Aegean Offset Printers, Greater Noida, U.P.

ISBN 978-93-90095-87-2 (HB)

Disclaimer: The views and opinions expressed in the book are the individual assertion of the Authors and not necessarily of SPMRF. The Publisher does not take any responsibility for the same in any manner whatsoever. The same shall solely be the responsibility of the Authors.

www.pentagonpress.in

CONTENTS

List of Contributors

Abel Didier Tella, from Benin, is the Director General of the Association of Power Utilities of Africa. He holds a Master of Science in engineering, a Graduate Degree in "Renewable energies, a Certificate of Very High Voltage Line Techniques", and an MBA. Before his current position, he had worked for 25 years at the Benin national power utility. Abel has 40 years' experience in the power sector and was a member of the scientific committees of the Regional Solar Energy Center (CRES) in Bamako (Mali) from1986 to 1989. He led the initiative of the African Network of Centres of excellence in Electricity. He speaks, reads, and writes fluently French, English, Spanish, Russian and some Portuguese.

Aditya Sinha is a public policy professional and is an alumnus of the London School of Economics and Political Science and the Tata Institute of Social Sciences. Currently he is working with the Economic Advisory Council to the Prime Minister. He also consistently imparts insights on issues of national and international significance to prominent media outlets. Aditya's scholarly endeavours have resulted in a multitude of research papers and book chapters on a variety of domains. His academic research deals with challenges in formulating regulations for emerging technology in emerging markets.

Andres Carvallo is a Professor of Innovation in the College of Science and Engineering, a Materials Applications Research Center (MARC) Fellow and Co-Director of Connected Infrastructure for Education, Demonstration and Applied Research (CIEDAR) Consortium. Outside of Texas State, he is the founder and CEO of CMG Consulting, a strategic planning and advisory firm focusing on Smart Grids, Smart Utilities, Smart Cities, and Smart Buildings. Andres is known as the "Godfather of the smart grid" for designing and building the very first smart grid in the US at Austin Energy, the author of "The Advanced Smart Grid" and has published 40 titles in Power Engineering, Telecom/IoT, and Building Technologies. He received a B.S. in Mechanical Engineering degree from the University of Kansas, post-graduate certificates in Business Management from Stanford University, in Quality Management from the Wharton School of the University of Pennsylvania, and in Power Utility Management from the University of Idaho.

Anirban Ganguly is Hony Director of Dr Syama Prasad Mookerjee Research Foundation. He is Member of BJP's, National Executive Committee (NEC), and has extensively worked in the areas of public policy and political research. He was a Member of the Central Advisory Board of Education (CABE), Ministry of Education, Government of India, Member of the Indian National Commission for Cooperation with UNESCO (INCCU) Ministry of Education, GoI, Member of the Governing Board of Auroville Foundation (Ministry of Education), Member of the Visva-Bharati Samsad (Court), Santiniketan. Anirban has authored/edited/co-edited the following books, *K.R. Malkani & The Motherland* (2022), *Modi 2.0: A Resolve To Secure India* (2021), *Dattopant Thengadi: The Activist Parliamentarian* (2020), *Amit Shah and the March of BJP* (2019), *Making of New India: Transformation Under Modi Government* (2018), *Syama Prasad Mookerjee: His Vision of Education* (2017), *The Modi Doctrine: New Paradigms in India's Foreign Policy* (2016), *Redefining Governance: Essays on One year of Narendra Modi Government* (2015), *Swami Vivekananda, Buddha & Buddhism* (2014) *Debating Culture* (2013), and *Education: Philosophy & Practice* (2011).

Arvind Kumar is President and Founder of India Water Foundation a non-profit organisation and think tank, Former Governor, World Water Council. He is a strategist and key-influencer in development sector with more than 28 years of experience, author, columnist, Water pro-activist, specializes in ecosystem-based adaptation, water-energy-food nexus, with specific emphasis on Transversality approach of inter-linkages between water, environment and SDGs. He has published over 500 research articles and is a Ph.D. in Defense Studies. Arvind is Member Technical Advisory Committee for India's Third National Communication and Biennial Update Reports to UNFCCC.

Bhupender Yadav is a Bharatiya Janata Party (BJP) leader from Rajasthan. He is currently Union Minister Environment, Forest and Climate Change & Minister of Labour and Employment. In 2000, He was appointed the General

Secretary of the Akhil Bharatiya Adhivakta Parishad and held the position till 2009. In 2010, he was appointed as National Secretary of BJP and in 2014, he took charge as National General Secretary of the BJP. He was BJP's election co-in-charge for the Assembly polls of Rajasthan (2013) and Jharkhand (2014) and in-charge for Gujarat. He was in-charge for the 2019 Lok Sabha election & 2020 Bihar Legislative Assembly elections. Bhupender Yadav is a Member of Parliament in the Rajya Sabha, representing Rajasthan, since 2012. He was re-elected to the position in April 2018. He received his Bachelor of Laws degree from Government College, Ajmer. Over the years, Bhupender Yadav has come to be the chairman of the following parliamentary committees: Personnel, Public Grievances, Law and Justice (2018), Joint Committee on the Financial Resolution and Deposit Insurance Bill (2017), Select Committee of Rajya Sabha on the Constitution (One Hundred and Twenty Third Amendment) Bill (2017), Committee on Commerce Member, General Purposes Committee, Joint Committee on the Enforcement of Security Interest and Recovery of Debts Laws and Miscellaneous Provisions (Amendment) Bill (2016), Select Committee of Rajya Sabha on the Enemy Property (Amendment and Validation) Bill (2016), Joint Committee on the Insolvency and Bankruptcy Code (2015), Select Committee of Rajya Sabha on the Prevention of Corruption (Amendment) Bill (2013), Select Committee of Rajya Sabha on the Constitution (One Hundred and Twenty Second Amendment) Bill (2014), Select Committee of Rajya Sabha on the Mines and Minerals (Development and Regulation) Amendment Bill (2015), Select Committee of Rajya Sabha on the Repealing and Amending Bill (2014), Rajya Sabha Select Committee on GST Bill. Bhupender Yadav is the co-author of the book *Supreme Court on Forest Conservation* (2011) and regularly expresses his views on issues of critical importance in various newspapers and on news websites. His new book *The Rise of the BJP* was published in December 2021.

Bhupendra Kumar Singh is currently Director and Head, Energy Security at Confederation of Indian Industries (CII), New Delhi after serving for a short stint at the Ministry of External Affairs, Government of India. A PhD on India's Energy Security from JNU, New Delhi, he has also done EMBA. Bhupendra has written several books and articles in reputed peer reviewed journals. For his exemplary work on cross border power trade in South Asia, he was conferred with Nepal's prestigious IPPAN's Distinguished Person Award, 2021 by the Prime Minister of Nepal.

Bibek Debroy is presently the Chairman, Economic Advisory Council to the Prime Minister (EAC-PM) and President, Indian Statistical Institute (ISI). An economist, he was educated in Kolkata, Delhi and Trinity College, Cambridge. He has worked in Presidency College, Kolkata (1979-83), Gokhale Institute of Politics and Economics, Pune (1983-87); Indian Institute of Foreign Trade, Delhi (1987-93); as the Director of a Ministry of Finance/ UNDP project on legal reforms (1993-98); Department of Economic Affairs (1994-95); National Council of Applied Economic Research (1995-96); Rajiv Gandhi Institute for Contemporary Studies (1997-2005); PHD Chamber of Commerce and Industry (2005-06); Centre for Policy Research (2007-15); and Member, NITI Aayog (2015-19). Bibek has authored/edited several books, papers and popular articles.

Dinkar Srivastava joined the Indian Foreign Service in 1978 and was the Indian Ambassador to the Islamic Republic of Iran (2011-15). During his tenure, he led negotiations on Indian Participation in Chabahar Port. In the past, he has served as Indian Ambassador to the Czech Republic, Libya and India's High Commissioner to Malta. He has been a member of the Indian delegation to the UN, the World Conference on Human Rights, and the International Court of Justice. Post-retirement, he served on the Board of Directors of GAIL and India Ports Global Ltd. Dinkar has coordinated Vivekananda International Foundation Task Force on 'India's Energy Transition in a Carbon-Constrained World' and is the author of *Forgotten Kashmir: The Other Side of the Line of Control* (Harper Collins, 2021).

Hanif Qureshi is BTech (Electrical Engg), MTech (IT), MBA, and PhD from the University of Cincinnati, USA. He is a TEDx speaker and an active scholar. As Secretary, of Dept. of New and Renewable Energy, Haryana, he contributed towards many Green policies and programmes including PM Kusum scheme and Solar Rooftop programme. As Joint Secretary (Automobiles), Govt. of India, Hanif worked for the modernization of the Indian automobile industry including electric vehicles. He administers the FAME Scheme Phase II and the two PLI schemes in the Ministry of Heavy Industries.

Kumar Sanjay Krishna studied Physics in St Stephen's College and DelhiUniversity before joining in IAS in 1985. Allotted to Assam cadre, he heldvarious posts in Assam and Delhi, which included Deputy Commissioner in Sonitpur and Kamrup districts, Managing Director of Assam Tea

Corporation, Home Secretary in Assam, Director in PMO, Joint Secretary in Department ofEconomic Affairs, Additional Secretary in Agriculture Ministry. Hesuperannuated as Chief Secretary of state of Assam. Presently he is theChairman of Assam Electricity Regulatory Commission. Kumar Sanjay is known for his efforts in developmental works during his various filedpostings. He was also involved in negotiations for financing of various largeprojects such as Delhi Metro Phase II, Hogenakkal and Guwahati Water Supplyprojects, Hyderabad ring road project, and Chennai Metro.

Lydia Powell has been with the Observer Research Foundation for over 20 years working onpolicy issues in energy and the environment in the Indian context. Her current interests include energy access, carbon constraints on energy use, clean coal & natural gas for energy and environmental security. She has also worked for Norsk Hydro and for Orkla, two of Norway's largest conglomerates whose interests include energy. Lydia has three Post-Graduate Degrees—two on Energy Management from Norway and one in Solid State Physics from India.

Manohar Lal is the Chief Minister of Haryana from Karnal constituency in the Haryana Legislative Assembly since 2014. He is a former RSS Pracharak.

Panchamrita Sharma is a Post Graduate in Management from the Assam Institute of Management with specialization in Marketing and Finance. She joined Assam Electricity Regulatory Commission (AERC) in 2004 as Junior Consultant (Finance). During her almost two decades of service in the Commission, Ms. Sharma carried out different assignments related to—regulatory accounts, electricity tariff determination, framing of regulations, consumer advocacy and others. Panchamrita is presently working as Joint Director (Regulatory Affairs & Finance Planning), AERC.

Pathikrit Payne is a Public Policy & Strategic Affairs Analyst, Television panellist and Senior Research Fellow with Dr Syama Prasad Mookerjee Foundation. He is an alumnus of Nanyang Technological University (NTU), Singapore, and has over 18 years of professional experience in policy analysis, corporate consulting, along with several years of experience in frontline journalism from conflict zones. A popular face in Indian television news media, Pathikrit appears frequently as a Strategic Affairs Analyst on *CNN NEWS 18*, *Republic TV*, *NEWSX*, *Mirror Now*, *Sansad TV* and *India Ahead* to name a few. He occasionally writes guest columns for *News18*, *Pioneer*, *Millennium Post* and *Organiser*.

Pratim Ranjan Bose is an economic commentator and researcher with three decades of experience in financial media. He is a specialist in energy, infrastructure, regional trade and connectivity. He has written extensively on Northeast India and its neighbouring economies. Bose writes columns in leading media outlets and appears on national TV. He works with corporates in an advisory capacity. He participated in many research & advocacy projects, spearheaded by Indian and foreign think tanks. Pratim was a Deputy Editor in *The Hindu Business Line*. He is a post-graduate in economics from Jadavpur University, a Jefferson Fellow (2010) and a recipient of the US Grant (2016). He is a published author.

R.K. Pachnanda is currently the Chairman, Haryana Electricity Regulatory Commission. Prior to this he was Chairman, Haryana Public Service Commission, Security Adviser to the Chief Minister, Assam, Director General, Indo-Tibetan Border Police (ITBP), Director General, National Disaster Response Force (NDRF) and Commissioner of Police, Kolkata. He practiced law before the Punjab & Haryana High Court before joining the IPS. Ranjit has been awarded with the IPS Association Sword of Honour at the National Police Academy. During service he was awarded the President's Police Medal for Distinguished Service, the Indian Police Medal for Meritorious Service and six DG's Commendation Rolls. He was head of the Indian Delegation at the UN Chiefs of Police Summit at New York in June 2018. He has authored *Terrorism and Response to Terrorist Threat* (2001) and co-edited *Modi 2.0: A Resolve to Secure India.*

Reji Kumar Pillai is the President of India Smart Grid Forum established by Government of India and is also the Chairman of Global Smart Energy Federation, a global umbrella organisation of smart energy associations and utilities from 18 countries headquartered in USA. He is an advisor to Arab Renewable Energy Commission and work closely with the Association of Power Utilities in Africa and International Smart Grid Action Network, an intergovernmental organisation of 28 countries including India. Reji is an internationally renowned expert with over four decades of experience in the electricity sector in diverse functions covering the entire value chain and across continents. He has played pivotal role in several ground breaking initiatives related to renewable energy, electric grid modernization, electric mobility, energy storage and digitalization in India during the past two decades. He is spearheading a mission to leverage technology to transform the electric grids and provide clean and reliable electricity to every citizen 24x7 at affordable cost; and actively working for the "Right to Electricity Act" that will ensure lifeline supply of electricity to all; and advocating for the "Right to Sleep Act" to provide climate-controlled sleeping pods in low-income communities.

Richard Schomberg is International Electrotechnical Commission (IEC) Special Envoy for Smart Electrification. Recipient of the IEC 2011 Lord Kelvin award, he chairs the IEC Systems Committee on Smart Energy.He owns a consulting practice (Industrial Strategy, Complex Systems Engineering, Cybersecurity, Standardization) and is Board member of the G3-PLC Alliance. Richard was EDF VP Corporate Standardization, and had the responsibility of EDF R&D activities in North America. Richard is Emeritus member of the US DoE Gridwise Architecture Council, System Engineering Professor at Supelec (Paris) and Chair of Intelligrid Strategy Committee (Electric Power Research Institute—Chauncey Starr Award 2005).

Uttam Kumar Sinha is a leading commentator on trans-boundary water issues, climate change and the Arctic region. He works at the Manohar Parrikar-IDSA, and is the managing editor of the Routledge-published *Strategic Analysis*. Uttam is a recipient of many fellowships including senior fellow at the Nehru Memorial Museum and Library (2018-2020); academic visitor at the Harvard Kennedy School (2015); Chevening 'Gurukul' leadership at the LSE (2008); and a visiting fellow at the Peace Research Institute Oslo (PRIO). He is the author of several books including *Indus Basin Interrupted: A History of Territory and Politics from Alexander to Nehru* (Penguin Random House, 2021), and regularly writes for the *Hindustan Times*.

INTRODUCTION

Under the leadership of Prime Minister Modi, India has become one of the fastest-growing major economies as well as the fastest-growing energy consumer in the world. In the last two decades, India's energy use has doubled with rising incomes and improved standard of living. However, with a share of 17.7 per cent of the world population, India's energy use, on a per capita basis, is less than half the world's average (in 2014, it was one-third of the world's average). On the other hand, there are social development goals to achieve including electrification of all un-electrified households in rural areas and all poor households in urban areas of the country; and ensuring that all households have access to clean cooking fuel. An expanding economy, increasing population, high urbanisation, and industrialisation means that India will see a quantum increase in energy demand, like any other country, till 2040. The energy choices that India considers will not only have a direct bearing on its growing population but will also, in interconnected ways, effect the global energy market, carbon emissions, and flows of technology and capital.

Energy security remains a key priority of the Prime Minister Narendra Modi-led NDA government. But the prime minister also has a clear policy articulation that India's energy development is inextricably tied to its climate goals, a sentiment that continues since the UN Climate Change Conference (COP 21) in Paris in 2015. At the COP 26 in Glasgow in 2021, the prime minister presented India's '*Panchamrita*' (a mix of five nectar elements) of climate action and raised India's credibility as a climate-conscious country. The *Panchamrita* is bold and proves the determination and value of commitment to a climate action pathway:

- India will reach its non-fossil energy capacity of 500 GW by 2030.
- India will meet 50 per cent of its energy requirements from renewable energy by 2030.

- India will reduce the total projected carbon emissions by one billion tonnes from now onwards till 2030.
- By 2030, India will reduce the carbon intensity of its economy by less than 45 per cent.
- By the year 2070, India will achieve the target of Net Zero.

There is also an energy path that India has established with seven key drivers:

- Accelerating efforts to move towards a gas-based economy.
- Cleaner use of fossil fuels particularly petroleum and coal.
- Greater reliance on domestic sources to drive bio-fuels.
- Achieving the renewable target of 450 GW by 2030.
- Increasing the contribution of electricity to de-carbonize mobility.
- Moving into emerging fuels, including hydrogen.
- Digital innovation across all energy systems.

Climate Factor in Energy Choices

Climate change and energy security are interconnected and are two sides of the same coin. The increasing share of non-hydrocarbon or non-fossil energy, as evidence suggests, will help in significant reduction in carbon emissions. There is now broadly a global drive to expand energy sources and increase energy efficiency, both in distribution and consumption in order to mitigate climate change, reduce energy dependency, and minimize energy price volatility.

One is entitled to ask that since climate has always changed, so why such a fuss over it now. This change, however, is no ordinary event. Starting from the post-industrial period, human activity, directly or indirectly, has altered the composition of the global atmosphere. Human-induced actions are now being referred to as the Anthropocene. While this is now the evidenced truth, the dispute is of acceptance and responsibility. Developed countries having scarcely acknowledged that the roots to the Anthropocene climate change lie in their high per capita emissions trajectory. The economic system and the mode of production since industrial times that resulted in development, wealth, and comfort were equally exploitative. The colonial powers with their prized colonies, while establishing control and profit, plundered the landscape with wanton disregard to local considerations or the sustainability of the ecosystem. Resultantly, the world today is already encountering the climate future.

The concentration of CO_2 in the atmosphere has consistently been above 410 per parts million for several years. This means the world is adding 40 billion tons of CO_2 pollution into the atmosphere every year. How confident are states and societies in transiting towards a carbon diminishing world? To limit the global temperature rise to 1.5°C and no more than 2.0°C the entire systems of production, management and governance calls for a radical transformation including behaviour, consumption pattern, and lifestyle alteration. Energy use will be central to this.

Given the current policy approach, four noticeable trends to India's climate-energy security can be charted. First, the clean energy momentum is enabling India to fulfil its 2015 Paris climate pledges. The carbon emission intensity of India's economy is expected to improve by 40 per cent in 2030 which will exceed the target of 33-35 per cent. The share of non-fossil fuels in electricity generation is likely to reach 60 per cent, again above the defined target of 40 per cent. India will see a wide deployment of clean energy technologies in solar, wind and lithium-ion battery as also emerging technologies such as green hydrogen. It indicates that the industrial and commercial opportunities from clean energy are humongous. Second and consequent to the first, India's coal dependency in the power sector will reduce by almost 10 per cent in 2040. Third, energy demand in the road transport sector is projected to be more than double over the next two decades. Fourth, the intake of electricity from different energy sources, including battery storage, will transform existing power system operation and make distribution grids flexible and robust.

Energy transition will be the most important pillar for climate action. India is rapidly crafting a robust ecosystem to enable the transformation through technology readiness, capacity upgrade, climate finance, regulatory reforms and new and innovative business models, which will together help in achieving climate and sustainable development goals.

Leadership

India has shown the world what it takes to be a climate leader. The UN Environment Programme in 2018 recognized Prime Minister Modi for his bold environmental leadership on the global stage. "Under Modi's leadership", the UNEP noted, "India pledged to eliminate all single-use plastic in the country by 2022. Prime Minister Modi also supports and champions the International Solar Alliance, a global partnership to scale up solar energy."

The prime minister's initiative of the 'One sun, One Earth, One grid' along with UK's Green Grid Initiative caught the attention of the world at the COP26 in Glasgow. Bilateral cooperation focuses on the transition of renewable energy at a global level.

Not one to shy away from value-creating solutions, Modi, on India's Independence Day in 2021, launched the National Hydrogen Mission with an aim to meet climate targets by producing 5 million tonnes of green hydrogen by 2030 and bolster the development of renewable energy capacity, and, as he optimistically expressed, "...a quantum leap to energy independence by 2047." The momentum that the renewable energy pathway has set for this decade suggests that with careful planning India can achieve its net-zero goals in the long-term. In the mid-term a significantly higher mix of renewables can help a large part of India's coal stock reach its natural end of life between 2030 and 2040 and be replaced by more cleaner and renewable energy sources.

On 15 August 2022, while addressing India's completion of 75 years of independence, Modi stated an era of a new India on its path to becoming a leader in thought and action: "We have to become self-reliant in the energy sector. How long will we be dependent on others in the field of energy? We should be self-reliant in the fields of solar energy, wind energy, and various other renewable energy sources like Mission Hydrogen, bio fuel and electric vehicles."

Soon after, India updated its Nationally Determined Contribution (NDC) goals after approval from the Cabinet. It reaffirmed India's low-emission growth pathways and "To put forward and further propagate a healthy and sustainable way of living based on traditions and values of conservation and moderation, including through a mass movement for 'LiFE'—'Lifestyle for Environment'—as a key to combating climate change." The updated NDC "...takes forward the Hon'ble Prime Minister's vision of sustainable lifestyles and climate justice to protect the poor and vulnerable from adverse impacts of climate change." Overall, the decision demonstrates India's commitment at the highest level for decoupling of economic growth from greenhouse gas emissions. It projects "...increase in green jobs such as in renewable energy, clean energy industries, in automotives, manufacturing of low emissions products like electric vehicles and super-efficient appliances, and innovative technologies such as green hydrogen, etc."

Progress

The UN Emissions Gap Report 2020 concluded that India is well on the way of achieving its NDC targets with policies focused on minimizing the presence of oxides of sulphur, nitrogen, and traces of mercury in the air besides carbon emission. Actions to reduce carbon emission and build resilience and adaptive capacity to cushion the adverse impact are well thought. With its plan to reduce the carbon emission intensity of GDP, India is well positioned to create an additional carbon sink of 2.5 to 3 billion tonnes. The carbon emission intensity has reduced by 24 per cent between 2005 and 2016 and 27 per cent by 2020. A significant contribution to this is the increase in forest and tree cover between 2015 and 2019.

The Climate Action Tracker also acknowledges the fact that India is the only G20 country whose NDCs are 2°C compliant and is poised to achieve the 1.5°C goal of global warming. A major contributor to global warming is emissions from coal-fired thermal power plants. The target is to achieve minimum 40 per cent cumulative power generation installed capacity from non-fossil fuel energy resources by 2030. The share of non-fossil sources, in installed capacity of electricity generation, was 39.2 per cent by August 2021, including hydro and nuclear. Solar energy increased from 2.63 GW in March 2014 to 50.78 GW in August 2021 and wind energy amounted to 40.13 GW in August 2021. The total renewable energy in August 2021 was 152.90 GW.

The prime minister's initiatives for climate action include setting up of 450 GW renewable power generation capacity, land degradation neutrality, the National Hydrogen Mission, self-reliance in energy production by 2047, 100 per cent electrification of Indian Railways by 2024, net zero by 2070, 20 per cent ethanol blending target advanced to 2025, 5,000 compressed biogas plants, faster adoption and manufacturing of hybrid and electric vehicle (FAME II) scheme and promoting key sectors with a strong backward and forward linkage.

Several measures have been taken to increase the proportion of renewable energy in the energy mix including co-firing terrified biomass pellets in thermal power generating plants, to encourage innovation, to provide concessional financing for solar projects, higher norms for Renewable Purchase Obligations, permitting foreign direct investment up to 100 per cent, waiver of inter-state transmission system charges on solar and wind projects, framework for renewable energy certificates, special dispensation for wind and solar generators in the deviation settlement mechanism, introduction of green contracts in power exchanges, promotion of electrical vehicle charging stations, as also planning for electricity storage systems at an affordable cost, including pump storage power plants.

The use of hydrogen as an energy source is potentially a game changer. The National Green Hydrogen Mission (NGHM) has been established to develop a roadmap. In a recently released Harnessing Green Hydrogen Report by the Niti Aayog, it is estimated that green hydrogen can subside approximately 3.6 gigatons of cumulative CO_2 emissions by 2050.

To promote green hydrogen (and green ammonia), all inter-state transmission charges have been waived for 25 years for such projects commissioned before 30 June 2025. Banking of such power with the distribution companies has been permitted without any restrictions and banked renewable power (say wind, solar, biomass, etc.) can be used for green hydrogen. The Modi government approved the NGHM with an initial outlay of Rs. 19,744 crore. This programme aims to make India a global hub for production and export of green hydrogen and its derivatives. The target is to bring in an investment of Rs. 8 lakh crore and create over 6 lakh jobs. This will lead to a production capacity of green hydrogen to at least 5 MMT per annum by 2030 with concomitant reduction in fossil fuel import of over 1 lakh crore and an abatement of 50 MMT of annual greenhouse gas emissions. The government has announced that it would be using solar energy to split water by electrolysis process to produce green hydrogen to make India energy self sufficient. Green hydrogen will be an important solution to decarbonise sectors such iron and steel, chemicals, transportation, aluminium and cement. Green hydrogen is the clean energy molecule that is 'Made in India' and a bulwark against the climate crisis.

Given the commitment to sustainability, FinTech (finance and technology), both from within the country and by way of foreign direct investment (FDI), is of crucial importance, including large-scale deployment of renewable asset management software tools and artificial intelligence. Modi has encouraged an investor-friendly policy in infrastructure, including the power sector. The energy transition from pre-dominantly coal-fired electricity generation to hydro power as well as non-fossil fuel power would itself create the requirements for scaling up investments in generation, transmission, and distribution of power and added employment opportunities.

Prime Minister Modi has encouraged an investor-friendly policy in infrastructure, including the power sector. The energy transition from predominantly coal-fired electricity generation to hydro power as well as non-fossil fuel power would itself create the requirements for scaling up investments in generation, transmission, and distribution of power and added employment opportunities. India's contribution to global carbon emissions is low. India has actually utilised just 1.3 per cent of total carbon space and India's utilisation in terms of per capita global carbon space would be about 17.5 per cent, logically 700 giga tonnes at 2°C of global warming.

The world community has shown faith in Prime Minister Modi's unflinching resolve. India has a well-established and independent regulatory framework with vibrant and dependable capital markets, a robust banking system, skilled work force and a large consumer base. Hence, the Indian economy, given its inherent resilience and strength, will continue to soar. India has been recognized by global institutions like the IMF and World Bank, to be one of the fastest-growing economies of the world—"a bright spot on this otherwise dark horizon". Addressing a joint sitting of both Houses of Parliament, the President of India stated that India, with a stable, fearless and decisive government at the helm, was emerging as a global provider and every citizen's confidence was peaking. Top leaders of the world have been praising India's growth and observed that India is "undeniably a global powerhouse."

Energy transition will be the most important pillar for climate action for the country and for this India is rapidly crafting a sturdy ecosystem to enable the transformation through technology readiness, capacity upgrade, climate finance, regulatory reforms and new and innovative business models, which will together help in achieving India's climate and sustainable development goals. The prime minister's initiative of the International Solar Alliance in line with the concept of "One sun, One Earth, One grid" shall usher a new dawn for all nations.

In continuation with the exercise of assessing a number of critical themes that have presented opportunities and challenges to India since 2015, the Dr. Syama Prasad Mookerjee Research Foundation decided to take stock of India's environment-energy policy outcomes and the leadership of Prime Minister Modi. This volume presents a well-integrated collection of chapters from distinguished decision-makers, influential opinion makers, and eminent experts creating in the process a synergy of views supporting India's transition to affordable and sustainable energy that not only reduces emissions, but spurs economic growth and promotes sustainable climate investments.

The editors would like to thank the authors for their coherent and in-depth analyses. We hope the context and content will make it a worthwhile read.

Editors

POLICY PERSPECTIVES

1

A Green Future for the World: India Showing the Way

Bhupender Yadav

The year 2022 was marked by record droughts, heatwaves, forest fires and floods. On 21 February this year, 1.79 million square kilometres of sea ice around Antarctica reached its lowest extent. The previous record low of 130,000 sq km in the region was reached on 25 February 2022. Estimates suggest the difference was equal to an area about the size of New York. Human-induced climate change is causing widespread disruption in nature and putting the lives of billions of people at risk around the world. Those taking the hardest hit of this unfolding disaster are ecosystems and people least able to cope and who made the least contribution to the crisis.

Prime Minister Narendra Modi was quick to realise that not only is it imperative for India to make sustainable development the hallmark of the country's policy framework, but also get the world to work for a sustainable future together. Prime Minister Modi was, in fact, one of the first leaders in the world to realise the importance of climate action and act on it. Modi could foresee the significance of environmental protection right when he was the chief minister of Gujarat. The state created a department dedicated to climate change as early as in 2009.

In his book, *Convenient Action: Continuity for Change*, Prime Minister Modi wrote, "Sustainability is ultimately a moral issue since it involves the protection of the interests of our future generations."

India today has aligned all its policies to address this moral issue. India believes that equity, international cooperation and the commitment to leave no one behind, hold the key to success, where those most fortunate must lead the way. No nation can undertake this journey alone. India's G20 presidency is centred on the theme of 'One Earth, One Family, One Future' and the country has that promised the presidency will be "inclusive, ambitious, decisive, and action-oriented". Our climate action is also imbued in the principles of equity, international cooperation, and the commitment to leave no one behind.

India has in fact taken several global initiatives to ensure a shared sustainable future. In 2015, India initiated the International Solar Alliance with 123 signatory nations, most being sunshine countries, which lie either completely or partially between the Tropic of Cancer and the Tropic of Capricorn. ISA, headquartered in Haryana, is working to harness solar power and reduce the dependence on fossil fuels. At the first assembly of the ISA in October 2018, Prime Minister Modi put forth the idea of a 'One Sun, One World, One Grid' (OSOWOG) with an aim to connect energy supply across borders. The OSOWOG initiative, envisages connecting different regional grids through a common grid that will be used to transfer renewable energy power and, thus, realise the potential of renewable energy sources, especially solar energy. At COP26 held in 2021 in Glasgow, Prime Minister Modi formally launched OSOWOG along with the then UK premier, Boris Johnson.

In September 2019, India took the lead in forming another global collective aimed at climate action. Prime Minister Modi launched the Climate and Disaster Resilience Initiative (CDRI) with the objective of promoting disaster-resilient infrastructure at the 2019 UN Climate Action Summit. As the voice of the Global South, India is mindful of the fact that the developing and underdeveloped world is most vulnerable to climate disasters and through CDRI, India has taken the lead in ensuring the effects of the vagaries of climate change are lessened, if not totally eliminated.

In September 2019 itself, India took another major initiative in collaborative climate action by instituting the leadership group for industry transition (LeadIT), which brings together countries, companies, and industry experts to achieve net-zero emissions from heavy industries by 2050. LeadIT, as a global body, fosters collaboration between public and private policymakers to enable the needed policy environment, finance flows, and exchange of best practices for an accelerated industry transition.

While India has been instrumental in forging these global alliances, it has acted responsibly on the domestic front, emerging as a bright spot in climate action, which is inspiring the world.

At COP26, Prime Minister Modi announced Panchamrit, a five-point climate agenda:

- India's non-fossil energy capacity to reach 500 GW by 2030
- India will meet 50 per cent of its energy requirements with renewable energy by 2030
- India will reduce its total projected carbon emissions by one billion tonnes from now to 2030
- By 2030, India will reduce the carbon intensity of its economy to less than 45 per cent
- By 2070, India will achieve the target of net zero emissions.

In August 2022, India became one of the few countries to communicate its updated Nationally Determined Contribution to the United Nations Framework Convention on Climate Change. India now stands committed to reduce emissions intensity of its GDP by 45 per cent by 2030.

From a power-deficit nation at Independence, the efforts to make India energy-independent gained momentum in 2014. Today, we are a power surplus nation with a total installed electricity capacity of over 4 lakh MW. Keeping in mind the sustainable development goals, India's power generation mix is rapidly shifting towards a more significant share of renewable energy. Today, India is the world's third-largest producer of renewable energy, with 40 per cent of its installed electricity capacity coming from non-fossil fuel sources. The country witnessed the highest year on year growth in renewable energy additions of 9.83 per cent in 2022. The installed solar energy capacity increased by 24.4 times in the last nine years and stood at 63.3 GW as in February 2023.

Budget 2023-24, identifies green growth as one of the Saptarishi priority areas that will guide India's march to Amrit Kaal. The prime minister outlined three pillars for green growth and energy transmission. First, increasing the production of renewable energy; second, reducing the use of fossil fuel in the economy; and third, rapidly moving towards a gas-based economy.

This strategy has underlined the announcement of measures like ethanol blending, PM KUSUM Yojana, incentives for solar manufacturing, rooftop solar scheme, coal gasification, and battery storage in the budgets of the past few years.

The union budget allocated Rs. 35,000 crore for priority capital investment towards energy transition and achieving India's goal of net zero emissions by 2070. The National Hydrogen Mission received an allocation of Rs. 19,700 crore. The Mission will achieve a green hydrogen production capacity of at least 5 MMT (million metric tonnes) per annum with an associated renewable energy capacity addition of about 125 GW in the country, creation of over six lakh jobs, cumulative reduction in fossil fuel imports of over Rs. 1 lakh crore, and abatement of nearly 50 MMT of annual greenhouse gas emissions.

The Modi government is working on all aspects of environmental protection and so budget 2023-24 saw multiple schemes towards preserving India's ecological health. The government has rolled out MISHTI, a programme to facilitate mangrove plantation along India's coastline and on salt pan lands. It initiated the Prime Minister Programme for Restoration, Awareness, Nourishment and Amelioration of Mother Earth (PM PRANAM) to incentivise states and Union Territories promoting alternative fertilisers and the balanced use of chemical fertilisers. The budget also unravelled Amrit Dharohar, a scheme to encourage optimal use of wetlands, and enhance bio-diversity, carbon stock, eco-tourism opportunities, and income generation for local communities. Over the coming years, these schemes will help enrich biodiversity, increase carbon sink, ensure sustainability for wildlife, improve water conservation, prevent soil erosion and contribute to the journey towards a sustainable future.

India's population size and developmental needs of the people present their own challenges when the course for sustainable development is being discussed. Prime Minister Modi has ensured that in India, development and environmental protection are not opposed to each other but exist as part of the sustainable development paradigm.

India, home to 17 per cent of the global population, accounts for only four per cent of global carbon emissions. Developed nations with the same percentage of population account for nearly 60 per cent of carbon emissions. This is because reverence for Nature is part of our ethos.

Modi as prime minister has remained committed to ensuring this delicate balance is not disturbed, but strengthened, despite our population size and food security concerns. At every global forum, India has fought hard to protect the interests of her farmers by not buckling to international pressure when it comes to diktats on subsidies and food crop choices. Back home, India is making all efforts to make agriculture sustainable and a viable livelihood option.

The National Agroforestry Policy (updated 2019) promotes the adoption of agroforestry practices in the country by providing financial incentives to farmers. The policy promotes research and development in the field of agroforestry.

The Pradhan Mantri Fasal Bima Yojana extends financial assistance to farmers in case of crop failure due to natural calamities, pests, or diseases. This scheme has been extended to cover crops grown under agroforestry.

The Modi government also distributes soil health cards for farmers to access information about the nutrient status of soil to farmers and recommends appropriate measures to maintain soil fertility. The scheme promotes the use of organic fertilizers and bio-fertilizers, which are compatible with agroforestry.

In 2015, the Indian government launched the 'Har Medh Par Ped' (one tree on every farm) as part of its agroforestry initiatives. The program helps to increase the country's forest cover and support farmers' livelihoods. As part of the initiative, the Modi government provides farmers with saplings of fruit trees, timber trees, and other useful plants for planting on their land.

The government also launched the 'Van Dhan Yojana' scheme in 2018 to ensure forest-based livelihood opportunities for India's Adivasi communities. The program helps to improve the income and living standards of tribal communities by helping them market non-timber forest products, such as medicinal plants, honey, and bamboo.

The Modi government also launched the 'Mera Van Mera Dhan' (My Forest, My Wealth) scheme, which seeks to promote agroforestry and increase forest cover in the country. The scheme extends financial incentives to farmers who plant trees on their land and also helps them market the produce from them. Due to its holistic efforts, India is well set to be able to improve at least 30 per cent of biodiversity rich land and water areas by 2030 (30x30), a target set under the Global Biodiversity Framework agreed upon at the UN biodiversity summit in December 2022.

India's ambition is matched only by its action in the field of climate action, biodiversity conservation and wildlife protection. In August 2022, India took a major step in correcting a historical wrong when it reintroduced cheetahs that had become extinct in India in the 1940s-50s. In 2018, India achieved the target of doubling the tiger population four years before the targeted year of 2022. The country is expanding its tiger reserves and Project Tiger, which has completed 50 years, has been successful in bringing tigers back in the country from the brink of extinction. There is no parallel of a species-focused project of such a grand scale in the world.

On an average, tiger reserves generate employment of more than 50 lakh man-days annually for the local people. They also provide alternative livelihood options through eco-development committees and self-help groups.

Interestingly, tiger reserves do not just protect tigers but serve as the epitome of biodiversity conservation. More than 350 sweet water streams/rivers either originate from them or have a majority of their catchment areas in tiger habitats.

If Project Tiger has completed 50 years, Project Elephant has completed 30 years. The Indian elephant (elephas maximus) is a keystone species and an integral component of ecosystems playing a crucial role in maintaining forest ecosystems and biodiversity. India recognizes the elephant as the National Heritage Animal of India and accords it the highest degree of protection under the Indian Wildlife Protection Act (1972). It is because of this importance that India has the largest population of Asian elephants with 30,000 wild and about 3,600 captive elephants.

All these efforts and policies put together are seeing India take firm and responsible steps towards a sustainable future with uniquely Indian solutions.

For long, climate action, however, has been seen as a policy matter that governments work on. India has extended the ambit of climate action to individuals through the mantra of LiFE, Lifestyle for Environment. The mantra given to the world by Prime Minister Modi is a clarion call for people to live lives that contribute to restoring the ecological balance *janbhagidari* (people's participation).

Prime Minister Modi's leadership, steering this journey, has ensured that India does not only buckle under the pressures of the Global North but also charts its own path. In doing so, India has emerged as an example for the world in aligning development and environmental concerns together and getting the world to act together for a Green Planet.

2

Narendra Modi: Leading a Green India

Manohar Lal

The Hon'ble Prime Minister, Narendra Modi, has the unique ability to turn crisis into opportunity. He has shown a new path to the world in the matter of green energy—the only solution to avoid global warming. The prime minister feels that green energy will protect and conserve the environment, develop a strong economy and increase employment. India ranks third in the world in established renewable energy. India's consumption from non-fossil sources including renewable sources has increased by more than 25 per cent in the last seven years. India plans to extend its non-fossil energy capacity to 500 GW by 2030. By 2030, India will meet 50 per cent of its power requirement with renewable energy. The day is not far off when India will become a nation leading the world in terms of green energy.

Prime Minister Narendra Modi announced the launch of the National Hydrogen Mission in his Independence Day Address from Red Fort on 15 August 2021. He said that a target has been set to make India a global hub in green hydrogen. With green energy, India will be the third largest economy in the world by 2030, up from its fifth position today. Green energy is a mission that will join the world in one thread. Prime Minister Modi's mantra about one world, one sun, one grid reflects India's attitude towards climate change to the world, in which it is said that *Sarvajan Hitay, Sarvajan Sukhaya*, that is, everyone should be happy and this is possible only when the world moves forward to save the world environment.

The primary objective for deploying green energy is to advance economic development, improve energy security, improve access to energy, and mitigate climate change. Sustainable development is possible by ensuring access to affordable, reliable, and sustainable energy for citizens. Strong government support and the increasingly opportune economic situation have propelled India to be one of the top leaders in the world's most attractive renewable energy markets. The Modi government has designed policies, programs, and a liberal environment to ramp up the country in the renewable energy market at a rapid rate. A mixture of push policies and pull mechanisms, accompanied by pinpointed strategies has helped in the development of renewable energy technologies in India.

Prime Minister Modi cares for Mother Earth and has taken several path breaking steps for the promotion of renewable energy in the last eight years. The country is engaged in expanding the use of clean energy sources and has already undertaken several large-scale sustainable energy projects to ensure a massive growth of green energy.

In 2016, India set a target of reaching 175 GW of renewable energy capacity by 2022, comprising 100 GW of solar, 60 GW of wind, 10 GW of biomass power and 5 GW of small hydropower. In spite of impediments caused by the COVID pandemic, around 57 per cent of the 100 GW solar target and 67 per cent of the wind target has been met. Accordingly, India has set itself a lofty target of taking its non-fossil energy capacity to 500 GW by 2030, of which 280 GW will come from solar energy. India has set a target of 5 million tons a year of green hydrogen capacity by 2030.

Prime Minister Narendra Modi had made a statement at the 'COP26 Summit' in Glasgow, which speaks of the commitment of the government to make the globe free of carbon emissions. Prime Minister Modi has declared that the huge railway system of India will make itself 'Net Zero' by 2030. As a revolutionary step in solar power, the prime minister has initiated the International Solar Alliance, which is a coalition for disaster resilient infrastructure for climate adaptation. This is a sensitive and vital initiative to save millions of lives. The prime minister has presented to the world five nectar elements, 'Panchamrit', to deal with the challenge of global warming and climate change, namely, first, India will take its non-fossil energy capacity to

500 GW by 2030; second, India will meet 50 per cent of its energy requirements from renewable energy by 2030; third, India will reduce the total projected carbon emissions by one billion tons by 2030; fourth, by 2030, India will reduce the carbon intensity of its economy by more than 45 per cent; and fifth, by the year 2070, India will achieve the target of Net Zero. These 'Panchamrits' will be an unprecedented contribution of India to climate action.

To realise these targets, the prime minister has suggested the following action points:

1) To ensure that better and affordable solar technology be easily and conveniently available to all.
2) To increase the proportion of solar energy in our energy mix.
3) To encourage innovation so that solar solutions can be provided for several requirements.
4) To provide concessional financing and less risky finance for solar projects.
5) To develop such regulatory aspects and standards that can provide a new momentum to the development and adoption of solar solutions.
6) To develop consultancy support for bankable solar projects.
7) To create a comprehensive network of centres of excellence that can consider local factors and situations.

Under the leadership of Prime Minister Modi, India's installed renewable energy capacity has increased four times in the last 8.5 years and stands at more than 160 GW (including large hydro), which is 40 per cent of the country's total capacity of 400 GW (as on 31 March 2022). Further, India has become the third-largest renewable energy producer in the world. The schemes launched for promotion of solar in India includes the development of solar parks and ultra mega solar power projects, setting up of over 5,000 MW grid-connected SPV power projects under IV of JNNSM Phase-II, central public sector undertaking (CPSU) scheme for setting up 12,000 MW solar PV projects through government producers using domestic cells and modules to facilitate national energy security and environment sustainability for government purpose, etc.

MNRE has approved 61 solar parks totalling 40 GW capacity. The Bhadla solar park in Rajasthan is the world's largest solar power plant. It ranks first for its capacity of 2,250 MW power generated and second for its area of 10,000 acres. Solar energy accounts for 10 per cent of Rajasthan's total power consumption. Karnataka is the second biggest solar state with over 7.1 GW in large-scale solar projects. The Pavagada solar park of 2,050 MW spanning over 13,000 acres is operational in Karnataka. The Kurnool ultra mega solar park with 1,000 MW capacity was made operational in Kurnool, Andhra Pradesh.

An offshore wind policy was announced on 6 October 2015. Thirty-four companies (most significant global and domestic wind power players) competed in the "expression of interest" (EoI) floated to set up India's first mega offshore wind farm with a capacity of 1 GW. The government has set a target of 5.0 GW of offshore wind installations by 2022 and 30 GW by 2030 which has given a new confidence to project developers in the Indian market.

MNRE is implementing green energy corridors to expand the transmission system. The green energy corridor is a comprehensive scheme for evacuation and integration of renewable energy (RE) capacity addition of 32,713 MW during 12th plan period. To evacuate the proposed capacity addition and transmission systems, both intra-state and inter-state, the Renewable Energy Management Centre (REMC) has been proposed to control infrastructure at a sanctioned cost of Rs. 409 crore. POWERGRID has been appointed as the project management consultant (PMC). Over 9,400 km of green energy corridors have been completed or are under implementation at a cost of Rs 10,141 crore. The inter-state transmission system assigned to POWERGRID for implementation has been completed. Also, 11 REMCs were commissioned by POWERGRID in February 2020. Additionally, one new REMC in Telangana and one EMC at Andaman and Nicobar Islands are under implementation and scheduled for completion by the year 2022-23. The Government of India has approved the green energy corridor-intra-state transmission system phase-II scheme on 6 January 2022. The project cost is Rs. 12,031.33 crore with central financial assistance (CFA) at the rate of 33 per cent of the project cost, that is, Rs. 3,970.34 crore. The transmission infrastructure under the scheme will be setup in seven states, namely, Gujarat, Himachal Pradesh, Karnataka, Kerala, Rajasthan, Tamil Nadu, and Uttar Pradesh.

MNRE is assisting states and, through them, farmers in setting up solar pumps (off-grid application). Under the PM KUSUM scheme, MNRE has promoted the installation of ground-mounted grid connected renewable power plants in rural areas, installation of stand alone solar powered agriculture pumps, and solarisation of grid-connected agriculture pumps to make farmers independent of grid supply and also enable them to sell surplus solar power to DISCOMs.

From 2014-2015 to 2017-2018, more than 2.5 lakh (0.25 million) biogas plants were set up for cooking in rural homes to enable families by providing them access to clean fuel.

As on 30 June 2021, over 800 projects with a total capacity of 10,170 MW (installed capacity of biomass IPP-1,836 MW, installed capacity of bagasse co-generation-7,562 MW and installed capacity of non-bagasse co-generation-772 MW) has been installed in the biomass power and co-generation sector, for feeding power into the grid.

The tariff policy was amended mandating purchase obligations (RPO) by generators and discoms. Wind and solar inter-state transmission charges were waived, and the RPO trajectory and renewable energy policy was finalized.

The Surya Mitra programme was conducted to train college graduates in the installation, commissioning, operation, and management of solar panels.

Other initiatives of Prime Minister Modi relating to green energy are the International Solar Alliance. The ISA is an Indian initiative that was launched by the Prime Minister of India and the President of France on 30 November 2015 in Paris, France, on the sidelines of the Conference of The Parties (COP-21), with 121 solar resource-rich countries lying fully or partially between the tropics of Cancer and Capricorn as prospective members. The overarching objective of the ISA is to collectively address key common challenges to the scaling up of solar energy in ISA member-countries. The International Solar Alliance (ISA) headquarters in India (Gurugram) will provide knowledge support to solar energy improvements in India.

Under the One Sun, One World, One Grid (OSOWOG) vision, India seeks to replicate its global solar leadership, that is, International Solar Alliance, by encouraging the phased development of a single globally connected solar electricity grid to leverage the multiple benefits namely, low costs and zero pollution. The underlying logic behind OSOWOG is that a grid spread across multiple time zones could balance intermittent renewables with other renewables: the setting sun in one part of the grid is made up for by solar, wind or hydropower produced in a distant place.

Prime Minister Modi has recently laid the foundation stone of various green energy projects of the National Thermal Power Corporation Limited worth over Rs. 5,200 crore, and launched the power sector's revamped distribution sector scheme as well as the national solar rooftop portal. In a historic initiative, the prime minister launched the Ministry of Power's flagship revamped distribution sector scheme, which is aimed at improving operational efficiencies and financial sustainability of the DISCOMs and power departments. With an outlay of over Rs. 3 lakh crore over a period of five years from FY 2021-22 to FY 2025-26, the scheme aims to provide financial assistance to DISCOMs for modernization and strengthening of distribution infrastructure, focusing on improvement of the reliability and quality of supply to end consumers. It also aims to reduce the aggregate technical and commercial (AT&C) losses to pan-India levels of 12-15 per cent and ACS-ARR (average cost of supply—average revenue realized) gap to zero by 2024-25 by improving operational efficiencies and financial sustainability of all state-sector DISCOMs. Shri Modi has also launched the National Solar Rooftop Portal, which will enable online tracking of the process of installation of rooftop solar plants, starting from registering of applications to release of subsidy in residential consumers' bank accounts after installation and inspection of the plant.

These reforms have transformed the electricity sector with the focus being on making affordable power available for all. Electrification of about 18,000 villages which did not have access to power earlier signified the commitment of the government towards ensuring last-mile outreach.

The prime minister has recently said that 'Energy for Sustainable Growth' not only resonates with the Indian tradition but is a pathway to achieve future needs and aspirations. He said that sustainable growth is possible only through sustainable energy sources. He reiterated the commitment made at Glasgow to reach net zero by 2070. He also reiterated the target of achieving 500 GW non-fossil energy capacity and achieving 50 per cent of installed energy capacity through non-fossil energy by 2030. "Whatever targets India has set for itself, I do not see them as a challenge but as opportunity. India is moving with this vision in the last few years and the same has been taken forward at policy level in this year's budget", he said. The budget for FY 2023-24 announced Rs. 19,500 crore of investment in high-efficiency solar module manufacturing which will help in making India a global hub for manufacturing and R&D of solar modules and related products.

The most recent initiative by Prime Minister Modi has been the National Green Hydrogen Mission which will make India a global hub for production and export of green hydrogen. This will generate employment for over 6 lakh people and will reduce imports and greenhouse gas emissions.

With the inspirational vision of the prime minister and under his leadership and guidance, the Government of Haryana is making all out efforts for implementation of various central schemes for achieving renewable energy targets in order to achieve sustainable growth. Haryana has been one of the top-ranking states in the last two years in the state energy efficiency index launched by the Ministry of Power, GoI.

Two paddy straw-based power projects of 15 MW each have been commissioned in 2021-22 at Kurukshetra and Kaithal while another two of 9.9 MW each at Fatehabad and Jind are likely to be commissioned soon to tackle the problem of straw burning in fields. Haryana is a front-runner state in the country in installation of solar pumps under the PM KUSUM Scheme Component (B) of the Ministry of New & Renewable Energy with about 30,000 solar pumps in 2020-21 and 2021-22. For 2022-23, a target of installing 50,000 solar pumps is proposed. The Government of Haryana has a proposal to install solar power plants in the next two years in all government offices, higher education institutes, and universities where the energy requirement is more than 10 kW.

Prime Minister Modi, speaking from the ramparts of the Red Fort in Delhi on the 76th Independence Day on 15 August 2022, said that India needs to become 'aatmanirbhar' (self-reliant) in the energy sector, and lead the world. He said that India will have to take these green energy initiatives forward and lead as an example in the world. He said, "We need to be aatmanirbhar in our energy sector. From solar energy to Mission Hydrogen to the adoption of EVs, we need to take these initiatives to the next level for energy independence".

We, as true Indians must support the prime minister in achieving his great vision for a green India and a green earth.

3

The Prime Minister's Push for a Green India

R.K. Pachnanda

In the post-budget webinar on green growth, Prime Minister Modi observed that "India has been the fastest in renewable energy capacity addition among major economies since 2014. The potential of solar, wind and biogas in India is no less than any gold mine or oil field for our private sector...India has huge potential to lead the world in Green Energy. It will forward the cause of global good apart from generating Green Jobs."

The prime minister outlined three pillars for green growth and energy transition: increasing the generation of renewable energy, reducing the use of fossil fuel in the economy and moving rapidly towards a non-fossil fuel gas-based economy in the country. This strategy has underlined the announcements of measures like ethanol blending, PM-KUSUM Yojana, incentives for solar manufacturing, rooftop solar scheme, coal gasification, green hydrogen and battery storage, in the budgets of the past few years. The prime minister highlighted schemes such as green credit for industries, PM Pranam Yojana for farmers, Gobardhan Yojana for villages, vehicle scrapping policy for cities, green hydrogen and wetland conservation.

While underscoring the rapid proliferation of renewable energy generation capacity, the prime minister stated that India has achieved the target of 40 per cent contributions from non-fossil fuels in the installed electricity capacity nine years before the target date. India achieved the target of 10 per cent ethanol blending in motor spirits five months before time and emphasized that the nation strives to achieve 20 per cent ethanol blending in motor spirits by 2025-26 instead of 2030.

Further, under the National Green Hydrogen Mission, India is targeting a production of 5 million metric tonnes (MMT) green hydrogen. An allocation of Rs. 19,000 crore has been made to incentivize the private sector in this field. India has the potential of producing 10,000 million cubic metres of biogas from 'gobar' (cow dung) and 1.5 lakh cubic metres of gas, which can contribute up to 8 per cent to the city gas distribution in the country. Due to this, the Gobardhan Yojana is an important component of India's biofuel strategy. In the present budget, the government has announced plans to set up 500 new plants under the Gobardhan Yojana. The private sector will get attractive incentives for producing CBG from agri-waste and municipal solid waste (MSW).

The Central Government has made a provision of Rs. 3,000 crore in this year's budget to scrap around 3 lakh vehicles owned by Central and State governments that are older than 15 years following the principle of Reuse, Recycle and Recovery.

In order to achieve a quantum leap towards promotion of green energy, the government has made it mandatory for all firms constructing coal-based thermal power stations from April 2023 onwards to set up renewable energy projects of 40 per cent capacity of such coal-fired projects. This would ensure rapid growth in setting up of renewable power generation capacity. Further, in order to address the surge in peaking power demand, energy storage in the form of battery or pump storage (4 per cent by FY 2029-30) have been notified by the Central Government in July 2022. This would enable storage of electricity during low demand periods and draw upon the same during peak demand periods, thereby reducing the need for additional capacity in transmission and generation.

Green growth is one of the seven top priorities of the Union Budget 2023-24 for ushering green industrial and energy transition, environmentally friendly agriculture, and sustainable energy in the country. It will also generate a large number of green jobs. The Union Budget has envisaged a number of projects and initiatives spread across various sectors and ministries, namely, green hydrogen mission, energy transition, energy storage projects, renewable energy evacuation, green credit programme, PM-PRANAM, Gobardhan scheme, Bhartiya Prakritik Kheti Bio-Input Resource Centres, MISHTI, Amrit Dharohar, coastal shipping and vehicle replacement.

Our energy strategy is acknowledged the world over, as rational and balanced, which is only due to the vision and laser focus of the prime minister to ensure 'energy justice'. India is accelerating its efforts to increase the share of gas as fuel from the present 6.3 per cent to 15 per cent by 2030.

At the recently-concluded India Energy Week 2023, India propelled its biofuel revolution by launching E20 or 20 per cent ethanol-blended petrol, which has grown from just 1.53 per cent in 2013-14 to 10.17 per cent in 2023. Now India is also setting up five second-generation ethanol plants that can convert agricultural waste into biofuel, further reducing pollution due to stubble/ cross-residue burning, and generate income for farmers. The National Green Hydrogen Mission has been launched with an outlay of Rs. 19,744 crore to develop the country's green hydrogen ecosystem and produce 4 MT of annual green hydrogen, leading to a saving of Rs. 1 lakh crore in cumulative fossil fuel import savings by 2030. Along with green hydrogen and biofuels, India is also supporting electric vehicles through a production-linked incentive scheme to make advanced fuel cells of 50 gigawatt hours. Customs duty exemptions have also been announced for the sector.

Apart from these measures, the Government of India has taken several steps to achieve 550 GW by 2030. First, Green Energy Open Access Rules, 2022, have stipulated that only transmission, wheeling, cross subsidy charges, banking charges, SLDC fee, scheduling charges and deviation charges shall be levied on green energy open access consumers. This is subject to the fact that additional surcharge will not be applicable for open access consumers paying fixed charges and cross subsidy and additional surcharge shall not be applicable, if green energy is utilized for green hydrogen or green ammonia. Moreover, there shall not be any capacity limit for installation of power plants from renewable energy sources by entities for their own consumption and such plants may be set up at any location in India (RPO benefit may be claimed in any other state) and power shall be transmitted by using open access. Furthermore, all applications for open access of green energy (having contract demand or sanctioned load of 100 kw and above), shall be allowed by the nodal agency within a period of fifteen days.

Second, general network access and connectivity regulations of CERC will ensure prompt connectivity to generators, for the specific quantum without upfront declaring injection and drawl point. The injection and drawl points are to be declared one day ahead of scheduling of the power (applicable for 50 MW individually or collectively through lead generator). Third, there is waiver of inter-state transmission charges by the Ministry of Power. For new hydropower projects, for which construction work is awarded and PPA (Power Purchase Agreement) is signed on or before 30 June 2025, after 1 July 2025 to 30 June 2028, 75 per cent/50 per cent/25 per cent waivers have been granted. The waiver/or concessional charges shall be applicable for a period of 18 years from the date of commissioning of the hydropower plants. There is also a waiver for solar and wind projects commissioned upto 30 June 2025, for 25 years, hydro pump storage (PSP) for 25 years and battery energy storage systems (BESS) commissioned upto 30 June 2025 for 12 years.

Fourth, the finance minister in the recent budget for FY 2023-24, has announced that battery energy storage systems (BESS) with capacity of 4,000 MW will be supported with viability gap funding (VGF). Fifth, under the PM-KUSUM Scheme, central financial assistance is granted to farmers for installing standalone or grid-connected solar agricultural pumps at the rate of 30 per cent by the Central Government and 30 per cent by the State Government. Sixth, rooftop solar, central financial assistance is granted to individual households. Earlier, it was 40 per cent subsidy for the first 3 kW and 20 per cent subsidy beyond 3 kW and upto 10 kW. Now, with effect from 5 January 2023, the same has been revised to Rs. 14,588/kW upto 3 kW, Rs. 7,294/kW beyond 3 kW upto 10 kW and fixed subsidy of Rs. 94,822 for rooftop solar capacity exceeding 10 KW. Seventh, the National Bioenergy Programme was launched on 2 November 2022 for the period from FY 2020-21 to 2025-26. Under the programme, financial assistance has been provided for waste-to-energy projects, biomass projects, biomass co-generation (non-bagasse) and biogas projects. Eighth, renewable purchase obligation (RPO) has been fixed for various obligated entities ranging from 27.08 per cent to 43.33 per cent of energy consumption. Further, RPO has also been fixed for energy storage.

In this way, India shall comfortably achieve and exceed the target of non-fossil energy capacity of 500 GW by 2030 and net zero carbon emissions (carbon neutral) by 2070, as envisioned by Modi. As we implement our 'Amritkaal' strategy to achieve a USD 26 trillion economy by 2047, we will also methodically ensure energy security and independence and be a trail blazer of green energy in the world.

4

INDIA'S CONTRIBUTION TO GREEN ENERGY

Hanif Qureshi

The UN Climate Change Conference in Glasgow (COP26) brought together 120 world leaders for two weeks to deliberate on all facets of climate change—the science, the solutions, the political will to act, and clear indications of action.

While countries reaffirmed the Paris Agreement goal of limiting the increase in the global average temperature to well below 2°C above pre-industrial levels and pursuing efforts to limit it to 1.5°C, they also stressed the urgency of action 'in this critical decade,' when carbon dioxide emissions must be reduced by 45 per cent to reach net zero around mid-century.

The pace of economic growth in India has led to a steep rise in demand of power. The per capita electricity consumption has increased from 592 kWh during 2003-04 to 1,208 kWh during 2019-20. There is an increasing need to plan capacity addition optimally in view of the limited availability of fuel resources for generation, new sources of generation and environmental concerns.

India's five-point climate action plan, described by the Government of India as 'Panchamrit (five values),' is set to give a firm push to India's plans for increasing renewable energy, and switching to electricity and hydrogen fuels for transport. These are:

i. **Net zero by 2070**

Net zero refers to the balance between the quantity of greenhouse gases emitted and the quantity of such gases removed from the air. There is unanimity among energy experts that India's dependence on coal will have to be cut drastically in the next 10-15 years to achieve its net zero target and the country will have to swiftly switch to cleaner fuels. Net zero was a hotly debated subject at the COP26 talks in Glasgow.

ii. **500 GW of non-fossil fuels by 2030**
The commitment for achieving 500 GW of non-fossil based power generation by 2030 is an ambitious target set by the Government of India to achieve greater utilization of renewables.

iii. **Fifty per cent of energy requirement through renewable energy by 2030**
This would mean India will produce half its energy requirements from renewables, which India committed at the COP 26 summit. According to the CEA, India's total installed electricity capacity will be 1,100 GW by 2030, which will necessitate RE capacity of 550 GW by that time. This target is achievable if India makes swift transition to clean energy sources.

iv. **Cutting carbon emissions by 1 billion tonnes**
India is commit/ted to reduce projected carbon emissions by 1 billion tonnes (Gt) between 2021 and 2030. As of today, India's per capita emissions is 1.98 tonnes of CO_2. If you compare this with the world emissions by 2030, the US per capita emissions will be 9.42 tonnes, EU 4.12 tonnes, India's will be 2.7 tonnes, and China's will be 8.88 tonnes per capita.

v. **Reducing carbon intensity by 45 per cent**
Carbon intensity measures emissions of CO_2 per unit of the gross domestic product (GDP). Achieving 45 per cent will not be difficult considering India would be meeting half its energy demand from cleaner technologies by 2030, and there is a broad hydrogen road map for the country to adopt over the next 10 years. India has taken measures to reduce emissions from the transport sector, and the energy intensive industrial sector—especially cement, iron and steel, non-metallic minerals and chemical, which contribute about 30 per cent of the total emissions.

India's Solar Potential

India is endowed with vast solar energy potential. About 5,000 trillion kWh per year energy is incident over India's land area with most parts receiving 4-7 kWh per sqm per day. Solar photo-voltaic power can be harnessed effectively, thus providing huge scalability in India. Solar power also provides the ability to generate power on a distributed basis and enables rapid capacity addition with short lead times. Off-grid decentralized and low-temperature applications will be advantageous from a rural electrification perspective and meeting other energy needs for power and heating and cooling in both rural and urban areas. From an energy security perspective, solar power is the most secure of all sources, since it is abundantly available. Theoretically, a small fraction of the total incident solar energy (if captured effectively) can meet the entire country's power requirements.

There has been a visible impact of solar energy in the Indian energy scenario during the last few years due to the progressive policy interventions of the Government of India. Solar energy based decentralized and distributed applications have benefited millions of people in Indian villages by meeting their cooking, lighting and other energy needs in an environment friendly manner. The social and economic benefits include reduction in drudgery among rural women and girls engaged in the collection of fuel wood from long distances and cooking in smoky kitchens, minimization of the risks of contracting lung and eye ailments, employment generation at village level, and ultimately, improvement in the standard of living and creation of opportunity for economic activities at the village level. Further, the solar energy sector in India has emerged as a significant player in grid connected power generation capacity over the years. It supports the government agenda of sustainable growth, while emerging as an integral part of the solution to meet the nation's energy needs and an essential player for energy security.

The National Institute of Solar Energy (NISE) has assessed the country's solar potential of about 748 GW assuming 3 per cent of the waste land area to be covered by solar PV modules. Environmental issues along with the reduction in cost of renewable energy sources (solar PV and wind) have given a push to solar- and wind-based power generation technologies. The capital cost of renewable (solar PV and wind) technologies for power generation is becoming competitive day by day with coal-based generation. These technologies are carbon free and will help in achieving the sustainable development goals of the country. However, the intermittency associated with RE technologies is a limitation, which needs to be addressed in the power system. One of the options that can help in large-scale integration of RE generation sources can be adoption of grid scale energy storage technologies, which can complement RE generation sources. Storage hydro plants/pumped storage plants can be highly useful for facilitating integration of high variable RE power into the power system. While other new storage technologies are in nascent stages of development, grid scale battery energy storage systems are becoming attractive globally due to rapidly reducing cost with technological advancement. The world is anticipating that grid scale energy storage technologies may help in absorbing more RE economically into the power system in the near future. The recently held I2U2 summit has already laid a roadmap for a hybrid renewable energy project in Gujarat consisting of 300 mw of wind and solar capacity complemented by a battery energy storage system. The US Trade and Development Agency funded a feasibility study for the $ 330 million project and UAE companies will be investment partners. Such projects have the potential of making India a global hub for alternate supply chains in the renewable energy sector, said the foreign secretary.

Solar Energy Programmes

India started its journey towards clean energy goals in mission mode when it launched the National Solar Mission in 2010 with a target of 20 GW by the year 2022, which was later scaled up in 2015 to 100 GW. Solar energy has taken a central place in India's national action plan on climate change with the National Solar Mission as one of the key missions. The NSM is a major initiative of the Government of India with active participation from the states to promote ecological sustainable growth while addressing India's energy security challenges. It will also constitute a major contribution by India to the global effort to meet the challenges of climate change. The mission's objective is to establish India as a global leader in solar energy by creating policy conditions for solar technology diffusion across the country as quickly as possible.

The National Solar Mission (NSM) has schemes for development of solar parks and ultra mega solar power projects with an outlay of Rs. 8,100 crore. The Government of India offers financial assistance of Rs. 20 lakh per MW for infrastructure and power evacuation facility development. In order to achieve the above target, the Government of India has launched various schemes to encourage generation of solar power in the country like solar park scheme, VGF schemes, CPSU scheme, defence scheme, canal bank and canal top Scheme, bundling Scheme, grid connected solar rooftop scheme, etc. Under the solar parks scheme, projects of 40,000 MW aggregate capacity have been sanctioned against which projects of about 10,000 MW capacity have been commissioned. The efforts of the government have resulted in installation of about 60 GW solar power generation capacity in the country.

Grid-connected rooftops and small solar power plants programme is another flagship programme of the Government of India that have helped solar energy reach households and small establishments with the benefits of net metering. About 4,000 MW capacity has been installed under phase-I of this programme through DISCOMs and about 2,500 MW aggregate capacity has been sanctioned to states in phase-II. In phase-II, CFA upto 40 per cent of the benchmark cost is provided to RTS projects upto 3 kW capacity and 20 per cent for RTS system capacity beyond 3 kW and up to 10 kW in the residential sector.

One of the major initiatives of the Ministry of New and Renewable Energy, Government of India, to harness solar energy is the Pradhan Mantra Kisan Urja Suraksha evam Utthaan Mahabhiyan (PM-KUSUM), which aims to add solar and other renewable capacity of 30.8 GW by 2022 with a total central financial support of Rs. 34,035 crore. The scheme consists of the following three components:

- **Component A:** 10,000 MW of decentralized ground mounted grid connected renewable power plants of capacity 500 kW to 2 MW will be setup by individual farmers/group of farmers/cooperatives/ panchayats/farmer producer organizations (FPO). DISCOMs will invite applications from interested beneficiaries for setting up renewable energy plants and purchase the renewable power at a feed-in-tariff (FiT) determined by respective state electricity regulatory commissions (SERC).
- **Component B**: Installation of 20 lakh stand-alone off-grid solar powered agriculture pumps of individual pump capacity up to 7.5 HP with central financial assistance of 30 per cent cost of the benchmark or tender cost of pump. Pumps of higher capacities can be installed but the CFA will be limited to 7.5 HP pumps. State

governments give a subsidy of minimum 30 per cent and the remaining share will be provided by the farmer.

- **Component C:** Solarisation of 15 lakh grid-connected agriculture pumps of individual pump capacity up to 7.5 HP including through feeder level solarisation. The farmer will be able to use the generated solar power to meet irrigation needs and the excess solar power will be sold to DISCOMs.

India has more than 30 million tubewells of which about 8 million are run on diesel. These pump sets annually consume more than 213 billion units of electricity and about 5.52 billion litres of diesel with emission of about 15.4 million tons of carbon dioxide. India imports more than 227 MMT of crude oil, which is continuously increasing year by year. The complete implementation of PM-KUSUM will result in reduction of CO_2 emissions by about 32 million tons annually and annual reduction in diesel consumption by about 1.38 billion litres.

So far, solar power plants of capacity more than 53 MW have been commissioned under component A, 349,781, off-grid solar pumps have been installed under component B and 1,047 grid connected pumps have been solarized under component C.

Besides, off-grid solar applications like solar lamps, solar street lights and solar home lighting systems are also being promoted in the country as clean energy options. Small solar power packs of over 216 MW capacity, over 84 lakh solar lanterns and study lamps, 17.23 home light systems and more than 9.34 lakh solar street lights have been installed.

Wind Energy

India has a wind energy potential of about 595 GW and its wind energy programme is led by the indigenous industry and has shown consistent growth. With over 40 GW wind energy installations, India has the world's fourth-largest wind installed capacity. The Government of India has designed the offshore wind energy policy to harness the potential of offshore wind energy along India's coastline spread over 7,600 km. The ministry is developing a strategy and roadmap for installation of estimated 70 GW offshore wind projects off the coasts of Gujarat and Tamil Nadu. One of the major advantages of wind energy is its inherent strength in supporting rural employment and uplift of rural economy. Further, unlike all other sources of power, wind energy does not consume any water, which in itself will become a scarce commodity. Overall, the future of wind energy in India is bright as energy security and self-sufficiency is identified as the major driver. The biggest advantage with wind energy is that the fuel is free, and it does not produce CO emissions. Wind farms can be built reasonably fast. The wind farm land can be used for farming as well, thus serving a dual purpose, and it is cost-effective as compared to other forms of renewable energy with the latest discovered tariff of Rs. 2.65 per unit.

Bio-Energy Programmes

To meet basic energy needs, mankind has always been using biomass as the primary source of energy. It is the cheapest form of energy, renewable, widely available, carbon-neutral and has the potential to provide significant employment in rural areas. About 32 per cent of the total primary energy use in the country is still derived from biomass and more than 70 per cent of the country's population depends on it for its energy needs. For efficient utilization of biomass, bagasse-based co-generation in sugar mills and biomass power generation have been taken up under the biomass power and co-generation programme. As per a recent study sponsored by MNRE, the current availability of biomass in India is estimated at about 750 million metric tonnes per year.

The following bio-energy schemes are being implemented by the ministry:

- Programme on energy from urban, industrial and agricultural wastes/ residues
- Scheme to support promotion of biomass-based co-generation in sugar mills and other industries
- Biogas power (off-grid) generation and thermal application programme (BPGTP)
- New national biogas and organic manure programme (NNBOMP)

The Ministry of New and Renewable Energy has been providing attractive incentives for the above projects to boost the green energy agenda of the Government of India.

Biomass produced from crop residue in north-west India is often burnt in fields by farmers to clear them for the next crop. Paddy straw produced in these areas of the country such as Rajasthan, UP, Punjab and Haryana is being encouraged to be used as a fuel in biomass power plants. Thermal power plants in the country have also been mandated to use 5 per cent biomass for co-firing, which will increase to 7 per cent by 2023 and is expected to create a market for paddy straw round the year and a source of additional income for farmers along with rural employment opportunities.

Small Hydro

In India, hydro power plants of 25 MW or below capacity are classified as small hydro, which have further been classified into micro (100 kW or below), mini (101 kW-2 MW) and small hydro (2-25 MW) segments.

India has an estimated potential of 21,135.37 MW from 7,135 sites for power generation in the country from small/mini hydel projects, which were assessed by the alternate hydro energy centre (AHEC) of IIT Roorkee.

The ministry has taken a series of steps to promote development of SHP in a planned manner and improve reliability and quality of the projects. By giving various physical and financial incentives, investments have been attracted in commercial SHP projects apart from subsidizing state governments to set up small hydro projects. The ministry is also placing special emphasis to promote the use of new and efficient designs of water mills for mechanical as well as electricity generation and setting up of micro hydel projects up to 100 KW for remote village electrification. These projects are taken up with the involvement of local organizations such as water mills associations, cooperative societies, registered NGOs, village energy cooperatives, and state nodal agencies.

National Hydrogen Mission

In his Independence Day speech on 15 August 2021, the prime minister announced the launch of the National Hydrogen Mission to aid the government in meeting its climate targets and making India a green hydrogen hub. This will help in meeting the target of production of 5 million tonnes of green hydrogen by 2030 and the related development of renewable energy capacity. Hydrogen and ammonia are envisaged to be the future fuels to replace fossil fuels. Production of these fuels by using power from renewable energy, termed as green hydrogen and green ammonia, is one of the major requirements for environmentally sustainable energy security of the nation. The Government of India is taking various measures to facilitate the transition from fossil fuel/ fossil fuel-based feed stocks to green hydrogen/green ammonia. The notification of this policy is one of the major steps in this endeavour.

One Solar, One World, One Grid

The sun is the source of all energy and solar energy and is available only during the day time and dependent on the weather. One Solar, One World, One Grid (OSOWOG) is the solution to this challenge. Its objective is to aid in developing a worldwide grid through which clean energy can be transmitted anywhere, anytime. It also aims to help in reducing storage needs and enhancing the viability of solar projects. Its ultimate goal is to reduce carbon footprints and energy costs. At the first assembly of the International Solar Alliance (ISA), in October 2018, Prime Minister Modi floated the idea of the OSOWOG initiative. The initiative may have a spill-over effect, as the cost-effective source of energy production could be used in other areas such as poverty alleviation, provision of drinking water, sanitation facilities and food security. Global collaboration will bring increased investment in research and development.

A tripartite memorandum of understanding (MoU) was signed between the Ministry of New and Renewable Energy (MNRE), the International Solar Alliance (ISA) and the World Bank on 8 September 2021 for a study on the OSOWOG initiative and any development in this area will open a plethora of opportunities for solar energy as a perennial source of energy for mankind.

Compressed Biogas Programme

India is among the fastest-growing economies in the world and its energy consumption is slated to increase rapidly. India's dependence on fossil fuels for its energy needs has two major concerns, that is, a growing import bill and carbon emission. The country now imports close to 85 per cent of crude oil, which roughly translates to 45 per cent of the primary energy demand and this is only going to rise in the near future. This trend has huge implications for the energy security of the country. The Government of India has set a target of reduction in import dependence by 10 per cent from 2015 to 2022.

India's import dependence on crude oil, natural gas, and a large share of carbon-intensive energy sources necessitates action to ensure energy security and economic sustainability in the long run. Also, through sustainable alternative towards affordable transport (SATAT), launched in October 2018, the GOI aims to set up 5,000 Bio CNG plants by 2024 and use disposable paddy straw.

Sofar, 3,350 Letter of Intents (LoIs) have been issued by oil marketing companies to project developers and 30 projects have been commissioned while 6,700 MT CBG has been sold.

Renewable Purchase Obligation

Under Section 86(1)(e) of the Electricity Act 2003 (EA, 2003) and the National Tariff Policy 2006, renewable purchase obligation (RPO), is a mechanism by which the obligated entities have to purchase a certain percentage of electricity from renewable energy sources as a percentage of the total consumption of electricity. RPOs are categorized as solar and non-solar RPO. To achieve the target of 175 GW of renewable energy by 2022, including solar energy capacity of 100 GW, the Ministry of Power (MoP) has notified the target RPO trajectory up to year 2022.

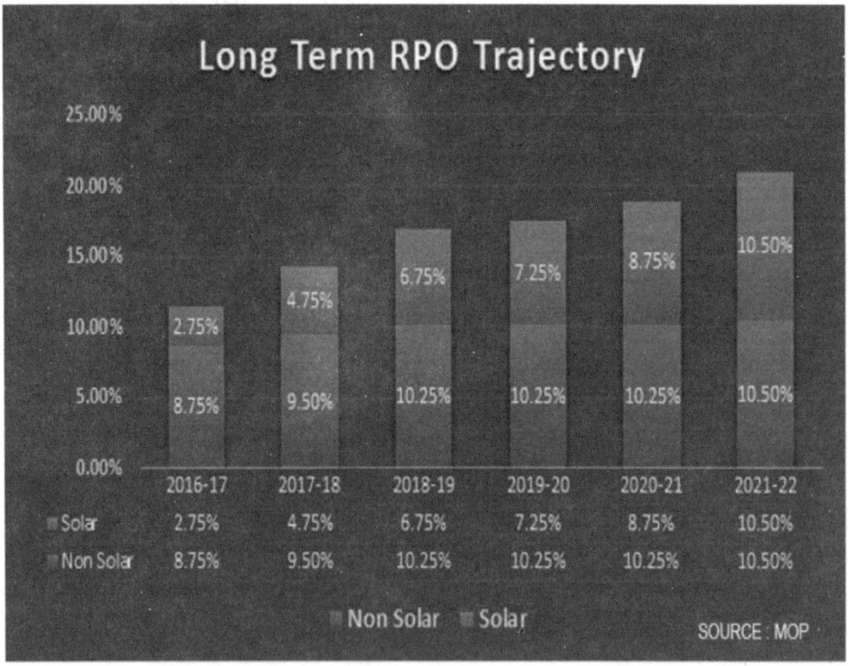

It can be a step towards meeting the INDCs, thereby contributing towards the global effort to meet the challenges of climate change. Pursuant to the enactment of the Electricity Act 2003, the SERCs are required to fix a minimum percentage of the total consumption of electricity in the area of a distribution licensee for purchase of energy from renewable energy sources. With the amendment of the tariff policy in January, 2016, the state electricity regulatory commissions (SERCs) are required to reserve a minimum percentage for purchase of solar energy, which shall be such that it reaches eight per cent of the total consumption of energy, excluding hydro power, by March 2022 or as notified by the Central Government from time to time. The Government of India in July 2018 notified the long term growth trajectory of renewable purchase obligations (RPOs) for solar as well as non-solar, uniformly for all states/union territories, reaching 21 per cent of RPO by 2022 with 10.5 per cent for solar-based electricity.

Electric Vehicles (EVs)

The availability of fossil fuels is limited, and their use is destroying our planet. Toxic emissions from petrol and diesel vehicles lead to long-term, adverse effects on public health. The impact of emissions of electric vehicles is much lower than that of petrol or diesel vehicles. From an efficiency perspective, electric vehicles can convert around 60 per cent of electrical energy from the grid to power the wheels, but petrol or diesel cars can only convert 17–21 per cent of the energy stored in the fuel to the wheels. That is a waste of around 80 per cent. To reduce the impact of charging electric vehicles, India is ambitious to achieve about 40 per cent cumulative electric power installed capacity from non-fossil fuel-based energy resources by the year 2030. Therefore, EVs are the way forward for Indian transport.

More than 17 states of India have come out with their EV policies to incentivize EV adoption by public and auto manufacturers. With research and collaboration with leading industries worldwide, the EV sector is poised for phenomenal growth in the near future. Hoping to convert more consumers into EV owners, the government is offering subsidies for purchasing EVs. A tax exemption of Rs. 1.5 lakh is also given for people buying electric cars on loan. The GST for the purchase of EVs is set at just 5 per cent with zero cess.

By 2030, 80 per cent of two and three-wheelers, 40 per cent of buses, and 30 to 70 per cent of cars in India will be EVs, says the NITI Aayog. As the nation gears towards its 'zero-emission 2070' dream, funds and focus are directed towards electric mobility. In March 2022, the Minister for Road Transport and Highways, Nitin Gadkari, mentioned in Parliament that between 2019-2020 and 2020-2021, two-wheeler EVs rose by 422 per cent; three-wheelers by 75 per cent and four-wheelers by 230 per cent. The number of electric buses also increased by over 1,200 per cent.

India's road to a fully-electric ecosystem still has a few hurdles—high cost, inadequate infrastructure and lack of high performing EVs. The electric variants of the two- and four-wheelers are often priced much higher than regular fuel options. This is the most important reason for the slow adoption of electric mobility.

Under two phases of FAME or faster adoption and manufacturing of hybrid and electric vehicles scheme, the government has been trying to improve the infrastructure for EV manufacturing in the country. There is also a plan for 22,000 EV charging stations to be set up by oil marketing companies across the country.

Energy Conservation Building Code

With rapid urbanization, the building sector in India is experiencing unprecedented growth. It has 38 per cent (~208 mtoe) of India's total annual energy consumption and 31 per cent (296 TWh) of the total annual electricity consumption (IEA, 2017; NITI Aayog and Prayas, 2017). It is the need of the hour to put in place mechanisms that will help India meet its nationally determined contribution, sustainable development goals commitment.

Launched in 2007, the Energy Conservation Building Code is the first ever initiative by the Government of India (GoI) to address energy efficiency in the commercial building sector. Developed by the Bureau of Energy Efficiency (BEE), the code sets minimum energy standards for commercial buildings with a connected load of 100 kW or contract demand of 120 KVA and above. The enactment of the Energy Conservation Act (EC Act) in 2001, with the primary objective of providing the necessary legal framework for promoting energy conservation measures led to the formation of BEE and subsequent development of ECBC.

More than 20 states have adopted ECBC and set up ECBC cells to assist stakeholders in designing and constructing their buildings as per the ECBC.

Energy Audit and its Implementation Scheme

To identify areas where excess energy consumption or wastage of energy is taking place in buildings, the Department of New and Renewable Energy, Haryana is implementing a scheme to carry out investment grade energy audits. This energy audit of buildings involves measuring the actual energy consumption of various electrical gadgets used in the buildings, comparing it with an estimate of the minimum energy required to undertake the process, establishing technically and economically feasible means to achieve the same and suggest best ways to optimize the energy consumption leading to energy saving and money saving in electricity bills.

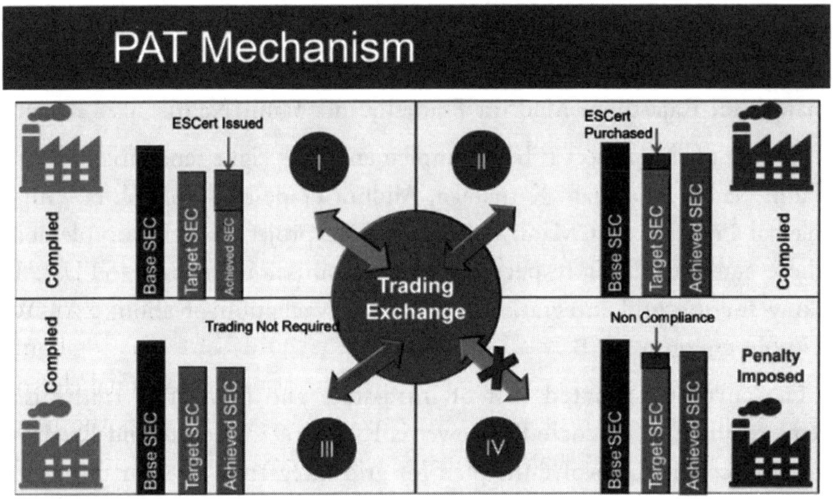

SEC (Specific Energy Consumption): Energy Consumed per unit production

Under Prime Minister Narendra Modi's vision, the Government of India is providing financial as well as technical support to enhance energy efficiency of energy intensive sectors like SMEs and designated consumers through cluster approach and Perform, Achieve and Trade (PAT) Mechanism of the National Mission on Enhanced Energy Efficiency (NMEEE). The mechanism involves rigorous energy auditing, M&V and reporting. BEE has rolled out six PAT cycles till 31 March 2020, with a total of 1,073 DCs covering 13 sectors. It is projected that total energy savings of about 26 MTOE translating into avoiding of about 70 million tonnes of CO_2 will be achieved by March 2023. In the first two PAT cycles, savings of about 22 MTOE energy and CO_2 reduction of 93 million tones was achieved.

The Green Energy Corridor

All states of India do not have similar renewable energy potential and power needs. To ensure hassle-free flow of power to load centres from generation points, the green energy corridor concept was visualized with the objective to synchronize electricity produced from renewable sources, such as solar and wind, with conventional power stations in the grid. Prime Minister Narendra Modi launched the intra-state transmission system (InSTS) project in 2015-16 for evacuation and integration of the renewable energy (RE) capacity addition of 32,713 MW. Total fund requirement of Rs. 34,141 crore was initially assessed for the development of the transmission system and control infrastructure for the addition of RE capacity in the renewable rich states of Andhra Pradesh, Gujarat, Himachal Pradesh, Jammu and Kashmir, Karnataka, Maharashtra, Rajasthan, Madhya Pradesh, and Tamil Nadu.

Phase-1 of the project is being implemented by eight renewable-rich states of Tamil Nadu, Rajasthan, Karnataka, Andhra Pradesh, Maharashtra, Gujarat, Himachal Pradesh, and Madhya Pradesh. The project is being implemented in these states by their respective state transmission utilities (STUs). It is working for the grid integration and power evacuation of about 24 GW of renewable energy.

The current estimated cost of intra-state and inter-state transmission systems required to evacuate RE power is Rs. 12,693.94 crore and Rs. 15,455 crore, respectively. To evolve the plan for grid integration of solar power parks in 21 states, a comprehensive transmission plan was evolved for evacuation of about 20,000 MW capacity envisaged through intra-state and inter-state systems and transmission schemes for solar parks, namely, Ananthapur (1,500 MW), Pavagada (2,000 MW), Rewa (750 MW), Bhadla-III (500 MW), Bhadla-IV (250 MW), Essel (750 MW), Banaskantha (700MW) and Fatehgarh (1,000 MW) have been commissioned.

It is a step towards contributing to the long-term energy security of India and will promote ecologically sustainable growth by reducing the carbon footprint. It will facilitate in generating large direct and indirect employment opportunities for both the skilled and unskilled personnel.

The programmes and initiatives of the Government of India, powered by the vision of the Prime Minster, are testimony to its commitment for green economy through net zero goals for which a well-laid road map has been envisioned and all states are working in harmony with the national government to realize the goals.

ENERGY-ENVIRONMENT CONNECT

5

NARENDRA MODI: RE-IMAGINING ENVIRONMENTAL CONSCIOUSNESS AND RELAYING THE BUDDHA LINK

Anirban Ganguly

"I have always believed that I have a special connection with Lord Buddha. I experience that I am connected to his thoughts and his path of love and compassion", Prime Minister Narendra Modi once confessed in one of his addresses to a convention commemorating Buddha's life and message. This special connection must have been forged in his childhood days in Vadnagar, which had been a vibrant Buddhist centre of learning civilisationally. Decades later, as Chief Minister of Gujarat, Narendra Modi, evinced keen interest in Vadnagar's Buddhist antiquity and ordered excavations leading to the discovery of Buddha's sacred relics. As Chief Minister, Narendra Modi had organized an international Buddhist Assembly which saw delegates from more than 20 countries participating. He was perhaps the first chief minister of an Indian state to convene such a Buddhist assembly. Prime Minister Modi refers to this dimension of his relationship with Buddha and Buddhism as a "wonderful coincidence"—that of Vadnagar, his birthplace, being "a great centre of Buddhist learning centuries ago."

Prime Minister Modi's fascination and his ever-renewing effort and outreach to rekindle and re-state the Buddha legacy and heritage are thus not a new phenomenon that has taken off after his becoming prime minister. Like a number of his flagship and path-breaking national initiatives, this too he had envisaged and started working out on a limited scale in Gujarat as chief minister and later gave it a global scale and shape as prime minister. Reinstating and disseminating the Buddha legacy, infusing it with a new scope and dimension and making India conscious of her civilizational role and responsibility towards preserving and disseminating the Buddha legacy and message has been one of Prime Minister's Modi's principal outreach. In his words, 'From Kandy to Kyoto, from Hanoi to Hambantota, Lord Buddha is omnipresent through his thoughts, relics and culture..." it is this civilizational, cultural and spiritual connect that Narendra Modi has sought to relay and re-imagine for the present.

He has himself travelled on the global Buddhist circuit, leaving no opportunity to visit centres and sacred sites connected to Buddha, his life, and his message and that of the great teachers and masters of Buddhism. Prime Minister Modi's outreach to Mongolia, his continuing connection with the Buddha legacy of that country, is second only or equal to that once initiated by venerable Kushak Bakula Rinpoche. For decades after that, this link lay inert, till Prime Minister Modi infused new energy and direction to it. His taking of a sapling of the sacred Bodhi Tree and gifting it to the iconic Gandan Monastery in Ulaan Batar renewed and rejuvenated the sacred civilizational tie. The Gandan Monastery is the custodian of a portion of the sacred relics of one of the greatest teachers of Buddhism, Atisa Dipankara from Bengal. The recent outreach with the sacred relics of Buddha from India being taken across Mongolia at the behest of the International Buddhist Confederation, created a sensation among the people of Mongolia. The Buddha spirit and link connecting our two countries for centuries received a new impetus and direction. There are many such instances where Prime Minister Modi has initiated international efforts, with the India and Buddha legacy at the centre.

The latest can be surmised through his insistence on connecting the message of Mission LiFE—Lifestyle for Environment—one of his special global initiatives aimed at mitigating the multidimensional environmental challenge with the philosophy and message of Buddha. While inaugurating the International Buddhist Summit in Delhi convened by the International Buddhist Confederation, he remarked that the herculean problem of climate change could be addressed if people became conscious of their lifestyle and if the movement towards change begins with the individual. "Mission LiFE is influenced," he said, "by the inspirations of Buddha and it furthers Buddha's thoughts." Over the years, in every global Buddhist forum that he has addressed, Prime Minister Modi has spoken of this fundamental approach. "One of the biggest challenges is that of climate change", he once observed, "reckless life-styles of the present threaten coming generations. Weather patterns are changing, glaciers are melting. Rivers and forests are in danger. We cannot let our planet remain wounded. Lord Buddha put emphasis on a way of life where respect for Mother Nature is paramount." This aspect of the Buddha philosophy has now become the sustaining vision of Mission LiFE.

While inaugurating the flagship global outreach 'SAMVAD', an initiative of Prime Minister Modi and the late Prime Minister Shinzo Abe of Japan in 2015, Modi described the deep and intrinsic link between Buddhist traditions and the environment. "In India," Modi reminded an international gathering at New Delhi's Vivekananda International Foundation which was hosting SAMVAD, "faith and nature have had a deep link since ancient times. Buddhism and environment are deeply correlated. The Buddhist tradition in all of its historical and cultural manifestations encourages greater identification with the natural world because from a Buddhist perspective, nothing has a separate existence." Drawing a metaphysical schema, connecting the ideational and spiritual dimensions of environmental consciousness and conservation, Modi observed:

> The impurities in the environment affect the mind and the impurities of the mind also pollute the environment. In order to purify the environment, we have to purify the mind. The eco-crisis, in fact, is a reflection of imbalance of the mind. Lord Buddha therefore accorded importance to the need for preserving natural resources, created tools for water conservation and forbade monks from polluting water resources. Nature, forests, trees and the well-being of all living things play a great role in the teachings of Lord Buddha.

Modi's concern with the environment, climate change and the future is not something which he has grown into as prime minister. As Chief Minister of Gujarat, he had evolved an elaborate and refreshingly new programme for mitigating the effects of climate change and environmental degradation. His "convenient action" in the field of environmental conservation, perhaps made him stand apart as a chief minister as it makes him stand apart today as prime minister and as a global leader. It was his reading of "Vedic literature" that educated him "about the strong bond between humans and Mother nature." As Chief Minister of Gujarat, Narendra Modi's action on the environmental front was documented in a book he authored, *Convenient Action – Continuity for Change*. Elaborating on the theme of "Climate Ethics", Modi recalled how respect and compassion for the environment is integral to Indian ethics and civilizational values:

> With my humble moorings in a small village ensconced in the rural hinterland of Western India, I grew up in an atmosphere that was more in harmony with nature than the inhospitable, polluted and haphazard landscapes of big cities to where I shifted in due course. Respect for nature was inextricably embedded in our culture at home, so much so that we were told by my mother to fold hands and ask for Mother Earth's forgiveness after getting up in the morning before putting our feet down on the ground. This, I realised, a few years later in life, was the social integration of the philosophy of the Vedas in India...

Modi has argued for the need to "link to the consciousness of the Earth", while formulating or taking into account, "our social and economic policies" since "our actions are likely to be limited and potentially harmful." Since his early days as an elected head of an Indian state, Modi demonstrated this imperative—that of linking environmental consciousness with policy making:

> A few years ago, I used to read a lot of sceptic views on Climate Change, whether or not it was actually happening. Having been in public life I am aware of behind-the-scene lobbying by vested interests that normally accompany any such carefully orchestrated campaigns. But even in those days of uncertainty and confusion, I based the formulation of public policy of my conviction of complementary relationship between man and nature. This helped me to clarify my thoughts and to choose a developmental path that would lead to empowerment of the poor and downtrodden in a way that would make the sustainable use of the bounties of nature...

This approach saw Modi transform the water climate of an arid and water-challenged state like Gujarat; it saw him enthuse people to become part of this environmental movement and turn into in a people's movement which saw the creation of "353,937 check-dams and village ponds/tanks" in the State benefitting over 13 million people in rural areas. Micro-water harvesting structures were created across Gujarat as Chief Minister Modi undertook an interesting and innovative approach to water-harvesting and conservation in rural Gujarat. It demonstrated a uniquely creative mind in tackling the effects of climate. Modi had written:

> During my various interactions with small and marginal farmers in the State, I have been using socio-religious analogies for inculcating upon them the culture of water conservation. Social ethos in rural areas is more prone to be pro-actively driven for a particular cause by invoking religious beliefs and, therefore, I have been encouraging these farmers to make "Water Temples' (*Jal Mandir*) by digging farm ponds and village ponds. This religious simile of equating water ponds with temples has lent religious reverence for the preservation and conservation of water through these ponds.

Modi also encouraged farmers to keep "earthen pots full of water" for the purpose of drinking at home. He told them that village and farm ponds were "like water pots for Mother Earth for quenching her thirst" and that farmers were "duty bound to create" them, "as an obligation towards Mother Earth." Modi's approach and creative appeal led eventually to the creation of intricate "micro-harvesting structures in different parts of Gujarat." Modi's environmental message and approach is thus based on concrete, visible, and transforming experiments on the ground.

Modi is also perhaps the first global leader who has spoken of "climate justice." Launching SAMVAD, he had argued that the present generation "has the responsibility to act as a trustee of the rich natural wealth for future generations." The issue for him was not merely about "climate change", it was also about "climate justice." "I repeat", he emphasised, "it is not the issue of climate change but about climate justice. In my view, the most adversely affected by climate change are the poor and the downtrodden. When a natural disaster strikes, they are hit the hardest. When there are floods, they are rendered homeless. During an earthquake, their homes are destroyed. During droughts they are affected and during extreme cold the homeless suffer the most." Modi called for a change, a shift of focus from "climate change" to "climate justice."

In connecting the Buddha legacy throughout the Buddhist world, in connecting and revivifying the Buddha legacy in India and in imparting a contemporary direction to Buddha's message for addressing present challenges of "climate, conflict and calamity" as he articulates it, Prime Minister Modi has emerged as an enlightened trustee and leader of the global Buddha heritage.

The more than 360-crore layout for shaping a Buddha circuit in India, the inauguration of the Kushinagar international airport to facilitate the inflow of "crores of Buddha followers from all over the world" and to ensure that their journey is smooth and less tedious, the development of the India International Centre for Buddhist Culture and Heritage in Lumbini, the regular convening of international Buddhist conclaves, the huge effort of aiding India's neighbours to protect and preserve their Buddhist heritage, the restoration of the Buddhist sanctuary of Bagan and the Ananda temples, the conservation of temples in Cambodia and Laos and My-Son temple in Vietnam, India's aid and succour outreach, be it vaccine aid or aid during disasters and calamities, like in Nepal and, more recently, in Turkey, is driven on the one hand by the ageless philosophy of *Vasudhaiva Kutumbakam* and on the other hand by 'Compassion' which is the core of Buddha philosophy. All of these have seen India emerge as a responsible and compassionate preserver of Buddha legacy and heritage globally. India's Buddha outreach led by Prime Minister Modi has no strings attached to it, is not calculative or domineering; it is based on and driven by 'Metta', compassion and consideration. It seeks to bring together, to weave in a cohesion, as Prime Minister Modi said, countries which are "like-minded and like-hearted."

India's proactive effort in laying the contours of the Buddha circuit under Prime Minister Modi's stewardship brings to mind the words and hopes of Dr. Syama Prasad Mookerjee, who, as president of the Mahabodhi Society of India in the early years of freedom, had called for preserving the Buddha legacy and heritage. "There are many holy places in India," Dr. Mookerjee had observed, "which are sanctified by their association with the life and activities of Lord Buddha and they would naturally attract pilgrims and visitors from all Buddhist countries throughout the world. I fervently hope that these places would not only be preserved and protected by our government and the peoples of India but in and around them, would develop institutions and monasteries which should become active centres of beneficent activities both in social and cultural spheres, inspiring masses of people and also attracting those who want to devote themselves to the cause of higher studies and research." Decades after that hope was evinced, Prime Minister Modi, as Dr. Syama Prasad Mookerjee's foremost heir, is fulfilling it in letter and in spirit.

The International Buddhist Summit in New Delhi, convened by the International Buddhist Confederation in April 2023, the first of its kind and inspired by Prime Minister Modi, set a new agenda for the Asian Century. It is an agenda which is driven and based on Buddha's message. The Asian Century will be shaped by India and other "like-hearted countries" and it will have, as one of its principal centres, Buddha. "Those who imagine the 21st century to be Asia's," said Prime Minister Modi, "probably forget one aspect. There can be no 21st century belonging to Asia without Buddha. There can be no 21st century without Buddha. It is Buddha only who can inspire the world..."

That Asian Century has begun taking shape and India, under Modi, is imparting it with a lasting philosophical foundation inspired by Buddha's civilizational message. An awakened collective environmental consciousness, driven by an awakened and active sense of 'climate justice', will also play a crucial role in shaping that century.

REFERENCES

Hindu-Buddhist Philosophy on Conflict Avoidance & Environmental Consciousness, New Delhi: Vivekananda International Foundation & Wisdom Tree, 2017.

Narendra Modi, *Convenient Action—Continuity for Change*, Gurgaon: Lexis Nexis, revised and expanded edition, 2015.

Lessons from Lord Buddha: a collection of speeches by Hon'ble Prime Minister Narendra Modi, New Delhi: Press Information Bureau, Government of India, 2023.

6

Many Shades of India's Climate Diplomacy

Uttam Kumar Sinha

Energy-climate Link

In an interdependent and globalised world, energy security greatly defines climate agenda. Not only does energy security depend on how states manage their relations with one another but also how they come to terms with stability of energy supply, its affordability, and environmental sustainability. Together, it constitutes what is described as a 'trilemma'. Searching for alignment or compatibility between the three (stability, affordability, and sustainability) is a policy nightmare. We also know, dreadfully so, that climate crisis is one of the greatest challenges of the 21st century. The crisis refers to long-term shifts in temperatures and weather patterns. Energy sources from fossil fuels (coal, oil, and gas) are the largest contributors to global warming and climate shifts, accounting for over 75 per cent of global greenhouse gas emissions and nearly 90 per cent of all carbon dioxide emissions.[1]

Nations are seen to be getting their act together and weighing in their priorities in dealing with fossil fuel-linked climate consequences. For example, the Paris Climate Agreement in 2015[2] was a success because of its universal acceptance. Such unanimity is unprecedented, and was last seen in 1945 when the world signed the UN Charter. Recently, the idea of achieving net zero emissions[3] with over 90 countries, to date, having communicated their 'net zero targets' is impressive. However, achieving carbon neutrality without ensuring energy security is unproductive. The energy sector holds the key to responding to climate challenges. Even the most reluctant, are conceding that clean energy, as part of climate action, is not only smart for the planet but is smart for businesses as well. Already the big players in the Paris Agreement—China, the European Union, India and Johnny-come-lately, the USA, have moved forward with plans to meet their climate targets and energy policies. The actions of the 'Big Four' are significantly important as they constitute two-thirds of the global energy demand.

Despite the positivity, and as things stand, the world is on course for a much warmer existence. The Earth is now about 1.1°C warmer than what it was in the 1800s. According to the UN-IPCC 6th Assessment Report (March 2023), the planet will breach the threshold of 1.5 °C above pre-industrial levels (average temperature between 1850 and 1900) by 2040 and there is a 50 per cent chance that the world may temporarily breach 1.5 °C of warming in one of the next five years. As many as 3.6 billion people or 45 per cent of the world population live in areas of high vulnerability to climate change impacts such as droughts, floods, heat waves, extreme weather events and sea-level rise.

India's Climate Diplomacy

India's climate diplomacy combines the civilization and heritage reflected in its ancient texts. It has intellectual and philosophical sophistication. For example, there is the Sanskrit word *Vasudeva Kutumbakam* (the world is one family) and the principle of a *Dharma*-based society where the strong protect the weak, where giving precedes taking and where ecology is sustained and nurtured. And, last but not the least, it has, in contemporary times, a global outreach suggesting collective action and partnership.

Beginning with the UN Conference on the Human Environment at Stockholm in 1972, India set three fundamental narratives. First, the rich versus poor debate in which India called for paying attention to poor nations and arguing strongly that over-population was an 'over-simplification' of the climate problem.[4] India forcefully argued that rich 'North' countries with a small population consumed the bulk of natural resources. Second, India argued for a global solution, since environment issues were interlinked and there was no alternative to a cooperative approach. Third, it lent a credible voice to the developing countries or the 'Global South' by reminding the rich industrialised countries of their levels of prosperity and pollution as an outcome of their past colonial exploitation. It strongly built the narrative of under-development as the cause of climate change and simultaneously called out the industrialised countries for their lack of sincerity in dealing with the issue. It set the North-South debate in global environmental politics.

Interestingly, the Stockholm Conference gave birth to the United Nations Environment Programme (UNEP), a "global authority for the environment with programmes focusing on climate, nature, pollution, sustainable development, and more." Kenya had strongly bid for the UNEP headquarters to be located in Nairobi. New Delhi was also being considered along with New York, London, Mexico City and a few others. In order to build a strong African connection, India threw her weight behind Kenya and eventually Nairobi became the UNEP headquarters.

One cannot discount larger foreign policy objectives and climate diplomacy as a subset of that. One foreign policy objective was to rebuild diplomatic and economic relations with African countries starting with Ethiopia, Kenya, Libya, and Nigeria that had whole-heartedly supported India during the 1962 war with China. Having supported Kenya for the UNEP headquarters, India actively sought to deepen its African relationship and its victory over Pakistan and the liberation of Bangladesh in 1971 gave India a new status and helped rebuild India's image in the eyes of African states. Furthermore, the conclusion of the Indo-Soviet treaty in 1971 and India's strong diplomacy in keeping at bay the US threatening gestures at the height of the East Pakistan crisis enabled India to regain its anti-imperialist image. All these developments helped re-establish India's geo-strategic presence in Africa.

At the Rio Earth Summit in 1992, the agenda of 'equity and climate justice', became the negotiating foundation of India's policymakers. India recognised global warming but minced no words in expressing the problem and the solution as unequal. The historical responsibility of developed countries in carbon emissions during their respective drives for 'industrialization' and 'development' became the principal discourse articulated as 'common but differentiated responsibility and respective capability'.

The per capita emission became a strong and convincing argument. India's carbon emission even today is about one-third of global emissions. At 2.4 tCO_2e (tonne carbon dioxide equivalent), India's per capita greenhouse gas emissions are far below the world average of 6.3 tCO_2e. Per capita emissions in the USA (14 tCO_2e) are far above the global average, followed by Russia (13 tCO_2e), China (9.7 tCO_2e), Brazil and Indonesia (around 7.5 tCO_2e each), and the European Union (7.2 tCO_2e). "No climate crisis would exist if the world's per capita emissions were equal."[5]

However, at the 2009 Copenhagen climate summit, India's climate role exhibited a voluntary reduction of its carbon emissions and changes in domestic climate policies. There were discernible changes from what can be regarded as 'hardened position' on climate negotiations in 1992, to 'conditional acceptance' in 2007, and to offering 'consultations and analysis" in 2009.

Later, at the Paris Agreement in 2015, India pledged to cut GHG emissions by 33 to 35 per cent relative to the 2005 level by 2030. At the COP26 in Glasgow in 2021, Prime Minister Narendra Modi further pledged to cut emissions to net-zero by 2070, by reducing carbon emissions 1 billion tonnes by 2030 and also sharing 50 per cent of renewable energy among others.

Modi's Holism

Prime Minister Modi strongly comes across as a problem-solving leader and has consistently based his vision on a holistic approach–'how to think' rather than 'what to think'. The energy sector is a testimony to such innovative thinking and practical implementation, and forms a critical pillar of Modi's climate diplomacy, which in turn is an important subset of his foreign policy. Some broad strands are observable:

- Emphasis on multilateralism
- Maintaining peace and security
- Domestic actions and global ambition
- International climate-energy cooperation

Taking these broad strands together can potentially transform new challenges into opportunities. The energy sector, in particular, becomes an effective tool to commit to the functioning of an international climate regime. The crucial element of India's climate diplomacy under Modi, as can be observed, is that it prioritises climate action both in the domestic context as well as with external players.

A good way to analyse this is by using Robert Putnam's two-level game approach. He writes, "Domestic politics and international relations are often somehow entangled.... It is fruitless to debate whether domestic politics really determine international relations or the reverse. The answer to that is clearly both sometimes. The more interesting questions are 'when?' and 'how?'"[6]

What has made India change its climate approach, how do India's domestic policies weigh in global climate governance, what is India's political leadership investment on climate. Before explaining the four Ds of Prime Minister Modi's climate diplomacy (De-escalating global tension, Digitalisation, De-carbonsisation and Democratisation of climate action), the following section will briefly capture India's climate pledge.

India's climate action and environmental protection is constitutionally derived. Article 48A states that India shall "endeavour to protect and improve the environment" and "safeguard forests and wildlife". In 2002, the COP8 meeting in New Delhi adopted the Delhi Ministerial Declaration, which called for developed countries to transfer technology needed to cutemissions and adapt to climate change to developing countries. This is a key priority for India's climate diplomacy. The issue of fairness or equity remains a strong concern. In 2006, the National Environment Policy aimed to integrate environmental protection into the development process. A few years later, the PM Council on national action plan for climate change was set up bringing climate change issues as a high priority concern to the attention of the top leadership. Globally, India is part of four negotiating blocs on climate talks. These are BASICS, a coalition of the four major emerging economies (Brazil, South Africa, and China); the like-minded developing countries (LMDC); the G77+China; and the Coalition for Rainforest Nations (CfRN).

During Modi's first term, India ratified the Paris Agreement choosing Gandhi Jayanti (2 October 2016) to do so. It came almost exactly a year after it submitted its climate pledge, or "nationally determined contribution" (NDC). The pledge is for a 33-35 per cent reduction in emissions associated with each unit of economic output (emissions intensity) by 2030, compared to 2005 levels. It further outlines plans to increase tree cover to create an additional cumulative carbon sink of 2,500-3,000 $MtCO_2e$ by 2030—roughly on par with its total emissions across one year.

While the domestic actions show commitment and sincerity, it also forewarns the inadequate response of developed countries to global warming. The message is clear, "India, even though not a part of the problem, has been an active and constructive participant in the search for solutions,"[7] India is clear that implementation of its climate pledge will depend heavily on climate finance, technology transfer, and capacity building support from developed countries. In all, it estimates it will need at least $2.5 trillion up to 2030, from both domestic and international funds.

4 Ds

De-escalating Global Tension

Sustainable peace and security is important for climate stability. The visceral images of environmental cost of war and conflict are instructive. The defence sector across the world is the largest institutional consumer of oil and thus tops the list of GHG emitters. Air pollution from war zones adversely affects public health. Investing in peace and security means investing in climate action. In the midst of the Ukranian conflict, when Prime Minister Modi met Russian President Vladimir Putin and said "Today's era is not of war" it was not one of criticism of Putin's action but of understanding the value of peace and prosperity.

India has emerged as a diplomatic power reaching out to countries in all directions and establishing in the process that a world of 'multiple poles' gives greater choices—an equidistant diplomacy. While this seems to be a sensible strategy requiring great skills in a competitive international system with cross-cutting fissures, it can also rebound.

That said, there is self-confidence in India's diplomatic approach. With political stability, electoral delivery, and high trust of the leader, India is now a proactive global climate player. Further, India's economy is in a 'sweet spot'. Last year saw good economic growth and India is poised to grow at 6.9 per cent in 2023. The baseline growth estimate has been put at 6.5 per cent for the financial year 2024.

Again, because of rotational leadership, India has been actively taking the lead in climate matters in global formations like BRICS in 2022, G20 in 2023 along with chair of the SCO. Under its G20 leadership, India is setting the theme for "human-centric globalisation".

The G20 members represent around 80-85 per cent of the global GDP, over 75 per cent of the global trade, and about 60 per cent of the world population. They are responsible for 75-80 per cent of global GHG emissions (in absolute terms). All but one (Iran) of the top ten carbon emitting countries are G20 members. At the same time, the G20 economies account for the largest share of global wealth and therefore possess the financial wherewithal to spearhead the green transition required to limit the rise in global temperature to 1.5 degrees Celsius. Moreover, the G20 countries are home to many of the world's most significant carbon sinks, such as the Brazilian Amazon Rainforest, and the Sundarbans in India.

G20 countries also account for 45 per cent of the world's coastline. The emphasis on Blue Economy, which is expected to be worth USD 3 trillion by the end of the decade, is a critical area of climate diplomacy by bringing in a model of a more sustainable blue economy. India's human-centric globalisation and call for global South and North-South dialogue is a strong counter to East-West rivalry.

Digitalisation

There is a general understanding that sustainability has to be won byte-by-byte. India, like many others, is pushing for massive digitalisation as part of its ambitious Digital India plan. This revolution has also transformed diplomacy and is being referred to as DigiPlomacy. Global digitalisation is growing, and is estimated to reach USD 2.4 trillion by 2024 from the 2019 level. Early analyses suggest the benefits from digital transformation are significant, potentially reducing:

- Carbon dioxide emissions by at least 20 per cent
- The use of natural resources in products by 90 per cent
- Waste and detoxifying supply chains by a factor of 10-100X

Digitalisation is widely seen as a major bridge towards a new carbon-neutral world. India records 11 times more digital payments compared to the USA and Europe and four times more than what China does. However, there is an urgent need to focus on 'greening' the digital chain itself, right from the design stage. Experts point out that the carbon emission of the internet itself is nearly twice as much as the (pre-pandemic) airline industry and its annual water footprint is equal to one million Olympic swimming pools.

Climate ambitions cannot be met without climate finance and for that a reformed financial architecture is a prerequisite. While India has brought up an extensive public digital infrastructure and it deftly carried out the transformative paperless vaccination, there are 133 countries in the world that do not have access to basic digital mechanisms. This presents an opportunity for countries to work together with India towards digital transformation.

De-carbonisation

India has a five-point strategy to achieve net zero by 2070, which includes enhancing non-fossil energy capacity, leveraging renewable energy to generate power for meeting national energy requirements, a one billion tonne reduction in carbon emissions by 2030 and a reduction in the carbon intensity of the economy. India's de-carbonisation diplomacy can be described as 'going green and going digital'.

India has successfully built a globally competitive renewable energy industry and is looking at innovative measures to reduce capital costs for green projects such as renewables to reduce solar power prices to INR 1/unit in the next five years. India has taken a confluence of major initiatives—the production linked incentive (PLI) schemes for advanced cell chemistry (ACC) battery storage and solar panels, promotion of electric vehicles through schemes such as FAME, establishment of the International Solar Alliance, and most recently, the National Green Hydrogen Mission.

Democratising Climate Change

Relationships between democracy and, more particularly, democratization on the one side and climate change and responses to that on the other are complex. That said, Prime Minister Modi's statement at a World Bank event 'Making it personal: how behavioural change can tackle climate change'[8] is of particular interest. He said, "Individuals making the right decisions for our planet are key in the battle for our planet. This is the core of Mission LiFE". He further mentioned, "Climate change cannot be fought from conference tables alone. It has to be fought from the dinner tables in every home" and "Mission LiFE is about democratising the battle against climate change."[9]

In 2022, Modi launched the LiFE movement. As an environment-conscious lifestyle, the mission enhances the idea of 'pro-planet people' (P3), while simultaneously reinforcing Mahatma Gandhi's environment trusteeship, which claims 'The Earth, the air, the land and the water are not an inheritance from our forefathers but on loan from our children.' While addressing climate change requires national and international action; communities, households, and individuals have a vital role to play too. One could argue that LiFE is a typical diversionary by putting the onus on the individual and absolving the government of its role. Where does the responsibility lie has been a recurring debate in the relationship between the state and its people. Clearly both are needed—system change and lifestyle change.

Some analyses in fact point out that lifestyle carbon footprints need to be reduced by 91-95 per cent by 2050 in high-income countries, compared with 76 per cent in lower-middle income countries, that could account for a quarter of the emission reductions required to keep the global heating down to 1.5°C.

What India leadership is positing is a redefinition of human life and values. Individuals matter and they are important in affecting change by making choices about protecting the environment. The LiFE expression is simple: If democracy can work because of people's participation, then so can environment action, and since humans collectively have damaged the environment, then logically they can equally fix it in other words, 'mindful and deliberate utilisation' instead of 'mindless and wasteful consumption'.

Central to LiFE, indisputably, is reining runaway consumption. Consumption patterns also reflect inequality between the developed, emerging economies and the developing world. However, there is one common factor and that is the high-consuming lifestyle-linked greenhouse gas emissions of the rich and wealthy across the world. Addressing the way the affluent live by utilising the carbon emission space is fundamental to allowing everyone equitable opportunities for a life of dignity. Calculations show that the emissions share of the top 1 per cent highest-income earners is greater than the total emissions of the bottom 50 per cent combined.

To reach a 'fair consumption space' a number of government actions like easing subsidies for fossil fuels and tax incentives on low carbon technologies along with increasing the prices of carbon-intensive products and activities can be considered and several policies have already been undertaken. Individual actions that are neither expensive nor reducing well-being can be initiated based on environmental consciousness and choice. A number of studies and survey indicate that there are several behavioural shifts at the individual level; for example a plant-base diet without wasting food, reducing buying of clothing every year, upgrading light bulbs, recycling, extending the use of electrical and electronic items, optimising public transport and holding on to personal vehicles longer. Another environment conscious approach is to trade-off individual carbon footprints. For example, if one is using personal cars, then a good practice would be to offset it by other low-carbon emission action like moving to green energy. Even if at least one carbon-reducing specific action is taken at an individual level, the impact collectively will help fight climate change.

Conclusion

India's climate diplomacy is credible, legitimate, and salient. It can be seen as a constructivist outlook of reality determined by its interactions, interpretations and experiences, as well as functionalism that calls for cooperation and coordination amongst states. From being reluctant to even rigid in its early climate positioning, it has now, under Prime Minister Modi, taken a proactive climate leadership role that bolsters its larger foreign policy objectives and strengthens its domestic requirements.

ENDNOTES

1. United Nations, 'Causes of climate change', see https://www.un.org/en/climatechange/science/causes-effects-climate-change#:~:text=Causes%20of%20Climate%20Change&text=Generating%20electricity%20and%20heat%20by,and%20trap%20the%20sun's%20heat
2. The central aim of the Paris Agreement is to strengthen the global response to the threat of climate change by keeping a global temperature rise in this century well below 2 degrees Celsius above pre-industrial levels and to pursue efforts to limit the temperature increase even further to 1.5 degrees Celsius. Additionally, the agreement aims to increase the ability of countries to deal with the impacts of climate change, and at making finance flows consistent with low GHG emissions and a climate-resilient pathway. To reach these ambitious goals, appropriate mobilization, and provision of financial resources, a new technology framework and enhanced capacity-building is to be put in place, thus supporting action by developing countries and the most vulnerable countries, in line with their own national objectives. The Agreement also provides for an enhanced transparency framework for action and support. See https://unfccc.int/most-requested/key-aspects-of-the-paris-agreement
3. According to UN Climate Actions, "Net zero means cutting greenhouse gas emissions to as close to zero as possible, with any remaining emissions re-absorbed from the atmosphere, by oceans and forests for instance." See, https://www.un.org/en/climatechange/net-zero-coalition
4. Indira Gandhi, former prime minister of India, attended the Stockholm Conference in 1972, the only woman and head of government to do so. In her speech, she raised the question, "Are not poverty and need the greatest polluters?"
5. Bhupender Yadav's statement at COP27 in Egypt, 18 November 2022.
6. Robert Putnam, "Diplomacy and Domestic Politics: The Logic of Two-Level Games", *International Organisation*, 2(3), 1988.
7. India's Intended Nationally Determined Contribution, 15 October 2015.
8. The World Bank event was held on 15 April 2023.
9. Prime Minister Modi's video message on 15 April 2023. https://pib.gov.in/PressReleaseIframePage.aspx?PRID=1916725

ENERGY STRATEGY

7

India's Pursuit of Energy Security: Potential and Prospects

Arvind Kumar

The significant developments recorded in human history have, in one way or the other, been linked to better pathways to produce and use energy. The unbridled incessant human quest for developing new sources of energy along with the benefits accruing thereof has proved instrumental in bringing humankind currently to a crossroads. The 'benefits-outweighing-the-damages' approach to energy has spurred multiple problems relating to climate change that, inter alia, comprise greenhouse gas (GHG) emissions that are problem-multipliers and trigger the depletion of natural resources like coal, crude oil, and natural gas. The requirements of an exponentially growing population now outstrip the ability of Planet Earth to meet those needs. Various reports published by the Intergovernmental Panel on Climate Change (IPCC) have frequently warned that unabated emission of GHG gases entails the potential of enhancing the likelihood of severe, pervasive, and irreversible impact for the people and ecosystems.

New records set in 2021 by the four key drivers of climate change—greenhouse gas concentrations, sea-level rise, ocean heat, and ocean acidification—indicate that anthropogenic activities are triggering planetary-level changes on land, in the ocean, and in the atmosphere, entailing intense and long-lasting ramifications (WMO, 2022). There is an increasingly growing thinking that tackling the climate change crisis direly needs to end human dependence on energy generated from fossil fuels like coal, crude oil, and natural gas. Being at the heart of the climate challenge, if energy is the cause of the climate crisis, it is the key to the solution as well. Fossil fuels are by far the biggest contributors to global climate change, accounting for 75 per cent of global greenhouse gas emissions and about 90 per cent of all carbon dioxide emissions. Avoidance of the worst adverse impacts of climate change warrants reduction of emissions by almost half by 2030 and reaching net-zero by 2050. This is being facilitated, albeit gradually, by ending reliance on fossil fuels and switching over to alternative sources of energy—renewable energy sources that are clean, affordable, sustainable, and reliable.

Undoubtedly, fossil fuels still reign supreme in the realm of energy with more than 80 per cent of energy production worldwide; nevertheless, cleaner sources of energy are gaining global traction, and about 30 per cent of electricity is reported to be currently generated from renewable resources. Renewable energy sources—the sun, wind, water, waste, and heat from the Earth—are available in plenty, are replenished by nature, and emit negligible-to-no greenhouse gases or pollutants into the air. The increasing use of renewables has undeniably started to transform the global energy landscape in an irretrievable way.

Concept of Energy Security

Apart from being vital to human existence, energy is one of the essential components for economic growth, and as such, energy and economic development are interlinked. An incessant and hassle-free supply of energy is indispensable to keep up the momentum of economic growth. In other words, energy security is very crucial for economic development. Energy security entails four dimensions—availability; accessibility; affordability; and acceptability (Yao and Chang, 2014). These dimensions entail further three categories that comprise three main aspects of energy security—physical energy security, economic energy security, and environmental sustainability. Physical energy security embraces both the availability and accessibility dimensions, such as the availability of electricity supply to meet immediate requirements or the availability of a specific fuel resource as input for electricity generation (Gyamfi et al., 2015). Economic energy security focuses on the affordability of energy resources like the cost per unit of electricity generation, etc., and environmental sustainability entails the acceptability dimension, especially the impacts of energy on issues pertaining to the environment like greenhouse gas emissions accruing from the utilization of a specific fuel resource (Kruyt et al., 2009).

The concept of energy security entails multi-faceted perspectives on defining energy security, unfolding almost unanimously on the complications inherent in such definition-building. An extensive meta-study of diverse energy security approaches by Ang et al. (2015) culminates in the conclusion that there exists no widely accepted definition of energy security in terms of a narrowly defined construct. On the basis of their findings, the authors envisage the emergence of five dominant themes pertaining to energy security—securing energy availability; securing energy infrastructure; securing the affordability of energy supplies; societal aims such as the eradication of energy poverty; environmental security and sustainability; energy security governance; and the improvement of energy efficiency—and the call for a more comprehensive conceptualization of energy security is given by von Hippel and colleagues (2011) who argue that security of supply is one of many pillars that also embrace economic, technological, environmental, socio-cultural and military security dimensions. Nevertheless, the incorporation of three additional challenges of human security, international implications, and state capacity to execute particular energy security policies is suggested by Vivoda (2010). Furthermore, more recent approaches have come to emphasize on the obvious linkage between energy security and sustainability (Narula, 2019).

The notion of energy security has come to be construed in terms of the uninterrupted availability of energy sources at an affordable price (IEA, 2021). In other words, energy insecurity can crop up either on account of the interruption of energy supply or sudden price fluctuations entailing the potential of rendering supply unaffordable. According to Chester (2010), this sort of conceptualization of energy security comprises two main traits: (a) a narrow focus on the security of oil and natural gas as two key sources of energy, and (b) applying this conceptualization of energy security as the mainstay of geopolitical and foreign policy decision-making. This elaboration of the notion of energy security is said to be compatible with the 4 As of energy security—Availability of energy resources; Accessibility; Acceptability of associated environmental impacts; and Affordability of investment (Asia Pacific Energy Research Centre, 2007). Application of the logic of key security questions—security for whom, for which values, and from what threats—by Cherp and

Jewell (2014) has facilitated the problematisation of the 4 As approach, and these authors opine that energy security conceptualizations answering these questions are prone to entail the potential of explaining and informing policy options. For the purpose of the present paper, the definition of energy security as envisaged by IEA (2021) is deemed appropriate.

Geopolitical Aspects of Energy Security

The geopolitics of energy is an endeavour to explore the intersection of energy, security, and international politics. It is an attempt to discern how energy demand and supply influence international politics and vice versa. Both conventional and alternative sources of energy influence and get influenced by geopolitical realities. It is a widely recognized fact that energy has long shaped the international system, determining the alliance of the great powers, and outcomes of wars. If decisions pertaining to energy taken today will influence what the world looks like tomorrow, in an identical way, the political and security events of today will mould the energy realities of tomorrow.

Until a few years ago, the emphasis was on the geopolitical tensions engendered by fossil fuel scarcity and the probability of peak oil supply (Klare, 2012); nevertheless, a dramatic transformation has taken place in current times in the global energy landscape and energy geopolitics. Undeniably, humankind currently has inherited a world of relative fossil fuel abundance, which has become a primary challenge in the wake of increasing emphasis on reducing consumption of fossil fuel and speeding deployment of low carbon technologies, along with energy demand reduction and emphasis on energy efficiency. In the wake of these developments, the global focus of attention is increasingly shifting to the geopolitics of renewable energy. There has emerged an unorthodox 'whole systems' approach to take into account the geopolitical dimensions of the required energy system transformation (EST), and this transformation is specified as a twofold process, which is focused on transition in fuel supply—emphasis on low-carbon non-fossil energy sources, and a 'high-carbon transition' that envisages a diminution in demand for fossil fuels. Viewed in a broad perspective, a more thorough understanding of the convoluted relations between the constituent elements of EST is facilitated by the 'whole systems' approach, rather than concentrating on only a specific aspect like oil in the past or renewables today.

Geopolitics in common parlance is delineated as a study of the relationship between geography and the international politics of great powers, and during the Cold War, geopolitics was construed in terms of the contest between the then superpowers for influence and control over states and resources (O' Tuathail, 1998); in the post-Cold War period of the twenty-first century, conventional geopolitics has remained predominantly focused on unearthing and examining the role of geopolitical factors like territorial location and access to resources, in influencing national and international politics (Hogselius, 2019:7). Interestingly, conventional geopolitics still continues to wield its influence in the domain of energy geopolitics, and Bradshaw (2009: 1920) has delineated energy geopolitics as 'the influence of geographical factors, such as the distribution of centres of supply and demand, on state and non-state actions to ensure an adequate, affordable, and reliable supply of energy.' In the aftermath of the oil shocks of the 1970s, competition and rivalry over fossil fuel resources, especially oil, has often dominated the narrative in conventional geopolitics. Besides, disputes and tensions in regions endowed with abundant oil reserves—the Persian Gulf, the Caspian, and the Arctic—along with chokepoints such as the Strait of Hormuz and the Straits of Malacca have also been the focal points of conventional geopolitics. Nevertheless, the coal market having been largely confined to the domestic realm, has failed to emerge as the focal point. The current discourse is on the geopolitics of renewables that warrants recognition of energy as more diverse and demonstrates how geo-technical traits of different energy sources entail the potential of having political repercussions (Criekemans, 2018). Nonetheless, conventional state-centric and realist approaches to energy geopolitics still rule the roost, and many scholarly works have focused on such aspects. For example, Scholten (2018: 8) only takes into account interstate (renewable) energy relations, while Vakulchuk et al. (2020) focus on great power competition over access to strategic locations and natural resources.

Modern scholarship on geopolitics emphasizes the emergence of the field of critical geopolitics wherein geopolitics is best construed as a social construction that is reiterated through diverse and competing narratives of state and non-state actors (Dalby, 2008; Dodds, 2019). The 'whole systems' approach to geopolitics affords a synthesis of the critical and conventional strands of geopolitics, contending that geographic arrangements are prone to alter overtime, subject to politico-economic and socio-technological change. This creates room for more extensive ascertainment of the complex relationship between changing energy systems, geography, and international politics. Fast forward to 2030, the emerging new energy order is forecasting a world after oil, though still decades away, and the energy systems transformation entails the potential of addressing the existential threat of extreme climate change.

Geo-economic Aspects of Energy Security

The construal of geo-economics as the intersection of economics and finance with worldwide political and security considerations spurs the investigation of mechanisms of interaction between politics and economics that help actors exert power and influence in the context of geographical spaces. The ongoing process of energy transition from fossil fuels to renewables has seemingly been instrumental in triggering a fast shift of focus from the geopolitics of energy to the geo-economics of energy. A vast majority of countries, including some developed countries, have to spend a bulk part of their domestic budgets on importing fossil fuels along with providing subsidies domestically to keep up the momentum of economic growth, thereby causing a substantial drain on financing other development activities. Broad estimates by IPCC (2018) reveal that an annual investment of $ 2.4 trillion is required in the energy sector alone until 2035 to limit temperature rise to below 1.5^0 C from pre-industrial levels. According to IMF estimates, global fossil fuel subsidies were to the tune of $ 5.9 trillion in 2020, accounting for 6.8 per cent of GDP, which is expected to rise to 7.4 per cent of global GDP by 2025. This demonstrates the uneconomical nature of the use of fossil fuels aside from the environmental damages caused by them.

Relatively, the increasing use of renewable energy resources is cost-effective with almost negligible or zero emissions. Two-thirds of 163 gigawatts (GW) of newly-installed renewable power in 2021 incurred lower costs than the world's cheapest coal-fired option in G-20 countries. There has been a continued fall in the costs of renewables in 2021—the cost of electricity from onshore wind fell by 15 per cent, offshore wind by 13 per cent, and solar PV by 13 per cent compared to 2020. In the wake of current high fossil fuel prices, the renewable power harnessed in 2021 entails the likelihood of saving nearly $55 billion from global energy generation costs in 2022 (IRENA, 2022). The critical role played by cost-competitive renewables in addressing contemporary global energy climate emergencies by speeding up the energy transition line in consonance with the goals of the 2015 Paris Agreement suggests the importance of geo-economics of energy over the geopolitics of energy.

Besides, a vast majority of the global population, about 80 per cent, inhabit countries that are net importers of fossil fuels, which renders them vulnerable to geopolitical shocks and crises, as happened recently in the wake of the outbreak of hostilities between Russia and Ukraine that led to a tremendous spike in prices of fossil fuels. Nevertheless, renewable energy sources are available in all countries across the globe that can be harnessed to meet growing energy demands without external geopolitical pressures.

India's Energy Diplomacy

Energy diplomacy is defined as 'the use of foreign policy to secure access to energy supplies abroad and to promote (mostly bilateral, that is, government-to-government) cooperation in the energy sector' (Goldthau, 2012). India, currently the world's second most populous country and set to become the most populous country surpassing China by 2024, has a major presence on the global stage. India is one of the world's fastest-growing economies and the fifth largest economy in the world, wherein the energy sector has come to play a very crucial role in keeping up the trajectory of growth in India ongoing. India's energy demand has risen from 4 per cent of the global total to over 7 per cent recently and the growth in the economy is prone to fuel demand for more energy warranting more than 10 per cent of the global energy per year to double by 2040 (IEA, 2021). India's energy mix of primary energy comprises fossil fuels accounting for 90 per cent and the remaining 10 per cent consists of nuclear and renewable resources. India still imports 80 per cent of its crude oil from the Middle East, Central Asia and other countries and the import of crude oil by India is likely to increase to 90 per cent soon. Primary energy consumption in India registered an increase of 6 per cent in 2021 as compared to 2020 (BP, 2022).

India's energy diplomacy, a vital component of India's foreign policy, aims at ensuring energy security for the country. For this purpose, public sector oil and gas companies are encouraged to actively pursue equity oil and gas opportunities overseas by seeking engagement with foreign countries and international organizations in the hydrocarbon sector in a sustained manner. India has fostered active engagement in bilateral and multilateral cooperation with countries concerned. Encouraging PSUs in the oil and gas sector to develop a global vision in their pursuit of hydrocarbon assets to facilitate the strengthening of India's energy security underlines the major emphasis of India's energy diplomacy. Making investments in other countries and creating a mutually beneficial relationship is another characteristic of this energy diplomacy. This strategy of making investments abroad aims at acquiring quality oil and gas assets that paves the way for fetching equity oil to the country along with affording opportunities to Indian companies to work with global majors in the sector. The USA and its allies immediately imposed sanctions on Russia after armed hostilities between Russia and Ukraine broke out in the final week of February 2022, focusing on the country's financial sector. Early in April 2022, the USA tightened its sanctions by imposing full-blockade measures to cut off Russia from international trade and exports, particularly energy. However, India's diplomatic efforts were successful in getting a waiver from these sanctions so that it could import cheap Russian crude oil. Before February 2022, India's import of Russian crude oil was almost negligible, but it suddenly experienced a quantum jump of about five times, and in February and March 2022, India's imports of crude oil from Russia reached a record 1.6 million barrels per day; in the first few months of 2023, they exceeded the combined imports of crude oil from Iraq and Saudi Arabia. Currently, India purchases about 35 per cent of its imported crude oil from Russia, and India is exporting refined products (Dey, 2023).

The International Cooperation (IC) division of the Union Ministry of Petroleum and Natural Gas is entrusted with the task of strengthening India's energy security by sustaining and promoting engagements with foreign countries and global organizations in the oil and gas sector. While facilitating Indian PSUs in the oil and gas sector to aggressively explore opportunities for acquiring equity oil and gas assets overseas, the IC Division also encourages companies to diversify oil and gas sources to ensure the maintenance of a balanced portfolio (MoP&NG, 2022). India's active energy diplomacy has enabled India to emerge as the focal point in the realm of oil and gas as the third largest energy consumer in the world and to assert its market influence in the global arena to re-order the prevalent anomalies in the global energy markets.

India's Energy Transition

With the establishment of the Ministry of New and Renewable Energy at the Centre in the early 1980s, India had commenced its embarkation on the path of energy transition, and the installation of wind power plants in Maharashtra, Gujarat, and Tamil Nadu in 1986 had helped the country reaching total wind power installed capacity of 13 GW by 2010. The first solar power plant was installed in Punjab in 2009. The involvement of the private sector in power generation from renewable sources from 2003 onwards proved instrumental in eliciting foreign investment along with the participation of global players and large-scale FDI inflows in large non-conventional energy projects.

However, India's current energy scenario continues to be dominated by fossil fuels, as shown in Table 1, which reveals that the share of fossil fuels in power generation is almost about 60 per cent and non-fossil fuel resources contribute about 40 per cent. Keeping in consonance with its commitments under the 2015 Paris Agreement, India pledged to reduce the greenhouse gas emissions intensity of its GDP by 33 per cent to 35 per cent by 2030 relative to 2005, for which it has to abandon burning coal that contributes to global warming.

Table 1: Installed Power Generation Capacity (Fuel-wise) in India as on 22 July 2022

Category	*Installed Generation Capacity (MW)*	*% of share in Total*
Fossil Fuels		
Coal	204,080	50.7
Lignite	6,620	1.6
Gas	24,856	6.2
Diesel	510	0.1
Total Fossil Fuels	236,065	58.5
Non-Fossil Fuels		
Hydro	46,850	11.6
Wind	40,788	10.1
Solar	57,706	14.3
BM Power/Cogen	10,206	2.5
Waste to Energy	477	0.1
Small Hydro Power	4,888	1.2
Nuclear	6,780	1.7
Total Non-Fossil Fuels	167, 694	41.5

Source: Compiled from Ministry of Power (Government of India). (2022). Power Sector at a Glance, 22 July 2022. Available online at: https://powermin.gov.in/en/content/power-sector-glance-all-india

Accordingly, in 2017, India announced that it would enhance the share of natural gas in the energy mix to 15 per cent by 2030, and as of September 2021, natural gas comprised 6.5 per cent of the energy mix. Natural gas was considered as a 'transition fuel' in India's quest for harnessing renewable resources as the main power source to meet its energy needs and phasing out fossil fuel use. Besides, the nascent stage of development of renewable resources for power generation, their intermittent nature and heavy dependence on weather conditions are seemingly other significant factors that have propelled India to use natural gas as a 'transit fuel' till it manages to have a completely renewable-energy-based economy.

A draft LNG policy formulated by the Ministry of Petroleum and Natural Gas in February 2020 aims at developing the country's LNG infrastructure, including expanding the capacity of re-gasification plants that are capable of converting LNG back to natural gas, from the current 42.5 million tonnes per year to 70 million tonnes per year by 2030. Interestingly, in pursuance of its policy of 'One Nation One Gas Grid' announced in 2020, the Ministry of Petroleum and Natural Gas had envisaged expansion of India's LNG infrastructure, and more than 15,000 km of gas pipelines, encompassing 407 districts is scheduled to be completed by 2023 (MoP&NG, 2021). Nevertheless, India's planned enhancement in gas consumption is likely to require the country to significantly augment its imports, as domestic production has remained stagnant, and facilitate heavy investment in capital-intensive gas infrastructure, thereby exposing India 'to risks such as a carbon lock-in, stranded assets, and energy insecurity' (CAT, 2022). Thus, India needs to scale up its efforts to build its renewable energy capacity, rather than focus dependence on fossil gas, and the sooner the better.

Renewable Roadmap: Expectation and Reality

India has chartered an ambitious renewable roadmap for itself. While keeping in view India's steadfast commitment to the goals of the 2015 Paris Agreement and its pledge at the COP 26 summit in November 2021 to attain net-zero emission by 2070, India is firmly committed to considerably reducing its dependence on fossil fuels and is accelerating the process of switching over to non-fossil fuel resources. Hoping to achieve an installed non-fossil fuel electricity capacity of 500 GW by 2030, India is also contemplating to decrease its carbon emission by one billion tonnes by halting operations in the ongoing coal-based power plants. India set a target in August 2021 of achieving 300 GW of solar energy by 2030.

Solar energy can be expected to be the biggest contributor to the energy requirements of India in the near future in view of the fast pace of progress it has registered in recent years as can be observed from Figure 1.

Figure 1: Growth in India's Solar Power (in GW)

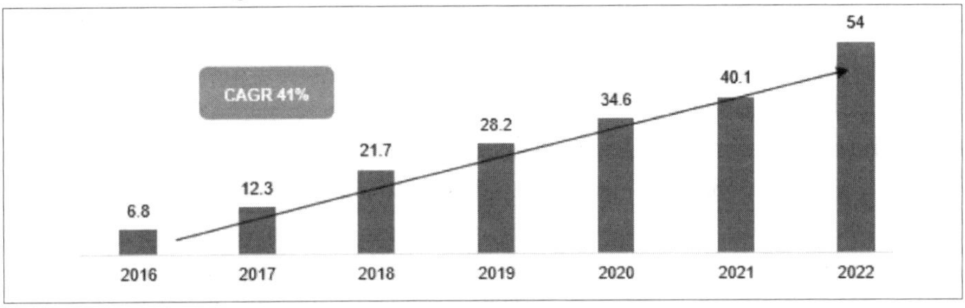

Source: IBEF (India Brand Equity Foundation). (2022). India's Energy Transition and Innovation Collaboration. Available online at: https://www.ibef.org/blogs/india-s-energy-transition-and-innovation-collaboration.

The priority accorded by the Modi Government to renewable energy has proven instrumental in envisaging a rapid increase in the country's installed solar power capacity from 2016 onwards, as shown in Figure 1. India's total solar capacity, which was 500 MW in 2011, increased to about 6.8 GW in 2016 and this capacity almost doubled every year in subsequent years. Total solar installed capacity, which stood at 28.2 GW in 2019, had increased to 54 GW as of March 2022, thereby ranking India among the top five global players, and recording a CAGR of 41 per cent in solar installation during the eight years of the Modi government.

Similarly, in wind energy also, India has recorded impressive progress in recent years. India, which had a cumulative wind power generation capacity of 1.17 GW, has registered rapid strides in wind power generation capacity over the years, and as of March 2022, as shown in Figure 2, India's wind power generation capacity stood at 40.4 GW, thereby recording a CAGR of 17.5 per cent.

Figure 2: Growth of Wind Power in India (in GW)

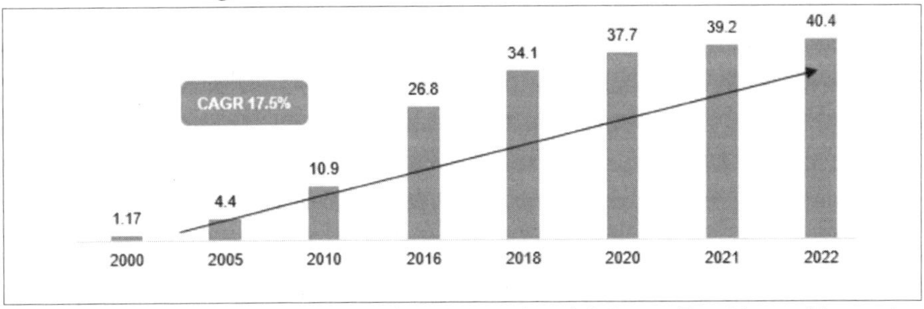

Source: IBEF (India Brand Equity Foundation). (2022). India's Energy Transition and Innovation Collaboration. Available online at: https://www.ibef.org/blogs/india-s-energy-transition-and-innovation-collaboration.

Adoption of progressive policies focusing on international collaboration and cooperation by the Modi government during the past eight years has enabled India to attract FDI and technology expertise from abroad along with the adoption of domestic policies emphasizing incentives to ensure ease of doing business for independent power producers and private global players. India signed a partnership agreement in January 2022 with the International Renewable Agency (IRENA) to strengthen its collaboration for renewable energy development in the country. India has also collaborated with the United States, European Union (EU), Italy, ASEAN, Israel, UAE, and others to invite investments along with technical expertise in its renewable energy sector.

The Way Forward

Irrespective of the fact that India ranks amongst the countries with high pollution levels and entailing a relatively high CO_2 intensity in its energy system, India still offers optimum hope of fulfilling its targets in consonance with the goals of the 2015 Paris Agreement and its commitment to achieve the net-zero goal by 2070 in the wake of the significant strides made by India in improving energy access in recent years along with sound regulations and political commitment towards energy transition (WEF, 2022).

REFERENCES

Ang, B.W.; Choong, W.L. and Ng, T.S. (2015). 'Energy security: Definitions, dimensions and indexes'. *Renewable and Sustainable Energy Reviews*. 42: 1077–1093.

Asia Pacific Energy Research Centre. (2007). 'A quest for energy security in the 21st century: Resources and constraints'. Available online at: https://aperc.or.jp/file/2010/9/26/APERC_2007_A_Quest_for_Energy_Security.pdf

BP (British Oil and Gas Company) (2022). *BP Statistical Review of World Energy 2022*. London: BP.

Bradshaw, M.(2009). 'The geopolitics of global energy security'. *Geography Compass*. 3(5): 1920–1937.

CAT (Climate Action Tracker). (2022). 'Natural Gas in India: A pathway towards reducing India's dependence on gas'. Available online at: https://climateactiontracker.org/documents/1050/CAT_2022-05-30_Report_NaturalGasinIndia_C6Dpm5s.pdf

Cherp, A., and Jewell, J. (2014). 'The concept of energy security: Beyond the four As'. *Energy Policy*. 75: 415–421.

Chester, L. (2010). 'Conceptualising energy security and making explicit its polysemic nature'. *Energy Policy*. 38(2): 887–895.

Criekemans, D. (2018). 'Geopolitics of the renewable energy game and its potential impact upon global power relations'. InD. Scholten (ed.), *The geopolitics of renewables*. Cham, Switzerland: Springer: 37–74.

Dalby, S.(2008). 'Imperialism, domination, culture: The continued relevance of critical geopolitics'. *Geopolitics*. 13(3):413–436.

Dey, Dipankar. (18 March 2023). millenniumpost.in, available online at: https://www.millenniumpost.in/sundaypost/in-retrospect/boomeranged-512104

Dodds, K. (2019). *Geopolitics: A very short introduction* (3rd edn). London: Oxford University Press.

Goldthau, Andreas (2012). 'A Public Policy Perspective on Global Energy Security'. *International Studies Perspective*. 13: 65-81.

Gyamfi, S.; Modjinou, M.; and Djordjevic, S. (2015). 'Improving electricity supply security in Ghana: The potential of renewable energy'. *Renewable and Sustainable Energy Reviews*. 43: 1035-1045.

Hogselius, P. (2019). *Energy and Geopolitics*. London: Routledge.

IBEF (India Brand Equity Foundation). (2022). 'India's Energy Transition and Innovation Collaboration'. Blog, ibef.org.blogs, Last accessed on 11 May 2022. Available online at: https://www.ibef.org/blogs/india-s-energy-transition-and-innovation-collaboration

IPCC (Intergovernmental Panel on Climate Change) (2018). 'Global Warming of 1.5°C. An IPCC Special Report on the impacts of global warming of 1.5°C above pre-industrial levels and related global greenhouse gas emission pathways, in the context of strengthening the global response to the threat of climate change, sustainable development, and efforts to eradicate poverty'. Available online at: https://www.ipcc.ch/site/assets/uploads/sites/2/2019/06/SR15_Full_Report_High_Res.pdf

IEA (International Energy Agency). (2021a). 'Energy security'. Available online at: http://www.iea.org/topics/energysecurit

——. (2021b). *India's Energy Outlook 2021*. Paris: IEA.

IRENA (International Renewable Energy Agency). (2022). *Renewable Power Generation Costs in 2021*. Abu Dhabi: IRENA.

Klare, M.T. (2012). *The race for what's left: The global scramble for the world's last resources*. London: Picador Publishing.

Kruyt, B.; Vuuren, D.P.V.; de Vries, H.J.M.; and Groenenberg, H. (2009). 'Indicators for energy security'. *Energy Policy*. 37: 2166–2181.

MoP&NG (Ministry of Petroleum and Natural Gas, Government of India). (2021). *Annual Report, 2020-2021*. New Delhi: MoP7NG.

——. (30 June 2022). About International Cooperation. Available online at: https://mopng.gov.in/en/international-cooperation/about-international-cooperation#:~:text=India%20is%20actively%20 engaged% 20in,to%20strengthen%20country's%20energy%20security.

Narula, K. (2019). *The maritime dimension of sustainable energy security*. Cham, Switzerland: Springer.

Ó Tuathail, G. (1998). 'Thinking critically about geopolitics'. In G.Ó. Tuathail, S. Dalby, and P. Routledge (eds.), *The Geopolitics Reader*. London: Routledge: 1–14.

Scholten, D. (ed.). (2018). *The Geopolitics of Renewables*. Cham, Switzerland: Springer.

Vakulchuk, R.; Overland, I.; and Scholten, D. (2020). 'Renewable energy and geopolitics: A Review'. *Renewable and Sustainable Energy Reviews*. 122: 109547

von Hippel, D.; Suzuki, T.; Williams, J. H.; Savage, T.; and Hayes, P. (2011). 'Energy security and sustainability in Northeast Asia'. *Energy Policy*. 39(11): 6719–6730.

Vivoda, V. (2010). 'Evaluating energy security in the Asia Pacific region: A novel methodological approach'. *Energy Policy*. 38(9): 5258–5263.

WEF (World Economic Forum). (2022). *Fostering Effective Energy Transition*. Geneva: WEF.

WMO (World Meteorological Organization). (2022). 'Four key climate change indicators break records in 2021.' *WMO Press Release*, Last accessed on 18 May 2022. Available online at: https://public.wmo.int/en/media/press-release/four-key-climate-change-indicators-break-records-2021

Yao, L. and Chang, Y. (2014). 'Energy security in China: A quantitative analysis and policy implications'. *Energy Policy*, 67: 595-604.

8

New India in a New Era: Strategy for Energy Security

Bhupendra Kumar Singh

Ensuring energy security is the topmost priority for India. It emanates from the need for continuous access of energy supply. While, for importing countries, it denotes ensuring continuous access of energy sources to sustain its commercial and economic activity, for exporting countries it means continuous access of the energy market to sell its energy products. However, for consumers it is a continuous access of energy sources at sustainable and affordable prices.

However, the COVID pandemic has altered the very notion of energy security. We are facing a challenging task to revive the Indian economy in the post COVID era. Energy sector is the backbone of the Indian economy but this sector faces many challenges. As the population is increasing and energy demand would increase in the post COVID-19 scenario coupled with increased climate change concern, producing more energy at lower cost with fewer emissions would be the primary challenge. Also, India has to develop in an energy constrained world and has to compete for global energy resources with many other developing and developed countries. Therefore, to mitigate these challenges, there is a need to come up with comprehensive, cohesive, and adoptable integrated strategies for ensuring India's energy security.

The Government of India has made its stance crystal clear on tackling these challenges with the main objective of making sustainable and clean energy accessible and affordable to all in India. It has launched various schemes to energize India under the ambient of 'Atmanirbhar Bharat'. They are as follows:

Oil and Gas

Pradhan Mantri Ujjwala Yojana (PMUY): In 2016, Prime Minister Narendra Modi launched PMUY to provide clean cooking fuel to deprived households in rural areas. The main objective of the scheme was to provide free LPG connections to deprived rural households in order to safeguard rural women's health and the environment. Under the scheme, the set target was to make available 8 crore LPG connections to rural households by 2020. The target has already been achieved in 2019 and this has helped the government in increasing LPG coverage from 62 per cent to 99.8 per cent in 2016-2021. Recently, Ujjwala 2.0 has been introduced in which the target is to achieve an additional 1 crore LPG connections and this time special preference has been given to migrant families. The social impact that PMUY has created, in empowering women through better health outcomes, reducing their poverty, and giving opportunities for economic activities, proved this scheme to be a successful one.

National Policy on Biofuels 2018: The Union Cabinet approved the National Policy on Biofuels in 2018 under the chairmanship of Narendra Modi. The aim of the policy is to mainstream the use of biofuels in the energy and transport sectors. The set targets are to achieve 20 per cent ethanol blending with petrol and 5 per cent ethanol blending with diesel by 2030. The notable features of the policy are: (i) it has divided the components of biofuels into three generations such as 1G, 2G and 3G biofuels for adequate fiscal financing to each category; (ii) expanded the raw materials by allowing the usage of sugarcane juice, starch, and sugar beet in producing ethanol; and (iii) allowing farmers to sell their surplus food production for ethanol blending with petrol. In addition to tax benefits, an estimated amount of Rs. 5,000 crore in viability gap funding scheme will be given to 2G ethanol biofuel refineries. Till 2020-21, a total of 332 crore litres of ethanol had been supplied and 8.5 per cent of blending had been done. The target of 10 per cent ethanol blending has already been achieved in 2022.

Pradhan MantriJi-Van Yojana: The scheme was approved in March 2019 for supporting integrated bio-ethanol projects financially. Under the scheme, the financial assistance of Rs. 1,969.5 crore is being allocated to setup 2G ethanol projects across the country for the period 2018-19 to 2023-24. The aim of the scheme is to improve the commercial viability of 2G ethanol production in India as well as promoting R&D and technology for the same. Four 2G bio-ethanol commercial projects of Rs. 150 crore each and one demonstration project of Rs. 15 crore, in four different states of India, have already been approved and are under construction in India.

Power

UJWAL Discom Assurance Yojana (UDAY): The Government of India launched UDAY in 2015 with an aim to provide 24x7 power to all in affordable and accessible prices. The objectives of the scheme are to support state-owned power distribution companies or DISCOMs financially and operationally and provide cost-side/revenue-side efficiency solutions. In the beginning, the scheme was supposed to go till 2019 only, but after understanding the impact and benefits it has created, the government introduced UDAY 2.0 in the Union Budget 2020-21.

Deen Dayal Upadhyay Gram Jyoti Yojana (DDUGJY): It was launched in 2014 with the aim of rural electrification and to improve transmission infrastructure for distribution of power. According to reports, 12,768,620 households have been covered under this electrification scheme. All inhabited un-electrified villages under census stand electrified as on 28 April 2018 as reported by the states. From 2014-15 to 2018-19, 18,374 un-electrified villages under census stand electrified due to DDUGJY.

Pradhan Mantri Sahaj Bijli Har Ghar Yojana 'Saubhagya': In 2017, the Government of India launched the Saubhagya Yojana with an estimated budget of Rs. 16,320 crore. The aim was to provide electricity to all non-electrified rural areas and economically poor urban households. It is considered as one of the world's biggest universal electrification initiatives. A total of 262.84 lakh households have been electrified under the scheme and states have reported 100 per cent electrification of all willing households identified before 31 March 2019.

Renewables

Recently, India submitted its updated NDC to UNFCCC, which aims at meeting 50 per cent of energy requirements from renewables, reaching non-fossil energy capacity of 500 GW by 2030, reducing the carbon intensity by 45 per cent by 2030 and achieving net zero emissions by 2070.

Pradhan Mantri Kisan Urja Suraksha Evam Utthaan Mahabiyan (PM-KUSUM): The scheme was launched in 2019 with an aim of increasing solar power generation and ensuring energy security for farmers in India to achieve India's targets of renewable energy capacity. An estimated central financial support of Rs. 34,422 crore has been set aside for this scheme. It is considered the world's largest scheme to promote clean energy in farming. The scheme is based on three components which are as follows:

- Individual renewable power plants of the capacity of 2 MW each will be installed to reach 10,000 MW of decentralized ground mounted grid connected renewable power plants.
- 17.50 lakh new standalone solar-powered agricultural pumps with capacity up to 7.5 HP each will be installed. The solarisation of 10 lakh grid-connected agricultural pumps will be done of individual pump capacity upto 7.5 HP.

Table 1: Achievements as on 30 September 2022

Total Installed Standalone Pumps (Nos)	147,367
Total Installed Solar Capacity (MW)	67.95
Total Installed Individual Pump Solar (IPS)	1,056

Source: Ministry of New and Renewable Energy, Government of India

Jawaharlal Nehru Solar Mission: The mission was launched in 2010 and has been modified twice till now as Phase II and Phase III. The main objective is to make India a global leader in solar power and to reach 100 GW of solar power by 2022. In Phase I (2010-2013) and II (2014-2017), the targets for grid connected PV (including rooftop) were 1,000 MW and 4,000-10,000 MW, respectively and the targets for off-grid solar PV applications were 200 MW and 1,000 MW, respectively. For Phase III, which commenced in 2017, the target is to make at least 25 solar parks and make ultra-solar power projects to target 40 GW of solar energy. For grid and off-grid connected solar PV, the targets are 100,000 MW and 2,000 MW, respectively.

Table 2: Targets

Phase	*Grid Connected PV (including rooftop)*	*Off-grid Solar PV Applications*
Phase I (2010-2013)	1,000 MW	200 MW
Phase II (2014-2017)	4,000-10,000 MW	1,000 MW
Phase III (2017-2022)	100,000 MW	2,000 MW

Source: IEA Database

National Wind Solar Hybrid Policy (2018): The Ministry of New and Renewable Energy introduced the National Wind-Solar Hybrid Policy in 2018. The objective of the policy was to utilize the transmission infrastructure and land by deploying efficient large grid-connected wind-solar PV hybrid systems. The policy also aims to bring less variability in renewable power generation, encouraging new technologies for improving hybrid projects and grid stability. The government has planned to support the research and development in wind-solar hybrid projects and the organizations that will help in making the hybrid system. The initiative is being taken to reach 175 GW of renewable energy capacity by 2022.

National Offshore Wind Energy Policy: Considering that India has a coastline of around 7,600 km, the Government of India introduced the National Offshore Wind Energy Policy in 2015. The policy aims to use the maritime space within the exclusive economic zone (EEZ) and work closely with state governments. The policy is responsible for seeing the overall offshore wind energy development in India. Currently, India has 24 GW of wind energy capacity. The target is to reach 30 GW of offshore wind energy by 2030.

One Sun, One World, One Grid Initiative: The One Sun, One World, One Grid (OSOWOG) is an initiative to introduce a transnational electricity grid that supplies power worldwide. The idea for this initiative was first proposed by Prime Minister Modi during the assembly of the International Solar Alliance (ISA) 2018. It aims to provide power to about 140 countries through a common grid that will ensure the transfer of clean and efficient solar power. This will, in a way, create a global system that will allow clean energy to be distributed anywhere, at any time (the power generated in one part of the world where there is day can be transmitted and used in other parts of the world where there is night).

The scheme can be divided into three main phases. In the first phase, the Indian grid would be connected to the grids of the Middle East, South Asia and South-East Asia to develop a common grid. This grid would then be used to share solar energy as per need, in addition to other renewable energy sources. The second phase would connect the functional first phase to the pool of renewable resources in Africa. The third phase would look to achieve true global interconnection. The idea will be to integrate as many countries as possible to create a single power grid of renewable energy.

Hydro

The Government of India brought a new hydroelectric policy aimed at boosting the sector, including according large hydro projects the status of renewable energy projects. According to the new policy, large hydro projects will also be designated as renewable energy projects. So far, only smaller projects of less than 25 MW in capacity were categorized as renewable energy. With the removal of this distinction, large hydro projects will be included as a separate category under the non-solar renewable purchase obligation policy. Under this policy, power purchasers will have to source a portion of electricity from large hydro projects.

Small Hydro Power Programme: The programme was started in 2017 and is still an ongoing programme in the country. The objective of the programme is to encourage states and independent private producers to set up small hydro projects in the country in the hope of realizing 21,000 MW power potential. Under the programme, IPPs have been advised to start working on projects, which should have an aggregate capacity of 1,000 MW and while achieving this amount of capacity, the next aim should be to reach at least 6,000 MW aggregate capacity by 2022. For remote and far-flung areas, the scheme is envisioned to help in setting up watermills for electrical and mechanical applications.

Electric Vehicles (EVs)

To decrease the level of pollution from the automobile sector and to encourage clean energy, the government has implemented many policies to promote the electric vehicle market in India. Electric mobility will help India in maintaining a greener environment and sustainable energy security. Enhancing electric mobility will be the key to reduce pollution and in improving the mobility infrastructure of India. The EV sales in 2020-21 was recorded at 0.32 million. Since 2011-12, over 638,000 EV registrations have been done by the Indian automobile sector. According to the Ministry of Heavy Industries, 0.52 million EV registrations have been done over the last three years. India Energy Storage Alliance (IESA) reported that the EV industry in India will grow at the compound annual growth rate of 36 per cent.[1] Fiscal incentives, investment in research and development, promoting manufacturing of EVs, demand incentives, etc., are included in these schemes.

Table 3: Targets for EV Penetration (Niti Aayog) by 2030

Vehicle Type	*% Penetration*
Buses	40%
Commercial Cars	70%
Two & Three Wheelers	80%
Private Cars	30%

Source: Niti Aayog.

National Electric Mobility Mission Plan (NEMMP): The Government of India launched NEMMP in 2013 with the aim of achieving national fuel security for India by promoting electric/hybrid vehicles. The ambitious target under the scheme was to achieve sales of 6-7 million of electric and hybrid vehicles by 2020. It was the first step towards promoting electric mobility in India. In 2013-14, approximately 20,000 hybrid and electric vehicles were sold.

Faster Adoption and Manufacturing of Electric Vehicles (FAME) India Phase I: The Government of India launched FAME India in 2015 with the aim of reducing the pollution caused by diesel/petrol vehicles and to encourage the manufacturing of electric/hybrid vehicles in India. FAME I was initiated with an outlay of Rs. 75 crore in 2015-16. The scheme envisages giving a boost to the early adoption of electric/hybrid vehicles manufacturing so that it can be presented as the first choice for buyers. This will help in decreasing the demand for petrol/diesel vehicles in the automobile sector. Under the scheme, 2.8 lakh hybrid/electric vehicles were supported through demand incentives and 425 electric and hybrid buses were deployed[2] across cities.

National Mission on Transformative Mobility and Storage: The mission was launched in 2017 keeping in view the potential of electric mobility and its benefits. The mission aims to transform the electric mobility of India by focusing on its manufacturing, fiscal incentives, R&D, regulatory framework, etc. The mission will define the measures for coordinating with the different ministries, and key stakeholders for integrated action in the electric vehicle market for a phased manufacturing plan for EVs.

Faster Adoption and Manufacturing of Electric Vehicles (FAME) India Phase II: FAME II was approved in 2019 with an outlay of Rs. 10,000 crore for a period of three years. The main objective of Phase II is to generate the demand for electric/hybrid vehicles and create a charging infrastructure across the country. It was redesigned in 2021 and extended up to 2024, which helped in increasing the sale of electric two wheelers to over 5,000 per week from 700 per week before redesigning.[3]

Table 4: Target for Electrification of Public and Shared Transportation under FAME II

Buses	40%
Vehicle Type	Target
E-buses	7,000
Electric three wheelers	500,000
Electric four wheelers	55,000
Electric two wheelers	1,000000

Source: Ministry of Heavy Industries

Till 2022, 469315 electric vehicles have been supported through the provision of demand incentives and 2,788 charging stations have been sanctioned under the scheme[4] in 68 cities across 25 states and union territories.

Focus on 'Neighbourhood First' Policy

The government has set its focus on a 'Neighbourhood First Policy', prioritizing an integrated neighbourhood. Improving connectivity among neighbours is one of the main goals under this objective. It shows the country's willingness to provide priority and support to its immediate neighbours in the form of resources, equipment, and training. Greater connectivity and integration, to improve the free flow of goods, people, energy, capital, and information is the core objective of the 'Neighbourhood First' Policy.

Act East Policy

The north-east frontier of India lies in the dynamic region of South-east Asia comprising Bhutan, Nepal, Bangladesh, and Myanmar. The economic potential of a region flagged by some vibrant economies is enormous and one would usually expect that a region like the North-east would be engaged in a healthy economic relationship with these neighbouring countries. The Government of India recently focused on the region with renewed interest for the development of the region through its Act East Policy in a way to capitalize on the unutilized potential for international trade and commerce and at the same time revitalize the region's economy.

Far East Policy

The government has also focused on seeking synergy between India's Act East Policy and Japan's 'Partnership for Quality Infrastructure' when both the countries developed a strategic deal in building high speed railways. Close collaboration between both the countries in the electricity and energy sector through measures such as the use of high-efficiency and environmentally friendly coal-fired power generation technology, and clean coal technology (CCT) has also been undertaken for the promotion of renewable energy and promotion of energy efficiency.

Focus on BIMSTEC and SASEC for expanding trade and commerce to regional and global markets with countries such as Myanmar, Bangladesh, Bhutan, Nepal, Sri Lanka and the Maldives. With reference to energy trade, India has signed power trade agreements with Bangladesh, Bhutan, and Nepal. While the prime minister's recent visit to Myanmar has encouraged further arrangements between both the countries in terms of building road connectivity and infrastructure, in the BIMSTEC region, India, Bangladesh, Bhutan, Nepal, Sri Lanka and the Maldives have come together for building strategic alliance and partnership in energy, trade and infrastructure, transportation and set regional goals.

Focus on Cross-Border Power Trade

Cross-border power trade in the Bangladesh-Bhutan-India-Nepal (BBIN sub-region) has also been brought into the limelight for power trade enhancement. The Ministry of Power, Government of India, has come up with recent cross-border trade guidelines in order to ease power trading between the BBIN countries. The guidelines have been met with appreciation and fervour by all the neighbouring countries. A bilateral agreement on power trading has already been signed and is underway between Nepal and Bangladesh and Nepal and India. Currently, cross-border projects between Bhutan-Bangladesh and India are underway.

The Future

Sustainable and accelerated economic growth requires commensurate growth in supply of energy and therefore, energy security is extremely crucial for India's planned growth. Declining oil reserves, uncertainties in future oil and gas supply, fluctuations in oil prices in the global market and growing concern for climate change, however, complicate its prospect for development.

Exploiting renewable energy at a larger scale, improving energy efficiency and conservation are important cost-effective ways of enhancing energy security as well as addressing climate change issues. Moreover, substituting resources that have higher carbon content with cleaner fuels could address climate change issues.

The long-term growth in the market for utilization of renewable energy technology will be determined by the socio-economic development of the country and its technological ability to compete with other energy options on a level playing field. Therefore, the main challenges are how to finance projects, how to gain access to necessary capital and how to spur investment in renewable energy. To encourage investment, the current investment policy should be relaxed.

Cross investments between oil-importing and exporting countries can play an important role in stabilizing the oil market. Strengthening market functions by improving the efficiency and transparency of the oil market, utilization of more credible benchmark oil, a flexible procurement method, and new market-based practices to determine adjustment factors are required. Free trade could provide an opportunity to improve market efficiency and transparency.

To address the challenges facing India's energy sector, it is imperative that the government develops and implements well defined, coherent energy policies, to ensure optimal utilization of domestic energy resources, development of adequate infrastructure—both upstream and downstream, acquisition of energy assets and diversification of imports of energy resources, development and harnessing of renewable energy resources, increase of energy efficiency, promotion of energy conservation and encouragement of innovation and development of technology, all of which are essential steps to ensure the country's energy security.

ENDNOTES

1. https://www.ibef.org/blogs/electric-vehicles-market-in-india, accessed on 30 November 2022.
2. https://static.pib.gov.in/WriteReadData/specificdocs/documents/2022/jul/doc202271169601.pdf, accessed on 24 November 2022.
3. https://static.pib.gov.in/WriteReadData/specificdocs/documents/2022/jul/doc202271169601.pdf accessed on 24 November 2022.
4. https://www.pib.gov.in/PressReleseDetail.aspx?PRID=1795444 accessed on 24 November 2022.

REFERENCES

Pradhan Mantri Ujjwala Yojana (PMUY), retrieved from https://www.pmuy.gov.in/ on 15 October 2022.

Pradhan Mantri Ji-Van Yojana, retrieved from https://pib.gov.in/PressReleasePage.aspx?PRID=1843441 on 15 October 2022.

Morimoto, S.; Gheewala, S.; Chollacoop, N.; and Anbumozhi, V. (2021). *Analysis of Future Mobility Fuel Scenarios Considering the Sustainable Use of Biofuels and Other Alternative Vehicle Fuels in East Asia Summit Countries.*

PM-KUSUM, retrieved from https://pmkusum.mnre.gov.in/ on 20 October 2022.

Jawaharlal Nehru Solar Mission, retrieved from https://www.iea.org/policies/4916-jawaharlal-nehru-national-solar-mission-phase-i-ii-and-iii on 20 October 2022.

National Wind Solar Hybrid Policy, retrieved from https://mnre.gov.in/img/documents/uploads/2775b59919174bb7aeb00bb1d5cd269c.pdf on 20 October 2022.

National Offshore Wind Energy Policy, retrieved from https://mnre.gov.in/wind/offshore-wind/ on 21 October 2022.

UJWAL Discom Assurance Yojana, retrieved from https://www.ibef.org/government-schemes/ujwal-discom-assurance-yojana on 21 October 2022

Deen Dayal Upadhyaya Gram Jyoti Yojana, retrieved from https://pib.gov.in/PressReleasePage.aspx?PRID=1811049 on 21 October 2022.

Pradhan Mantri Sahaj Bijli Har Ghar Yojana 'Saubhagya', retrieved from https://powermin.gov.in/en/content/saubhagya on 21 October 2022.

Small Hydro Power Programme, retrieved from https://mnre.gov.in/small-hydro/schemes on 25 October 2022.

National Electric Mobility Mission Plan (NEMMP), retrieved from https://pib.gov.in/newsite/printrelease.aspx?relid=116719 on 29 November 2022.

9

SECURING INDIA'S ENERGY SECURITY THROUGH RENEWABLES

Kumar Sanjay Krishna and Panchamrita Sharma

> *'...My words are not just words; they are announcements of a bright future for our future generations. Today, India ranks fourth in the world in installed renewable energy capacity. India's non-fossil fuel energy has increased by more than 25 per cent in the last seven years and now it has reached 40 per cent of our energy mix.'*

This was the statement made by Prime Minister Narendra Modi at the UN Climate Change Conference (COP26) Summit in Glasgow on 2 November 2021 while putting forward India's commitment to intensified climate action through a five-fold strategy termed as the 'Panchamrit' or 'The Five Ambrosia'. These five targets that India has set to play its part in helping the world reduce global warming include:

- Increase non-fossil energy capacity to 500 gigawatt (GW) by 2030.
- Meet 50 per cent of its energy requirements from renewable energy by 2030.
- Reduce the total projected carbon emissions by one billion tonnes from now onwards till 2030.
- Reduce the carbon intensity of its economy by less than 45 per cent by 2030.
- Achieve the target of net zero by the year 2070.

The climate action targets enumerated above are laudable given the fact that the effects of climate change are intensifying. The availability and affordability of both energy and food are at risk in many countries, contributing to a broader cost-of-living crisis in many parts of this world. To help mitigate these impacts, a massive scaling up of clean energy investment and deployment worldwide is needed. Besides, transition to sustainable land use is essential to protect our food systems against future shocks.

According to NASA, the global warming that has been seen over the past century has been breathtakingly rapid and is primarily due to human activities—specifically, the direct input of carbon dioxide and other greenhouse gases like methane into the Earth's atmosphere from burning fossil fuels like coal, oil and gas, or other human activities like industry, agriculture, construction, transportation, and deforestation. The electricity sector is the major source of the total global CO_2 emissions (approximately 40 per cent)—the primary heat-trapping, 'greenhouse gas' responsible for global warming, followed by the transportation, industry, and other sectors.

Despite mounting evidence of the dangers posed by climate change, global efforts to limit carbon emissions remain insufficient. The Kyoto Protocol adopted in 1997 called for industrialized nations to reduce their greenhouse gas emissions significantly. Talks begun by the Kyoto Protocol still continue, are complicated, and lack consensus among nations. Other accords, like the Doha Amendment, 2012 and the Paris Climate Agreement, 2015, have also tried to curb the global warming crisis.

The Indian Government, however, has been trying to balance the energy security concerns vis-a-vis climate action obligations and practising sustainable development. During the Paris Climate Agreement, 2015, India has set nationally determined contributions (NDC) to achieve 40 per cent (from 28 per cent) cumulative electric power installed capacity from non-fossil fuel-based energy resources by 2030, a commitment, which was fulfilled in November 2021 itself.

According to the Central Electricity Agency (CEA), India's installed renewable energy (RE) capacity including large hydro as on 30 November 2021 stood at 150.54 GW while its nuclear energy-based installed capacity was 6.78 GW adding to 40.1 per cent of the total installed electricity capacity of 392.02 GW.

In August 2022, India officially submitted its updated Paris Agreement targets, declared in COP26. Achieving these targets will require focus on three important areas: increasing renewable energy capacity, de-carbonizing emission intensive sectors, and creating more carbon sinks.

India's Current Energy Resources Scenario and Energy Security

While India is pursuing its commitment to reduce its carbon footprint, the nation is heavily dependent on fossil fuels to meet its energy needs. Considering that it is not well endowed with energy reserves, the country has a mammoth task of meeting its economic and social developmental goals, and lift its millions of people out of poverty.

India is the world's second-largest producer of coal after China. Coal has underpinned the expansion of electricity generation and industry, and accounts for 50 per cent of India's electricity production. Despite large deposits in the east and south, the quality of the coal in the country is not exceptional, and high-quality coal has to be imported from Indonesia, South Africa, Russia, and Australia. To enhance the production of coal in the country, the government has introduced commercial auction of coal on revenue-share mechanism.

A single window clearance portal was launched on 11 January 2021 to speed up operationalization of coal mines. Coal India Limited (CIL) has envisaged a coal production programme of one billion tonnes from CIL mines. Despite these measures, the entire demand for high-quality coal/coking coal (low ash coal) in the country cannot be met from domestic coal and import of coal has to be resorted to as power plants designed on imported coal, requires high-grade coal for blending purposes and cannot be substituted by domestic coal. An increase in the use of imported coal not only contradicts India's strategy of self-reliance for energy security but also compromises the quest for affordability. Despite this contradiction, and despite the emphasis on domestic production of coal and efforts to diversify the sources of energy, the demand for imported coal is likely to continue in future. Coal will remain an important energy source; however, the percentage of coal in India's energy mix is likely to decline in the future.

Oil accounts for 36 per cent of the country's primary energy use. India has just 0.8 per cent of the world's known oil and natural gas resources. Being the world's third largest importer of crude oil, India imported 212.2 million tonnes (MT) of crude oil valued at $119.2 billion in the last fiscal year, ending March 2022. It imports 52.7 per cent from Middle Eastern countries, 15 per cent from Africa, and 14 per cent from the USA. Of the total oil consumption for 2021, 41 per cent was used in transport, 32 per cent in industry (including non-energy uses), and 21 per cent in the residential, services, and agriculture sectors. The remainder is consumed in power plants (1 per cent) and in the hydrocarbon industry (5 per cent).

Natural gas currently accounts for only 8 per cent of India's primary energy use, and most of that gas comes from domestic sources, onshore and offshore. However, the position is likely to change drastically as India aims to increase the share of natural gas in its energy basket to 15 per cent by 2030, which is an increase from the current 163 MMSCMD to over 500 MMSCMD. Industry is the main consumer of gas with 48 per cent consumption in 2021 (mainly fertiliser plants). It is followed by electricity production (25 per cent) and, to a much lesser extent, transport (5 per cent) and the residential and services sectors (7 per cent). In 2020, the Petroleum and Natural Gas Board (PNGRB) authorized India's first gas exchange to achieve increased availability of gas through a free market.

An estimated investment of 100 billion dollars in oil and gas infrastructure has been lined up. The government approved viability gap funding/capital grant at 60 per cent of the estimated cost of Rs. 9,265 crore for the North-east gas grid project to develop a gas pipeline grid of 1,656 km in the eight states of the North-eastern region. India is aggressively working to build a city gas distribution network covering more than 400 districts of India. This network will serve 72 per cent of India's population with cleaner and affordable gas. To promote oil and gas production at the domestic level, the government has been encouraging Indian companies to increase their domestic production and multinational companies to participate in oil and gas explorations in India. Efforts have been made towards regulatory changes, a transparent gas pricing policy and re-development of uneconomical assets. The government came up with a scheme to make stranded gas-based power plants operational on R-LNG, which helped in reviving power plants of around 16,000 MW capacity. To incentivize gas production from difficult areas and discovered small fields, the government has granted marketing and pricing freedom for gas produced from such difficult areas.

Since increased domestic production alone will not be sufficient to meet the projected needs for either oil, gas, or coal, India is also expanding its efforts abroad. Eventually, this has made energy security one of the top foreign policy priorities of the Modi government. This is reflected in the prime minister's record number of high-profile foreign visits during which he has been cutting energy deals with energy rich countries. To ensure energy security, the Modi government has encouraged public sector oil and gas companies to aggressively pursue equity oil and gas opportunities overseas. Modi's skilful diplomacy on the world stage has increased India's global stature and brought in a flood of investment. Foreign direct investment into India in Modi's first term amounted to $193 billion, 50 per cent more than that of the preceding five years. Under Modi, India started purchasing crude and liquefied natural gas cargoes from the USA for the first time. In the last five years, he struck deals from Russia to the Middle East securing oil assets for India. He got the world's biggest oil exporter, Saudi Aramco, to agree to invest in India's largest oil refinery, and the UAE to fill up strategic oil reserves, reducing the strain on State finances.

As geopolitical environment changes have an impact on the hydrocarbon sector, and considering the dependency on the Middle East for India's oil and gas sourcing, there has been a conscious effort to diversify sourcing options. Modi has maintained relations with the Gulf countries crucial to India's energy security even as he strengthened ties with Iran. India has also taken steps to diversify its hydrocarbon exploration in the regions of Latin America, Africa, the Caspian Basin, Russia and in the waters of the Indo-Pacific region. Modi made a point of repeatedly meeting leaders such as Japan's former Prime Minister Shinzo Abe and Russia's Vladimir Putin, whose countries provide much-needed industrial investments and defence technologies. India, which used to import around 2 per cent of its oil needs from Russia, has enhanced its imports ever since war broke out between Russia and Ukraine this year, an effort which has been disapproved by critics.

India's energy security pursuit becomes more challenging with the growing concerns of global climate change and political instability in the energy-rich regions of the world. India has been relying mainly on coal and petroleum for its energy sources. With the fall in investments in global oil and coal due to environmental concerns and related activism, there is a strong possibility of an increase in prices, which will affect the economy at large.

India has built its strategic petroleum reserves in order to meet any supply shocks due to any external exigencies like wars, natural disasters, etc., in huge underground rock caverns at Visakhapatnam on the East Coast, and at

Mangaluru and Padur on the West Coast. These facilities, with a total capacity of 5.33 million tonnes, can meet about 10 days of India's crude oil requirements. Another 6.5 million tonnes of storage at Padur and Chandikholin Odisha are under consideration which will augment its supply to 22 days.

Sustainable development is the top order of business for countries and organisations worldwide. India, on its part, has been making concerted efforts towards energy transition and natural resources conservation by steadily adopting cleaner and greener energy choices.

India's move towards renewable energy sources alone will not suffice for its mounting energy demand. India also has to look towards energy sources with less carbon emission and which can provide base load power. In this context, gas and nuclear energy are significant. Owing to its difficult geographic location in South Asia, India faces strategic challenges for import of gas from its neighbouring nations as some of the proposed gas pipelines will pass through Pakistan and China. India failed to get onboard all interested parties in the IPI (Iran-Pakistan-India) gas pipeline and TAPI (Turkmenistan, Afghanistan, Pakistan, and India) gas pipeline for assured supply of natural gas.

China's One Belt One Road initiative can give China a definitive advantage if any conflict arises, by disturbing India's access to energy. China has been building infrastructure projects in Sri Lanka and Myanmar—countries that provide access to the Indian Ocean, and the vital sea lanes that ferry Beijing's oil imports and carry its exports to Africa, the Middle East, and Europe. Seeking to counter the Chinese, once hesitant, India embraced the Quadrilateral Security Dialogue (QSD) or QUAD, the informal alliance of India, the USA, Japan, and Australia. China responded to the Quadrilateral dialogue by issuing formal diplomatic protests to its members, calling it an 'Asian NATO'. The China-Pakistan Economic Corridor, and the 'String of Pearls' network are strategies to contain India. India responded with a 'Look East' policy—cultivating close relations with Southeast Asian nations. India and China are vying for a growing share of the global energy market in Russia, Latin American countries, and Africa. Chinese players 'have been outbidding Indian state-owned and private companies by discounts and exaggerated payments.' Renewable energy projects awarded to Chinese firms on Sri Lankan islands is a cause of concern for New Delhi. In turn, Beijing is alarmed by New Delhi's developing relations with Vietnam and its oil and gas exploration in the South China Sea.

Hydropower is nowadays referred to as 'the forgotten giant of clean electricity' as the share of hydropower generation capacity in the total installed generation capacity has been steadily declining. In June 2022, India's hydropower capacity of 46,512 MW (megawatts) accounted for roughly 11.7 per cent of total capacity—down from 37 per cent in 1947. The present installed capacity includes the 4,785 MW of pumped storage hydro projects, which are used as cost-effective devices for storing electricity. Another 2,700 MW of pumped storage hydro projects are under construction.

Factors such as long gestation periods, intensive capital requirements, long approval timelines, as well as environmental and social concerns have led to a slowdown in hydropower development in India. Massive flash floods caused by hydropower projects, causing thousands of deaths, destroying homes and incidents of damaged hydropower projects have made these projects unpopular. For instance, in September, 2022, the landslides caused by the flood water flowing above the construction of the main dam of the 2,000 MW Lower Subansiri hydro electric project caused devastation in the downstream areas. Workers engaged at the construction site are the most vulnerable and another collapse would spell disaster for the entire area.

Hydropower's ability to rapidly ramp up or ramp down power generation to follow load, meet peak demand, and make up for intermittent generation from RE sources whenever required make it important for maintaining grid stability. To encourage investments in hydropower, the Ministry of Power (MoP) has set hydro power obligation (HPO) at 0.18 per cent for 2021-22 and proposed increase to 2.82 per cent by 2029-30. Moreover, hydropower projects of over 25 MW capacity have been designated as renewable energy sources. Formerly, only projects with capacities of less than 25 MW were considered as renewable sources. During 2017-22, renovation, modernization, uprating and life extension works for 22 hydro power projects was planned which helped increase the aggregate capacity from 4,848 MW to 4,964 MW. Similar works are being planned for 57 projects during 2022-27.

While the benefits acquired from hydropower cannot be denied, however, the local environmental compromises also cannot be dismissed, as the damage done is often irreversible. Environmental impact assessment is a critical component in developing hydro power projects. It is important that government policies, in order to contribute to carbon reduction, do not ignore the cost imposed on the local environment and populations dependent on it.

Intensifying India's energy security through clean energy

In the past, India's energy security was mainly aimed at managing supply. After 2014, under the Modi regime, India's energy security policy has become more aggressive and comprehensive, and focuses on developing alternative energy sources such as nuclear, solar, and wind.

Nuclear energy has the potential to become 20 to 25 per cent of India's energy mix by 2050. India aims to increase its atomic power contribution from 1.68 per cent to 5 per cent by 2030, which will help the country lead towards a more sustainable and economic future. With over 23 nuclear reactors in seven power plants across the country, India currently produces 6,780 MW of nuclear power.

India has signed civil nuclear agreements with a number of countries including Argentina, Australia, Canada, the Czech Republic, France, Japan, Kazakhstan, Mongolia, Namibia, Russia, South Korea, the United Kingdom, the USA, and Vietnam.

Given India's non-signatory status of the Nuclear-Non-Proliferation Treaty, for any country dealing with India in nuclear energy and technology trade becomes an issue of a mutual trust and confidence which requires delicate diplomacy from India. In October 2018, India and Russia signed an agreement to construct six nuclear reactors. The USA-India nuclear deal was viewed by China as part of the US grand strategy to contain the growing power and influence of China in Asia. The India-China energy geopolitics resurfaced during India's bid for membership in the Nuclear Suppliers Group (NSG). China has been stridently opposing India's NSG bid primarily on the grounds that India is not a signatory to the Nuclear Non-Proliferation Treaty (NPT). Nuclear energy will play a significant role in India's efforts to shift to environment-friendly energy sources.

In the last seven-and-a-half years, installed capacity for generation of electricity from renewable energy sources (RES) has increased more than 22 times. RES has a share of 28.25 per cent as on 30 June 2022 in the total installed generation capacity in the country and India ranks fourth in the world for overall installed renewable energy capacity. In this renewable mix, solar and wind have made the greatest contributions of 50.59 per cent and 35.76 per cent, respectively.

India's push towards renewable energy is commendable, which is reflected in a number of path-breaking initiatives launched by the Indian Government since the signing of the Paris Agreement 2015, which have redefined India's commitment to sustainable energy.

These include increase in percentage of renewable purchase obligations (RPO); focus on sustainable urban infrastructure development through the Smart Cities Mission and Energy Conservation Building Code (ECBC), 2017; launching of the Unnat Jyoti by Affordable LEDs for All (UJALA) scheme—an energy efficiency scheme that distributed more than 36.89 crore LED bulbs and tube lights across the country by the end of October 2022, saving 47,880 million units per year and avoiding 9,585 MW of peak demand; the Pradhan Mantri Kisan Urja Suraksha evam Utthan Mahaabiyan (PM-KUSUM) scheme—which aims to add solar and other renewable capacity of 25,750 MW by 2022 including 17.50 lakh standalone solar powered agriculture pumps and solarisation of 10 lakh grid-connected agriculture pumps.

In April 2022, the MoP issued the revised scheme for 'Flexibility in generation and scheduling of thermal/hydro power stations through bundling with renewable energy and storage power.' This step by the government is expected to lead to faster energy transition. In May 2022, the MoP issued a year-wise trajectory for replacing nearly 58 BUs of thermal power generation in the country with renewable energy by 2025-26. The ministry has directed 81 thermal power plants in the central, state and private sectors to reduce their thermal power generation and offset the decline with 30,000 MW of renewable power. The move is aimed at conserving coal by 34.7 million tonnes per annum (mtpa) and reducing carbon emissions by over 60 mtpa.

Along with increasing renewable energy capacity deployments, the government focuses on ensuring a more inclusive growth of the power sector for future energy security. These include: enhancement of manufacturing capabilities through 'Make in India' and 'Aatmanirbhar Bharat' campaigns, addressing long-standing issues relating to transmission, open access, power procurement and distributed energy uptake. Newer areas of growth such as green hydrogen, offshore wind, and energy storage are also being explored and promoted.

Prime Minister Modi launched the National Hydrogen Mission on India's 75th Independence Day in 2021. Green hydrogen and green ammonia are envisaged to be the future fuels to replace fossil fuels. Production of these fuels by using power from renewable energy is crucial for environmentally sustainable energy security of the nation. The mission aims to produce 5 MT of green hydrogen by 2030 and aid the government in meeting its climate targets and making India a green hydrogen hub. This is projected to boost India's electrolyser manufacturing capacity to reach 8 GW per year by 2025. India will require at least 50 gigawatt (GW) of electrolysers or more to ramp up hydrogen production. MoP released the green hydrogen policy in February, 2022 which includes many encouraging provisions for green hydrogen and green ammonia manufacturers including waiver of inter-state transmission charges for a period of 25 years for projects commissioned before 30 June 2025.

The government has also encouraged faster adoption of electric vehicles (EVs) by offering upfront incentives on purchase of EVs and solar storage batteries. FAME, or Faster Adoption and Manufacturing of (Hybrid and) Electric vehicles, is currently India's flagship scheme for promoting electric mobility. Currently in its second phase, FAME-II is under implementation with effect from 1 April 2019 with a budget allocation of Rs. 10,000 crore. Greater adoption of EVs will reduce the import burden of oil substantially. EV penetration in India requires a substantial boost through development of EV charging infrastructure and reduction in price. Building consumer awareness is also important. Action has already been initiated by the government together with electricity regulatory commissions and other stakeholders to tackle the challenges associated with large-scale EV deployment like safety, load management, and EV tariffs.

Resilient infrastructure is a major element of a sustainable energy system. The Gati Shakti National Master Plan was launched in October 2021 to address issues concerning infrastructure projects, including power transmission. Cross-border power grid connectivity advances economic integration, sustaining development and energy security. The Central Electricity Regulatory Commission (CERC) notified the Cross-Border Trade of Electricity Regulations in 2019 in accordance with MoP guidelines. The Prime Minister's call for 'One Sun, One World, One Grid' has set the tone a for strong and reliable transmission system, which will support India's renewable energy (RE) ambitions. The green energy corridors initiated in 2015 are a key programme for renewable energy evacuation in the country. The distribution network is also being strengthened and the revamped distribution sector scheme (RDSS) is the latest among many schemes launched by the MoP, with an outlay of Rs.

3,03,758 crore over five years, that is FY 2021-22 to FY 2025-26. The state electricity regulatory commissions (SERCs) have been playing an important and progressive role in this process of transition and development through enabling regulations, monitoring implementation of schemes and prudent tariff determination.

In order to further accelerate the end goal of ensuring access to affordable, reliable, sustainable and green energy for all, the Green Energy Open Access Rules, 2022 was notified—whereby the limit of open access transactions has been reduced from 1 MW (1,000 kW) to 100 kW for green energy including the energy from waste-to-energy plants. The notified rules enable small consumers also to purchase renewable power through open access and simplified procedures.

India is emerging as a new normative player in the renewable energy regime, pursuing unwavering commitment to 500 GW of non-fossil fuel by 2030. India's energy security policytries to address social, political, economic, and environmental issues including concerns that are being internationally pursued. Despite dependence on fossil fuels, India's share in the growth of renewable energy is the second-largest in the world, after China.

The Way Forward: Energy Security Through Renewable and Clean Energy

India is on the way to achieve 20 per cent ethanol blending in petrol by 2025 and five per cent bio-diesel in diesel by 2030. To promote energy sustainability, India's new national biofuel policy targets generation of various types of bio-fuels from agriculture residue and municipal waste. India made great strides in recent years towards achieving universal access to modern energy, including clean cooking. In May 2016, the Ministry of Petroleum and Natural Gas (MOPNG), introduced the 'Pradhan Mantri Ujjwala Yojana' (PMUY) as a flagship scheme with an objective of making clean cooking fuel such as LPG available to rural and deprived households, which were otherwise using traditional cooking fuels such as firewood, coal, cow-dung cakes, etc. Approximately 95 million LPG connections have been released under the scheme until September, 2022.

Renewable energy, particularly wind and solar, has started playing an increasingly important role for augmentation of grid power, providing energy access, reducing consumption of fossil fuels and helping India pursue its low carbon development path. This high integration of intermittent sources in the grid has its own challenges and has created an urgent requirement for efficient grid-scale energy storage systems which would play a critical role for flexibility and balancing to ensure safe and smooth operations of the grid.

Among renewables, the solar power sector in India emerged as a fast-upcoming section in last few years, and its share of solar energy in the renewable portfolio increased from 2.6 GW to 57.7 GW. It supports the government agenda of sustainable growth, while, emerging as an integral part of the solution to meet the nation's energy needs and an essential player for energy security.

The International Solar Alliance (ISA), an initiative of India, is an alliance of 75 countries working to create a global market system to tap the benefits of solar power and promote clean energy applications and came into existence in November 2015 as proposed by Prime Minister Narendra Modi. The National Solar Mission (NSM), launched in January 2010, was the first mission of India to be operationalized under the national action plan on climate change (NAPCC). The mission's objective was to establish India as a global leader in solar energy by creating the policy conditions for solar technology diffusion across the country as quickly as possible.

Fifty-nine solar parks of 40 GW aggregate capacity have been approved. The world's largest renewable energy park of 30 GW capacity solar-wind hybrid project is under installation in Gujarat. The government significantly increased the budget allocation and expenditure for the renewable energy sector. An Additional allocation of Rs, 19,500 crore was made for the solar production linked incentive (PLI) scheme in the Union Budget 2022 and sovereign green bonds were also introduced in public sector projects. Green energy trading is in operation in the Indian Energy Exchange since August, 2020.

Presently, solar tariff in India is very competitive and has achieved grid parity. A target of installing 100 GW of grid-connected solar power by 2022 was kept, with 40 GW from rooftop solar (RTS). In order to achieve the above target, the Government of India has launched various schemes to encourage generation of solar power in the country like solar park scheme, VGF schemes, CPSU scheme, defence scheme, canal bank and canal top scheme, bundling scheme, grid connected solar rooftop scheme, etc.

Although utility-scale solar has seen tremendous progress with leading players lining up for projects, tariffs spiralling down and government agencies

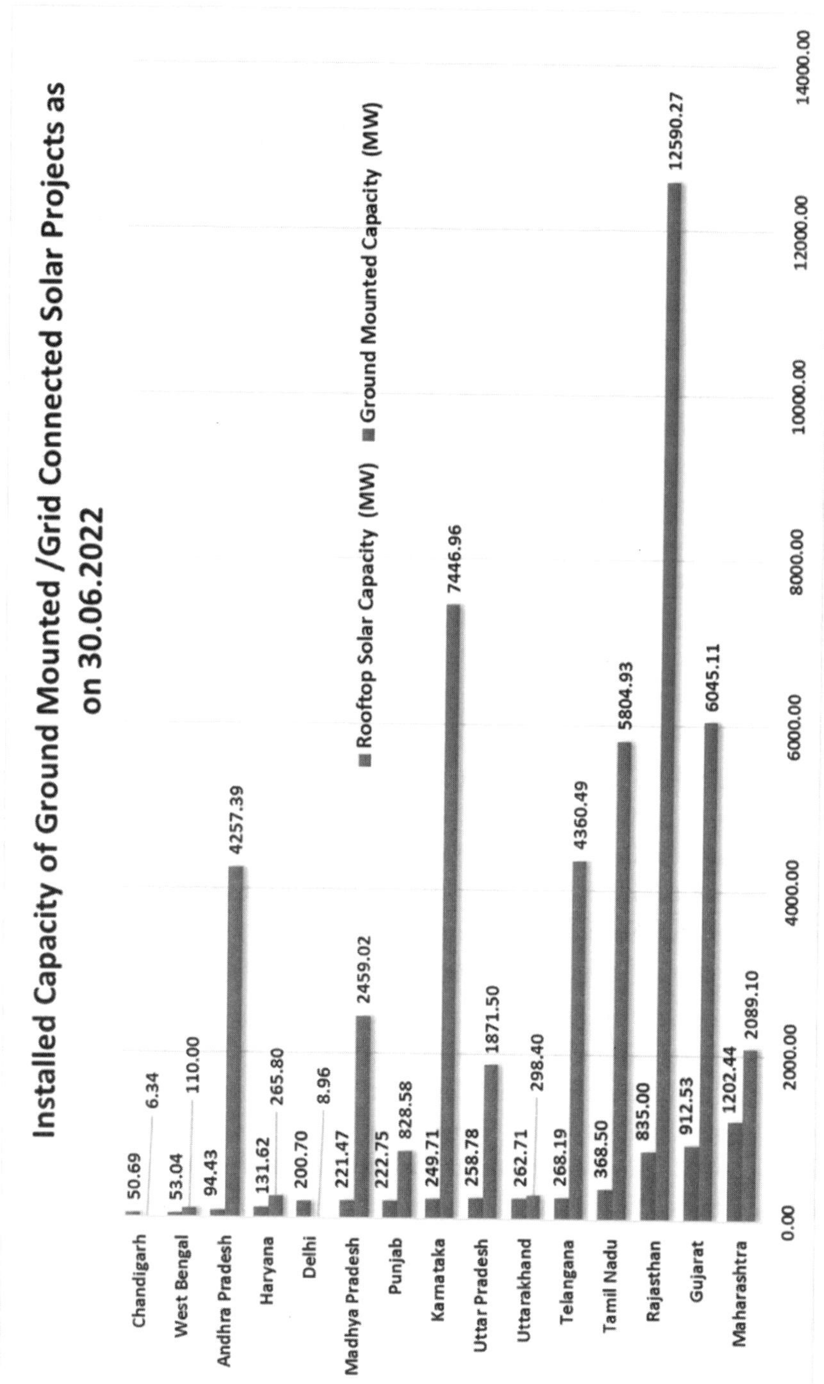
Installed Capacity of Ground Mounted /Grid Connected Solar Projects as on 30.06.2022
■ Rooftop Solar Capacity (MW) ■ Ground Mounted Capacity (MW)
Chandigarh 50.69 6.34
West Bengal 53.04 110.00
Andhra Pradesh 94.43 4257.39
Haryana 131.62 265.80
Delhi 200.70 8.96
Madhya Pradesh 221.47 2459.02
Punjab 222.75 828.58
Karnataka 249.71 7446.96
Uttar Pradesh 258.78 1871.50
Uttarakhand 262.71 298.40
Telangana 268.19 4360.49
Tamil Nadu 368.50 5804.93
Rajasthan 835.00 12590.27
Gujarat 912.53 6045.11
Maharashtra 1202.44 2089.10
0.00
2000.00
4000.00
6000.00
8000.00
10000.00
12000.00
14000.00

pushing mega projects, RTS capacity accounts for only 5.1 GW (10 per cent of total solar capacity installed).

The status of top fifteen states in installation of grid connected solar projects in India, as in June, 2022 shows that except in Delhi and Chandigarh, RTS did not receive the momentum it needed. The state rooftop solar attractiveness index, SARAL, has been developed by the MNRE to encourage states to deploy rooftop solar. Prime Minister Modi also launched the national portal for rooftop solar on 30 July 2022 in an effort to facilitate faster deployment of rooftop solar in different states.

The timeline for installation of a rooftop solar system is the least when compared to all other renewable energy sources. Besides, it is non-polluting and the demand exerted on the transmission network can also be minimized, if properly planned. However, for individual house owners, RTS is still not an attractive alternative. The upfront investment (cost of the solar panels) to set up a RTS system at home is still high for subsidized consumers. Lack of adequate information on the subsidies, panels available in the market, credentials of vendors, etc., also often deter potential consumers from installing a RTS system. However, the potential of increasing solar deployment through domestic RTS is huge in many Indian states.

For instance, Assam has an average peak demand of over 1,700 MW. Its own generation capacity is only 430 MW; therefore, it depends on allocated power from the central sector generating stations and sources from outside the state to meet its demand. The potential for solar generation in the state is estimated at 13.76 GWp and a 1 kWp solar PV panel can generate upto four units of electricity per day considering 5.5 hours of sunlight.

Assam is a smaller state having a land area of 78,438 km^2 compared to many solar-rich states like Rajasthan (342,239 km^2), Maharashtra (307,713 km^2), Gujarat (196,024 km^2), and Karnataka (191,791 km^2). Sixty-three per cent of the population in Assam depends on agriculture for their livelihood. As such, large-scale implementation of ground-mounted solar projects, which requires hundreds of acres of land is undesirable beyond a certain extent. Therefore, instead of depending on space-intensive solar PV projects, an easier alternative for the land-constrained state would be to install rooftop solar systems.

As per Census 2011, Assam has around 6.41 million households. Even if half of these households install a 1 KW system per house, this could add up to

3.2 GW of installed capacity, with commercial and industrial rooftop space being additional avenues for generation which signifies that self-reliance in power production is very much achievable. 'Make in India' and 'Housing for all by 2022' missions can accelerate the transition.

RTS with a battery option can be effectively designed as one of the most viable options to meet the growing peak demand in the future. While doing so, we may consider the experience in other parts of the world. California leads the USA in rooftop solar installations. A newly-passed bill in California in September 2022 is aimed at attracting community solar subscriptions for people who cannot put up panels on their roofs—and deliver clean power when the grid needs it the most. Compensation for community solar will be pegged to the actual value of electricity at the time it is delivered to the grid. Since California is awash in solar power during the day but desperately in need of power during evening hours, it is expected that market forces will push community solar projects to be built with batteries in order to allow projects to sell their power when it can command the best price.

The rollout of mass scale installation of smart meters and advanced metering infrastructure (AMI) in India is offering the opportunity to effectively manage the demand side in a far more granular manner in the key consumption zones of residential, commercial and industrial consumers. The country must utilize this opportunity in designing RTS implementation.

Given the compulsions of energy security, it is likely that many nations with large coal deposits will attempt to exploit them, despite concerns about global warming. Besides, the more a nation invested in energy mechanisms where it is at the mercy of third parties, the more likely it is liable to find itself held hostage by them. A recent example has been the Russian use of its natural gas monopoly to hold the European Union to ransom during the Russia-Ukraine War. There are a few concerns about India's energy future. India is likely to continue to be dependent on external suppliers, whether in oil, gas, or nuclear power. The only alternative may be coal, and until renewables come up in a big way, India will simply be energy-insecure. Therefore, India has to ensure self-reliance in renewable energy sources. Both wind and solar have proven to be of tremendous advantage in that they are locally available in abundance. However, there are still problems with storage and transmission, which needs to be overcome. It has to be ensured that a large chunk of solar modules is local and not imported and also that the locally-manufactured solar modules are of good quality. Currently, the domestic capacity of solar modules and components to produce these modules is limited. Pragmatic policy interventions need to be made to overcome these shortages in the next few years.

India has moved forward strongly and steadily in its journey towards renewable energy under the dynamic leadership of Narendra Modi. He was awarded the 'Champion of Earth' by the United Nations in 2018, which is additional power to India's growing normative leadership in this new energy source regime.

India is the first country to include the Lifestyle For Environment Movement (LiFE) in its nationally determined contributions. Mission LiFE seeks to mobilize at least one billion Indians and other global citizens to take individual and collective action for protecting and conserving the environment in the period 2022–28. Within India, at least 80 per cent of all villages and urban local bodies are aimed to become environment-friendly by 2028.

For a country that is still energy hungry, there is likely to be a dependence on coal for the next decade. However, careful planning and support of renewable energy sources can drive a new pathway that will go a long way in supporting India's energy security and net zero goals.

REFERENCES

1. Ministry of Power, Government of India (https://powermin.gov.in)
2. Ministry of New & Renewable Energy (https://mnre.gov.in),
3. Central Electricity Authority (https://cea.nic.in)
4. Coal India Limited (https://www.coalindia.in)
5. *Petroleum and Natural Gas Regulatory Board (https://www.pngrb.gov.in)*
6. International Energy Agency (https://www.iea.org)
7. Reports/articles in national newspapers, power magazines and the internet.

10

NEW NORTH EAST: FROM ENERGY DEFICIT TO EXPORT HUB

Pratim Ranjan Bose

Till 2014, when the Narendra Modi government assumed power in New Delhi, energy scarcity was a common theme in the eight North Eastern states of Assam, Arunachal Pradesh, Manipur, Nagaland, Mizoram, Meghalaya, and Sikkim; comprising nearly eight per cent of India's area and less than four per cent of the population (Census, 2011). Hilly, forested, remote, scarcely populated (Table 1), high seismic activity and once turbulent—there were structural hurdles in serving the region.

First and foremost, the status of the transport infrastructure was pathetic. Theoretically, the region had a higher per capita road infrastructure. In reality, it was inadequate for the terrain. The entire upper Assam—accounting for 70 per cent of the 45 million population in the North-east—did not have a single bridge to cross the mighty Brahmaputra which is five km wide on an average in the lean season.

Tripura, the second most populous state after Assam, was linked by a rickety and damaged road which was as narrow as 10 feet in places. Most parts of Arunachal, the largest state in the region in terms of landmass, remained inaccessible in the winter. The state did not have a single civil airport. Travelling from the state capital of Itanagar to Delhi required a day-long journey to Guwahati (Assam) to catch a plane or train.

On paper, there were seven airports in the region. In practice, barely four or five were operating and, most did not have a night landing facility. The rail connectivity project in the region was suffering prolonged delays. Agartala (Tripura) became the second state capital, after Guwahati, to be connected by rail (narrow gauge) in 2013.

Add to this the natural adversities. Parts of Arunachal remain snow-covered for nearly six months a year. The Brahmaputra and Barak rivers flood Assam two to three times a year. The muddy hills of Tripura and Meghalaya are prone to landslides in the rainy season which lasts for a good six months in the region.

Table 1: Key Indicators of the North-east

State	*Population (Census 2011)*	*Population as percentage of national population*	*Population density per sq km*	*Households (Census 2011)*	*Area as percentage of India total*
Arunachal Pradesh	1,383,727	0.11	17	270,577	2.6
Assam	31,205,576	2.58	398	6,406,471	2.4
Manipur	2,855,794	0.24	128	510,488	0.7
Meghalaya	2,966,889	0.25	132	548,059	0.7
Mizoram	1,097,206	0.09	52	222,853	0.6
Nagaland	1,978,502	0.16	119	396,002	0.5
Sikkim	610,577	0.05	86	129,006	0.2
Tripura	3,673,917	0.30	350	855,556	0.3
NER	45,772,188	3.78	175	9,339,012	8
India	1,210,854,977	100	382	246,740,228	100

Sources: 1) NER Factsheet, Ministry of Development of Northeast Region. 2) Basic Statistics of North-eastern Region 2015, North-eastern Council Secretariat, GOI.

With 98 per cent of the regional boundary shared with China, Myanmar, Bangladesh, and Bhutan; there are some distinct logistical limitations as well. From the eastern Indian metropolis of Kolkata; the capital city of Tripura in the far east and the national capital of Delhi are equidistant (over 1,500 km) by road. The Dibrugarh (Assam) to Kanyakumari (Tamil Nadu) Vivek Express is the longest train route of 4,200 km in India.

Last, but not the least, roughly a quarter of India's total forest cover[1] is concentrated in the North East. Nearly 75-85 per cent of Mizoram, Arunachal,

Meghalaya, Manipur and Nagaland are covered under thick vegetation. It means utility service providers need to run extra miles to reach out to the last man.

Days of Energy Starvation

Mitigating the energy crisis of the region, therefore, required a comprehensive approach with huge focus on infrastructure building and wider economic development. That was missing till 2014.

The result was telling. Media reports on petrol, diesel, liquefied petroleum gas (LPG) or cooking gas shortage were commonplace. India might have been a refining hub of the world, but fuel pumps in the region, particularly in hilly states, often used to go dry due to paucity of storage and transport infra.

The situation was similar for other petroleum products. Till March 2014, India issued 166 million LPG connections for 246.7 million households (Census, 2011). Adding another 10 million piped natural gas (PNG) connections to households in Gujarat, Delhi, Mumbai, etc; hardly 71 per cent of Indian households had access to cooking gas.

There are, however, serious questions about the quality of this data. Till 2014, the government used to follow a dual pricing model for LPG. Those for commercial usage (e.g., eateries, etc) were sold at market price. Domestic LPG was sold at a heavily subsidized rate. This led to a diversion of domestic cylinders to commercial. It means the historic data on domestic LPG is highly inflated.

The Modi government plugged the loopholes by ensuring one market price for LPG. The subsidy amount was reimbursed to domestic consumers through direct benefit transfer (DBT). The quantum of subsidies has also gone down in recent years, thereby reducing the arbitrage potential. It means the current data truly reflects household consumption.

Either way, the North-eastern scenario was distinctly inferior, when compared to the national scene, in the past. According to the Ministry of Petroleum and Natural Gas,[2] as on 31 March 2014, only 49 per cent of households in Congress-ruled Assam and 47 per cent in the Left-ruled Tripura had access to LPG. The North-eastern average was 52 per cent (Table 2).

Table 2: LPG Coverage in NE between March 2014 and January 2023

State	*Domestic LPG connections 31.03.2014 (million)*	*LPG coverage on 31.03.2014 as percentage of households*	*Active* Domestic LPG Connections 01.01.2023 (million)*	*LPG coverage on 01.01.2023 as percentage of households*	*No of households as per Census 2011 (million)*
Arunachal Pradesh	0.22	81.1	0.31	114.8	0.27
Assam	3.15	49.2	8.35	133.2	6.40
Manipur	0.36	70.5	0.65	127.4	0.51
Meghalaya	0.17	31	0.04	74	0.54
Mizoram	0.27	122.7	0.34	154.5	0.22
Nagaland	0.22	56	0.33	84.6	0.39
Sikkim	0.13	108	0.17	141.6	0.12
Tripura	0.40	47	0.79	92.9	0.85
NER	4.92	52.7	11.34	121.5	9.33
India	166.25	67.3	313.71	127.1	246,74

*Active indicates the subscribers take a minimum of two refills a year.

Source: Absolute LPG connection data from Indian Petroleum and Natural Gas Statistics 2014-15, and Petroleum Planning and Analysis cell of Ministry of Petroleum and Natural Gas, GoI; Household Data from Census, 2011. Compilation by author.

Cooking gas and electricity are useful metrics to understand the energy poverty of a society as it touches the life of the commonest of common citizens. The lack of access to cooking gas forces women to spend longer hours in collecting firewood and limits their ability to make gainful contributions to society. Mass use of firewood or high carbon-emitting energy like coal has negative impacts on forestry, environment, and respiratory health of women.

Bikash Singh, *The Economic Times* correspondent in Guwahati, the state capital of Assam, points out that notwithstanding the official data on LPG connections in the past, the availability of cooking gas was a major concern until recently. The point is valid. While numbers show high coverage of LPG in states like Arunachal or Manipur in 2014, in reality, supplies were never consistent.

Life used to come to a grinding halt in Nagaland for months every year, due to the fuel crisis. The rainy seasons were particularly bad as the poor transport infrastructure suffered further damage, cutting off the supply line. People in any of these hill states used to spend a considerable time of the year in search of petrol, diesel, or cooking gas.

"We used to file a lot of reports on fuel shortages in the past. Auto-fuel refill stations were limited beyond city limits. People selling petrol and diesel, at a premium, in plastic water bottles, was a common sight in the outskirts. Every year during the Durga Puja festival, the region was hit by an LPG crisis," Singh said.

Those days are gone. Singh now rarely files reports on energy shortages. In 2022, Assam suffered one of its worst flood situations in history. Multiple waves of flooding destroyed key rail[3] and road links, inundated cities[4] and towns and killed hundreds. The breach of a dyke in the Barak river kept Silchar (Assam) submerged for weeks. But, fuel supplies did not stop.

The oil marketing companies moved mountains to ferry LPG cylinders when road and rail links were snapped. They even reached out to the final consumer in inundated areas by boat.[5] "There was barely much issue with energy availability even in the face of a natural calamity of such a scale. That's a major change," Singh said.

The Paradigm Shift

The shift is captured in numbers. In less than seven years, between March 2014 and January 2023, India's LPG-household ratio increased from 67 per cent to 127 per cent in the Census 2011 household count. The actual coverage will be known once the reports of the latest round of census is out. Remember that the latest numbers are all about active connections, meaning the consumers take a minimum of two refills a year.

Considering a decadal (2001-2011) growth of 27 per cent in the number of households, India has anticipatedly achieved full coverage in cooking gas connections. Table 2 shows North-east India (121.5 per cent) kept up with the India story. From 49 per cent in 2014, Assam is now operating at 133 per cent. Even Meghalaya, which had a fascination for locally available coal, made a substantial switch to cleaner energy.

To sum up, the fuel crisis in the North-east has been mitigated. This is reflected in the growth of the per capita sales of petroleum products between the financial year 2013-14 (April-March) and the pre-COVID year of 2019-20 (see Table 3). The restrictions on mobility during the COVID years of 2020-21 and 2021-22, affected petroleum product sales across India.

Table 3: Per-capita Sales of Petroleum Products

State	*2013-14 (KG)*	*2019-20 (KG)*	*Growth (%)*
Arunachal Pradesh	123.7	190.5	54
Assam	60.3	90.6	50
Manipur	60.3	93.6	55
Meghalaya	158.1	185.7	17
Mizoram	94.7	129.2	36
Nagaland	60.8	86.6	42
Sikkim	156.7	214.1	37
Tripura	49.3	63.1	28
NER (simple average)	95.4	131.6	38
All India	122.9	157.5	28
Eastern Indian States			
Bihar	38.3	52	36
Jharkhand	76	103.6	36
Odisha	87.6	143.7	64
West Bengal	74.4	101.9	37
ER	69	100.3	45

Source: Indian Petroleum and Natural Gas Statistics for 2014-15 & 2021-22, Ministry of Petroleum and Natural Gas, GoI.

The tiny hill states of Assam have a distortionary effect on the regional average. Meghalaya and Sikkim are top tourist destinations in the region. Sikkim, Arunachal, and Mizoram have small populations each. Arunachal and Sikkim have a disproportionate presence of the armed forces.

Also, the petro-product consumption figures of Meghalaya are highly inflated. A substantial population of cars in Guwahati refill in Meghalaya due to major price arbitrage.

Meghalaya charges lower taxes on fuel. The state border starts right next to Guwahati (Assam), which is barely two hours from Shillong (Meghalaya) by road. Naturally, scores of tourist taxis plying on this route as well as many personal vehicles in Guwahati, the largest city in the region, refill in Meghalaya.

Leaving aside large hydel (Arunachal and Sikkim), thermal power plants (Assam and Tripura) and cement (Meghalaya), there is not much trace of heavy industrial activities in the region except in Assam, which has four refineries and a gas cracking unit.

In natural resources, Assam produces close to three million tonnes of crude and some coal. Tripura produces natural gas. Meghalaya has coal and dolomite. Nagaland, Manipur, Mizoram, and Arunachal barely have industry activities. Industry contributes a substantial chunk of Sikkim's gross state domestic product (GSDP) but that is due to hydel and pharmaceuticals.

In all, only Assam has some industrial base, in the traditional sense of the term, in the region. Over the last decade, the state attracted a few mid-sized investments in food, pharmaceuticals, etc. More importantly, with dramatic improvements in infrastructure, Guwahati emerged as the logistics hub of the entire North-east.

The rising industrial and commercial activity in Assam would not have been possible without energy security. This is proved by the numbers. Between 2013-14 and 2019-20, the per-capita sales of petroleum products increased by 50 per cent in Assam, almost double the national average (28 per cent).

The gap with the country has also reduced. From 49 per cent of the country average in 2013-14; per-capita petroleum product consumption in Assam stood at 57.5 per cent of the national average in 2019-20. The residual gap is attributed to lack of industrial activity.

A comparison with large eastern Indian states (Table 3) will offer better insights into improvement in fuel availability and the growth opportunities in Assam. Eastern India is low on business and industry (when compared to the north, south and western parts of the country) and reports lower per-capita sales of petroleum products than the national average.

The backwardness of Bihar is evident in its low demand for energy. West Bengal and Jharkhand are coal-producing states and have larger industrial bases than Assam, which is reflected in their energy consumption. All three states reported lower growth (36-37 per cent) in per-capita consumption than Assam (50 per cent)

Odisha is a rising industrial hub of India. It is rich in mineral resources, has top-of-the-order port infrastructure and is adding the only LPG terminal in the east. Naturally, it reported a higher growth (64 per cent) in energy consumption.

Changed Electricity Landscape

Mitigating demand for petroleum products is part of a bigger change undergoing in the North-east. Decades of negligence converted this once-prosperous land into a backward region, dependent on the rest of India for everything—from food and refined petroleum products to electricity.

Power availability was a serious concern in the region all along. Before 2014, Sikkim and Tripura became power surplus. Sikkim attracted investments in hydel. The gas-based 726-megawatt ONGC Tripura Power Corporation (OTPC) did the trick for Tripura. This apart, Assam and Manipur saw some distribution sector revamps.

However, a comprehensive approach was missing. The region was a net importer of electricity and the overall power availability scenario was pathetic. As of 2013, the average power supply in Assam "increased to 8-9 hours a day from 1-2 hours a day in 2000," reports an Asian Development Bank case study.[6] CEIC data suggests Assam used to witness 12-17 per cent peak-deficit when Modi came to power.

Low per-capita consumption of electricity was a foregone conclusion of the prevailing scenario (Table 4). Regional supply deficit apart, wide gap in rural electrification and dilapidated transmission distribution network were two major contributors to the dismal electricity consumption ratios.

Table 4: State-wise per capita Electricity Consumption (kWh)

State	*2015-16**	*2019-20**	*Growth (%)*
Arunachal Pradesh	600	631	5.1
Assam	322	348	8
Manipur	360	385	6.9
Meghalaya	835	861	3.1
Mizoram	503	629	25
Nagaland	346	367	6
Sikkim	687	929	35.2
Tripura	329	425	29
NER Average	498	572	14.8
National Average	1,075	1,208	12.3

*Figures rounded off

Source: All India Electricity Statistics, CEA, GoI.

This was most evident in Tripura. Despite being officially power surplus, the second-most populous state in the region had abysmally low per-capita consumption. Sikkim avoided a similar situation, partly by virtue of its low population base.

The correction began in 2015 when the Prime Minister launched Deen Dayal Upadhyaya Gram Jyoti Yojana[7] to reach electricity to nearly 20,000 (3.3 per cent) un-electrified villages. This was topped by the Saubhagya scheme in September 2017, to take electricity to 12 per cent (24.8 million) un-electrified households in the country by March 2019.

The significance of these two schemes cannot be measured by numbers. Firstly, most of the un-electrified villages were remotely located. Secondly, left-out households were almost entirely in rural India. Typically, the North-east was one of the biggest beneficiaries of the two projects.

Table 5 shows that in October 2017, over 20 per cent of North-eastern households did not have electricity. Nearly a quarter of Assamese families were outside the electricity map. Meghalaya, which reported higher per-capita consumption, kept nearly 32 per cent of households in darkness.

Table 5: Household Electrification in the North-east during September 2017–March 2019

State	*Status of household electrification on 10 Oct 2017 (%)*	*Status of household electrification on 31 March 2019 (%)*
Arunachal Pradesh	84.4	100
Assam	76.9	100
Manipur	77.4	100
Meghalaya	68.5	100
Mizoram	88.4	100
Nagaland	74.7	100
Sikkim	84.9	100
Tripura	82.7	100
NER	79.7	100
India	88.3	99.99

Source: Saubhagaya Dashboard,[8] GoI.

Except for a small pocket in Chhattisgarh, Saubhagaya took power to all by March 2019. For the first time in history, the North East became at par with the rest of the country in terms of household coverage of electricity. The results are evident in the growth in per capita consumption.

Table 4 clarifies that within two years of the launch of Saubhagya, the per-capita consumption of the region grew faster than the national growth. Tripura reported a mammoth 29 per cent growth in per-capita consumption of electricity riding on wider household coverage.

As a large, 31 million population (Census, 2011)-strong, multi-cultural state, Assam has distinct challenges when compared to say Tripura that can be travelled end-to-end in three to four hours and has a population equivalent to a district in West Bengal. It was, therefore, natural that Assam would take time to build momentum. The post-COVID growth trajectory in this state would be interesting to watch.

Meanwhile, the daily power availability in the entire region improved to 21 hours.[9] The peak deficit is on a systematic decline in Assam, indicating dramatic improvement in supplies. According to the "Resource Adequacy Plan and Load Generation Balance Report[10] 2022-23" of the Central Electricity Authority (CEA), the region witnessed 1.9 per cent peak deficit in 2021-22, distinctly lower than the eastern and southern regions. (Table 6).

Table 6: Actual Power Supply Position in the country during the year 2021-22

Region	*ENERGY*				*PEAK*			
	Energy Requirement	*Energy Supplied*	*Energy not Supplied*		*Peak Demand*	*Peak Met*	*Demand not Met*	
	(MU)	*(MU)*	*(MU)*	*(%)*	*(MW)*	*(MW)*	*(MW)*	*(%)*
Northern	416,065	412,484	3,581	0.9	73,305	72,935	370	0.5
Western	425,738	425,280	458	0.1	64,608	64,608	0	0.0
Southern	352,062	350,708	1,354	0.4	60,350	58,430	1,920	3.2
Eastern	163,456	162,562	895	0.5	26,019	25,145	874	3.4
North-Eastern	17,822	17,775	47	0.3	3,427	3,360	67	1.9

*March, 2022 data is anticipated

Source: Resource Adequacy Plan and Load Generation Balance Report 2022-23, Central Electricity Authority

From Power Deficit to Power Exporter: Focus Renewable

With the regional peak deficit reduced to a mere 67 MW, the North-eastern power scenario will henceforth undergo rapid changes.

An economy can claim to have a surplus when the domestic demands are met optimally. The rural electrification rush and improved supply, ensured universal access to electricity in the North-east. The government has now picked up the agenda of renewable energy generation.

Implementation of a slew of large hydroelectricity projects, which were pending for decades, should convert the North-east into a truly electricity-surplus, beginning 2023-24. To start with, Arunachal Pradesh became the latest electricity-exporting state in India.

More importantly, from now onwards, there will be a rapid increase in the share of green power generation in the region. This might help the North-east phase out some of the costly coal-power facilities in the medium and long term.

Until recently, the North-east was dotted with small and medium-sized hydro-electric and gas-based projects. The OTPC in Tripura and the 750 MW coal-based power station of NTPC at Bongaigaon in Assam were exceptions to this rule. Both the projects were implemented during the UPA (2004-2011) era.

While OTPC used the trapped gas in Tripura; setting up a large coal-power station in Assam was a bad decision. The region does not produce adequate coal to fire such a large plant. Dry-fuel is imported all the way from Jharkhand (700 km) leading to tariff impact. High tariff made the plant an economic liability.[11]

The solution came through hydropower. In 2022, the Prime Minister inaugurated the Arunachal-based 600 MW (4x150 MW) Kameng[12] hydropower station of the North-Eastern Electric Power Corporation Limited (NEEPCO).

Kameng is currently the largest hydel power station in the North-east. It will soon lose the tag to the 2,000 MW Subansiri[13] (Lower) hydroelectric project of the NHPC. The 8x250 MW project will be operational in phases between May 2023 and June 2024. Kicked off by the UPA government between 2005 and 2007, both the hydro-electricity projects suffered prolonged delays, till the Modi government picked them up literally from scratch.

From 1,242 MW in 2016[14] (against a potential of 58,000 MW) the installed hydroelectric generation capacity increased by 60 per cent to 2027 MW.[15] The installed capacity will cross 4,000 MW in 2024. In February 2023, the government approved the 2,880 MW Dibang[16] multipurpose project (MPP) in Arunachal.

Upon completion, Dibang will be the largest hydel facility in India. The project will be implemented by NHPC Ltd.

The North-east now occupies the central position in India's target to add 30,000 MW hydropower capacity by 2030.

Export-oriented Oil and Gas Economy

In February 2016, the government released the Hydrocarbon Vision 2030[17] for north-east India. It envisaged an investment of Rs.1,30,000 crore in upstream, midstream and downstream sectors in northeast India. The aim was to develop the region as a dominant hydrocarbon hub.

There are many facets to this plan, some of which—like 100 per cent household coverage of cooking gas—are either achieved or nearly achieved (Table 2). Production of bio-fuel through ethanol blending is a national agenda and is picked by the refineries in the North-east as well.

Overall, the vision document envisages two major changes. First, taking the North East along the path of energy transition by expanding the natural gas economy, thereby creating opportunity for future industrialization. Second, converting the region into a petroleum product exporter to the neighbouring economies of Bangladesh, Bhutan, and Myanmar.

The plan has already started taking shape and becoming a reality. On 18 March 2023, the prime ministers of India and Bangladesh jointly inaugurated[18] a 130-km long cross-country pipeline. The project will help the Assam-based Numaligarh Refinery (NRL) to export up to one million tonnes per annum (MTPA) diesel, a little over 20 per cent of Dhaka's annual imports.

Diesel exports to Bangladesh started in 2016 by rail.[19] The pipeline will expand the scope of the trade. A similar pipeline from the North East to Moreh, at the Myanmar border, is under active consideration. This is part of the market-making exercises before the region doubles refining capacity from the prevailing 7.35 MTPA—shared between two state-owned companies, Indian Oil[20] and NRL[21]—to roughly 15 MTPA by end-2024.

Interestingly, the North-east barely had half the crude available locally to utilize the prevailing capacity. Even after sourcing some imported crude through the Barauni-Bongaigaon pipeline, substantial capacity remained unutilised. It means past governments kept adding refining capacities in the region without much initiative to ensure the availability of crude.

Modi has a fool-proof plan. While efforts are underway to increase local crude production, the North-east will get adequate imported crude. A 1,600-

km crude pipeline is under construction from Paradip port (Odisha) to NRL, which will expand its capacity three times to 9 MTPA.[22] This pipeline is going to be the key to refinery expansion in the North-east and as on 31 December 2022, one-third of the project[23] was complete.

The story does not stop there. Natural gas is a critical resource, which is best used as industrial feedstock. The North-east has India's largest onshore gas reserve. However, lack of a utilization plan and necessary pipeline infrastructure, substantial part of the costly resource was either flared or wasted for heating in tea factories and power plants.

Flaring has reduced over the last two decades. Yet, the North East still wastes more gas than the rest of India. According to "Indian Petroleum and Natural Gas Statistics 2021-22", published by the Ministry of Petroleum and Natural Gas, among large onshore gas-producing states, Assam tops in flaring of this costly natural resource (Table 7). Roughly one-fourth of the total national flaring takes place in Assam.

Arunachal has a small gas production unit, which is almost entirely flared. Tripura checked flaring by directing almost the entire natural gas production in generating electricity. As a thumb-rule, gas-based electricity is distinctly costly when compared to coal-power, hydro-electric, solar, etc.

Table 7: Onshore Gas Production and Flaring in 2021-22

State	*Gross Production (MMSCM*)*	*Flare (MMSCM)*	*% Flared to Gross Production*
Andhra Pradesh	808.64	41.27	5.1
Arunachal Pradesh	57.70	46.64	80.8
Assam	3,371.45	213.95	6.3
Gujarat	1,017.29	48.13	4.7
Rajasthan	2,618.83	55.80	2.1
Tamil Nadu	1,066.52	23.20	2.1
Tripura	1,530.78	0.30	0.01
Jharkhand	4.04	0.00	0
Madhya Pradesh	290.10	0.40	0.1
West Bengal	389.25	12.01	3
India Total (Onshore+Offshore)	34,023.52	812.56	2.3

*MMSCM = Million standard cubic metres of gas.
Source: Indian Petroleum and Natural Gas Statistics 2021-22.

There are many pitfalls to this economic drain. Gas is a preferred feedstock for fertiliser and petrochemicals. The North East failed to attract investment in fertiliser. There was not much investment in petrochemicals either.

Till 2016, when Brahmaputra Cracker and Polymer Limited came into operation, the small Indian Oil Bongaigaon project was the only petrochem producer in the region. Brahmaputra Cracker took 32[24] years to become a reality. One cannot change history but one can surely create it. Modi did the second by launching an elaborate project, spearheaded by Indradhanush Gas Grid Ltd. (IGGL), to create a sprawling gas pipeline network in the North Eastern region. The IGGL network will be linked with the national gas grid by the Barauni-Assam link.

IGGL will essentially create pipeline infrastructure that can be used both for evacuation and supply. This should end the entire phenomenon of land-locked gas and the resulting misuse. The connection with the national grid will act as a huge security to future investments in the region against any potential gas crisis.

As of September 2022, IGGL achieved 48 percent[25] physical progress. They are expecting to complete 70 per cent of the work in 2023-24.

To start with, the North-east will receive additional supplies from the national grid. A substantial part of it will be consumed by NRL to replace costly naphtha to produce hydrogen, which will be essential in ramping up the refining capacity. The company is also awaiting the government's nod to set up a facility that will double the region's petrochemical production.

Conclusion: New North-east

Infrastructure and energy are two key growth drivers. For seven decades of Indian Independence, there was never any dearth of promises to the North-east to solve both. Every peace accord with militant groups in the region had economic components in it.

Unfortunately, the powers in Delhi were never keen to find a wholesome solution and integrate the region with the rest of the country. Public money was thrown to please specific interest groups without much economic benefit to the land. The now-abandoned plan to put up a state-owned steel plant in Assam (which is far away from iron ore mines) and the white elephant coal-power facility at Bongaigaon are reminiscent of that era.

Modi changed this perspective and that will change the North-east. Till date, the region depends on the rest of the country for cooking gas supplies. By 2024, it will be producing enough LPG to meet local demand and export to neighbouring economies. The huge refining and petrochemical capacity addition will trigger demand and create investment opportunities not only in the North-east but also in the adjoining economies.

Most importantly, the region will no more be backward in terms of infrastructure—including energy infrastructure—compared to the rest of the country. If the current trend of development is sustained, the regional infrastructure will be comparable to the best in India.

It is fully in tune with the energy transition agenda of India. One of the aims of Hydrocarbon Vision 2030 was to create CNG (compressed natural gas) highways. The sprawling gas transmission and distribution network will make it a reality.

ENDNOTES

1. "India State of Forest Report 2021," https://fsi.nic.in/forest-report-2021-details
2. "Indian Petroleum and Natural Gas Statistics 2014-15," Ministry of Petroleum and Natural Gas, http://petroleum.nic.in/sites/default/files/pngstat_0.pdf
3. "Assam flood: Road, rail links cut off, nearly 2 lakh people affected in state," *India Today*, 17 May 2022 https://www.indiatoday.in/india/story/assam-flood-landslide-rain-dima-hasao-bridge-washed-away-haflong-2-lakh-affected-rescue-ops-1950477-2022-05-17
4. "Silchar submerged: How illegal cutting of embankment led to floods," *Frontline*, 10 July 2022,https://frontline.thehindu.com/the-nation/silchar-floods-how-illegal-cutting-of-embankment-led-to-submerged-city/article65616524.ece
5. "IOC delivers cooking gas by boats in Assam amid devastating floods," *Business Standard*, 5 July 2022,https://www.business-standard.com/article/current-affairs/ioc-delivers-cooking-gas-by-boats-in-assam-amid-devastating-floods-122070500180_1.html
6. "Electricity and Power Supply in Assam State, Northeastern India," ADB, 29 April 2013, https://www.adb.org/results/electricity-and-power-supply-assam-state-northeastern-india#:~:text=By%202021%2D2022%2C%20peak%20demand,estimated%20to%20reach%203%2C985%20MW
7. https://www.ddugjy.gov.in/
8. https://www.ddugjy.gov.in/assets/uploads/1656499638k8xo7.pdf
9. "Availability of power in the country including North East goes up to an average of 21 hours," *The Economic Times*, 3 December 2021. https://economictimes.indiatimes.com/industry/energy/power/availability-of-power-in-the-country-including-north-east-goes-up-to-an-average-of-21-hours/articleshow/88075489.cms?from=mdr
10. LGBR 2022-23, CEA, https://cea.nic.in/l-g-b-r-report/?lang=en
11. "Why Assam wants a power plant unplugged," *BusinessLine*, 11 November 2019, https://www.thehindubusinessline.com/news/why-assam-wants-a-power-plant-unplugged/article29946596.ece

12. PIB Release, 19 November 2022. https://pib.gov.in/PressReleasePage.aspx?PRID=1877233
13. "Subansiri Lower expected to be completed in May this year," *The Economic Times*, 13 March 2013. https://energy.economictimes.indiatimes.com/news/power/subansiri-lower-hydro-electric-project-expected-to-be-completed-by-may-this-year/98592364
14. CSE Factsheet, http://cdn.cseindia.org/userfiles/factsheet-north-east-india.pdf
15. "Power potential in the North Eastern region," NEEPCO, https://neepco.co.in/power-generation/power-potential
16. "NHPC gets cabinet approval for... India's largest hydro project," 28 February 2023,https://economictimes.indiatimes.com/industry/energy/power/nhpc-gets-cabinet-approval-for-rs-1600-crore-investment-in-indias-largest-hydro-project/articleshow/98313745.cms
17. PIB Release, 9 February 2016, https://pib.gov.in/newsite/printrelease.aspx?relid=136255
18. PIB release, 18 March 2023,https://pib.gov.in/PressReleaseIframePage.aspx?PRID=1908377#:~:text=Prime%20Minister%20Shri%20Narendra%20Modi,Prime%20Ministers%20in%20September%202018
19. "India starts diesel exports to Bangladesh via rail," *The Economic Times*, 18 March 2016,https://economictimes.indiatimes.com/news/economy/foreign-trade/india-starts-diesel-exports-to-bangladesh-via-rail/articleshow/51445045.cms
20. "India's top refiner plans $22 bn expansion over 5 years," Reuters, 31 March 2018, https://www.reuters.com/article/us-india-ioc-idUSKBN1H70CW
21. NRL to invest Rs 35000 cr in major ongoing projects," *Money Control*, 20 September 2022,https://www.moneycontrol.com/news/business/nrl-to-invest-rs-35000-crore-in-major-ongoing-projects-9202151.html
22. Interview of NRL MD on capacity expansion plan, Iravati Research, https://www.youtube.com/watch?v=qOBrRunNEus&t=1s
23. "33 % physical progress of the pipeline by December 2022", NRL website, https://www.nrl.co.in/Current_Initiatives https://www.nrl.co.in/Current_Initiatives
24. "After 32 years Modi to inaugurate Assam gas cracker project today," *Hindustan Times*, 5 February 2016,https://www.hindustantimes.com/india/32-yrs-later-modi-to-inaugurate-assam-gas-cracker-project-today/story-hSpbEJg0UYcy1l1vUbuazJ.html
25. "IGGL achieves 42.94% physical progress," *The Economic Times*, 22 September 2022, https://economictimes.indiatimes.com/industry/energy/oil-gas/iggl-achieves-42-94-per-cent-physical-progress-rs-1556-46-crore-capital-expenditure/articleshow/94371193.cms

ENERGY TRANSITIONS

11

India's Responsive Governance: The Saga of Energy Transition

Bibek Debroy and Aditya Sinha

Introduction

In recent times, a growing number of scholars have raised serious concerns regarding the efficacy of democracy, claiming that elections do not always result in the election of responsive governments. One notable work in this field is Christopher H. Achen and Larry M. Bartels' acclaimed book, *Democracy for Realists: Why Elections Do Not Produce Responsive Government*, published in 2016. The authors boldly challenge the romanticized notion of democracy, known as the 'folk theory', which portrays voters as rational and informed decision-makers, carefully evaluating the available evidence and selecting the political party with the most robust policies to deliver on their promises. This conception originated from the Enlightenment era's emphasis on rational decision-making, but Achen and Bartels' critique has fuelled a lively debate on the very foundations of democracy and its effectiveness in delivering responsive governance.

However, like many Western scholars, Achen and Bartels (2016) underestimate voters' decision-making abilities, especially in developing countries. While there will always be an information asymmetry between voters and government/candidates, it is often over-stated. In India, too, elections have incentivized politicians to calibrate policy to voter preferences if voters reward good and punish poor policy performance electorally. Studies indicate that voter turnout also gets positively affected by fair and good governance (Miles, 2015). Moreover, voting is perceived as a quintessential public good by the populace. It is not solely restricted to the act of casting a ballot in favour of candidates and political parties who espouse policies that cater to the well-being of citizens. The act of voting demonstrates a citizen's endorsement of policies that benefit their day-to-day existence and showcases a pro-social and forward-thinking attitude, as evidenced by scholarly works by Bolsen, Ferraro, and Miranda (2014) and Nickerson and Arceneaux (2009).

One such pro-social strand which is emerging is public concern for environmental issues. The impact of global warming has started affecting median voters. Recent research has found climate change is shifting voter behaviour in the countries like India (Amirapu, Clots-Figuras, & Rud, 2023). One of the interesting results of this study is a significant increase in voter turnout with an increase in extreme heat. Further, this exactly mirrors the specific non-linear effect of temperatures on agricultural productivity. Thus, climate change seems to have an impact on both voter turnout and candidate preference. Undoubtedly, voters have recognized the pressing need to invest in green energy, a fact that has not gone unnoticed by policy makers. The evolving voting patterns have exerted pressure on policymakers to recalibrate their policies in line with this ground reality.

Much prior to the emergence of this research, the Union government, under the stewardship of Prime Minister Narendra Modi, had already embarked on the path of green energy. In recent years, the government has crafted a comprehensive energy transition agenda that caters to the needs of individual retail users and aims to achieve carbon neutrality by 2070, reflecting its commitment to becoming a responsible global power. This move is not merely a political manoeuvre to attract votes but an earnest effort to secure India's future. This chapter provides an analysis of India's energy transition journey, tracing its evolution and assessing its impact.

Energy Transition at the Grassroots

When discussing the transition towards sustainable energy sources at the national level, it is frequently overlooked that there has been a significant movement towards cleaner fuels at the grassroots level. Access to efficient and clean energy is critical for individuals to effectively engage in productive activities and enhance their overall quality of life. The absence of such energy sources can significantly hinder progress and limit opportunities for personal and economic growth. Over the past few years, the Indian government has been prioritizing investments in these critical resources to expand access and promote social and economic advancement. We would like to discuss two important schemes which have made this possible.

Pradhan Mantri Ujjwala Yojana: Advancements in Clean Cooking Fuel Delivery for Women's Health and Livelihood in India

There is no dearth of literature on the impact of traditional cooking fuel on the health of women (Matinga and Clancy, 2020; Silwal and McKay, 2015; Naeher et al., 2001). At the same time, collection, transportation and processing of fuels also have an impact on the health and livelhood on women. They experience poor health, face a considerable financial burden in the form of lost work days, ranging from three to seven days per month, attributable to fuel collection (Parikh, 2011). This burden is particularly pronounced among poor households. Despite widespread recognition of the challenges faced by rural women in accessing cooking fuels, successive governments have failed to take adequate action. For example, in 2006, the Planning Commission's Integrated Economy Policy called for the government to provide cooking fuels within one kilometre of rural households, thereby reducing the burden of heavy loads. Unfortunately, under the UPA government, little progress was made in this regard. However, under the current administration, significant strides have been made, with clean cooking fuel now being delivered directly to rural households.

The Pradhan Mantri Ujjwala Yojana (PMUY) was introduced on 1 May 2016, with the aim of providing deposit-free LPG connections in the name of female adult members of poor households throughout the country. The objective of issuing 80 million connections was accomplished by September 2019. To encompass the rest of the poor households, PMUY phase-2 (Ujjwala 2.0) was initiated in August 2021 with a goal of providing an additional one million PMUY connections, which was met by January 2022. The government subsequently resolved to provide an additional 6 million LPG connections under Ujjwala 2.0, and as of 1 January 2023, the target of 16 million Ujjwala 2.0 connections had already been achieved. The beneficiaries under Ujjwala

2.0 get a deposit-free LPG connection along with a free first refill and stove. The scheme also allows for online applications for new PMUY connections and a special provision for migrant families to obtain a new connection using self-declaration as proof of address and family declaration. Furthermore, the government also announced a targeted subsidy. In addition, w.e.f. 21 May 2022, the government announced an additional subsidy of Rs.200 per 14.2 kg cylinder for PMUY beneficiaries for up to 12 refills for the year 2022-23.

The government is often criticized that while beneficiaries under Ujjwala got free LPG cylinders, they are not opting to get the cylinders refilled on a sustained basis. However, the government is addressing this issue too. Apart from these special provisions, oil marketing companies (OMCs) have taken various steps to encourage better consumption of LPG and to reduce diversion and delay in supplies. These steps include deferring loan recovery from subsidy amounts for PMUY beneficiaries, offering a swap option from 14.2 kg to 5 kg to reduce upfront cash outgo, providing the option of a 5 kg double bottle connection, conducting Pradhan Mantri LPG panchayats to persuade beneficiaries to use LPG on a sustained basis, organizing mass awareness camps, providing up to three free refills to PMUY beneficiaries under the Pradhan Mantri Gareeb Kalyan package from April to December 2020, Aadhaar-based de-duplication, direct benefit transfer of LPG subsidy, and opening new distributorships.

Undoubtedly, the Pradhan Mantri Ujjwala Yojana has proven advantageous to individuals at the grassroots level. According to a research study (currently undergoing pre-review) by Ajay Nagpure, Ritesh Patidar, and Vandna Tyagi, there has been a substantial increase in the distribution and utilization of LPG as a cooking fuel (Sinha, 2022). This surge has resulted in the prevention of over 150,000 premature deaths caused by pollution in 2019 alone. It's worth noting that this estimation only pertains to indoor air pollution, and is limited to the year 2019. It's reasonable to presume that comparable benefits were gained in the following years as well.

From Diesel to Solar: Promoting Sustainable Agriculture in India through the PM-KUSUM Scheme

The notion of sustainable agriculture involves a complex equilibrium between maximizing crop yields and maintaining economic stability, while minimizing the depletion of finite natural resources and adverse environmental impacts.

Renewable energy systems, such as solar photovoltaic water pumps, offer a promising solution for sustainable agriculture. In order to encourage farmers to adopt solar energy systems, subsidies for solar water pumps, in conjunction with attractive purchase guarantees, may serve as an effective incentive to transition from diesel-powered pumps, as suggested by Al-Saidi and Lahham (2019). Solar energy provides various benefits, such as low operating costs, a modular design, relative reliability, and a lack of emissions, pollution, or soil contamination that may arise from fossil fuels.

That is exactly what India has been doing. The Pradhan Mantri Kisan Urja Suraksha evam Utthaan Mahabhiyan (PM-KUSUM) scheme was launched to achieve multiple objectives, including reducing diesel usage in the agricultural sector, ensuring water and energy security for farmers, increasing farmer income, and mitigating environmental pollution. The scheme operates on a demand-driven basis, and the allocation of resources to the three components of the scheme is based on the demand of the states/union territories. Component-A allows individual farmers, groups of farmers, cooperatives, panchayats, farmer producer organizations (FPOs), and water user associations (WUAs) to set up solar power plants with a capacity of up to 2 MW on barren, fallow, marshy, or cultivable land. Component-B and Component-C of the scheme enable individual farmers, groups of farmers, cluster irrigation systems, WUAs, FPOs, and primary agriculture credit societies (PACS) to install standalone solar pumps or convert their existing grid-connected agriculture pumps to solar energy.

The introduction of schemes has not only contributed to a decrease in carbon emissions but has also made electricity more accessible and affordable. According to the 2016-17 All-India agricultural input survey released by the Ministry of Agriculture and Farmer Welfare, there are approximately 11.2 million diesel agricultural pumps in India. In contrast, a total of 500,000 standalone solar pumps have been reported to have been installed cumulatively as of 31 December 2022, including those installed under the PM-KUSUM scheme. This data highlights the potential for a significant shift towards clean energy in India's agricultural sector, which is heavily dependent on diesel pumps. However, the proportion of solar pumps currently in use remains relatively small, indicating a need for further efforts to accelerate the adoption of solar technology in this sector.

The reason for a lower proportion of solar pumps can be attributed to the limited intake of some states of the scheme. The success of scheme implementation varies across different regions as it operates on a demand-based system where states and union territories must request assistance from the central government. A few states, such as Rajasthan, Haryana, and Maharashtra, have already witnessed tremendous advantages for farmers under the scheme. Therefore, it is imperative for states to take a proactive approach in encouraging farmers within their jurisdiction to capitalize on the benefits of the scheme.

Table 1: Year and State/UT-wise details of farmers benefitted under PM-KUSUM Scheme since inception, till 31.12.2022

S.No.	*State/UT*	*Farmers benefitted (Nos.)*			
		2020-21	*2021-22*	*2022-23*	*Total*
1	Arunachal Pradesh	0	0	91	91
2	Gujarat	93	366	824	1,283
3	Haryana	8,166	23,798	8,254	40,218
4	Himachal Pradesh	40	216	265	521
5	Jammu & Kashmir	0	103	359	462
6	Jharkhand	381	6,336	2,205	8,922
7	Karnataka	76	238	0	314
8	Kerala	0	0	30	30
9	Madhya Pradesh	7,234	0	3	7,237
10	Maharashtra	0	2,426	35,295	37,721
11	Manipur	0	28	0	28
12	Meghalaya	0	35	0	35
13	Odisha	110	647	381	1,138
14	Punjab	1,107	5,390	5,631	12,128
15	Rajasthan	3,514	19,978	32,012	55,504
16	Tamil Nadu	988	199	1,281	2,468
17	Tripura	63	358	753	1,174
18	Uttar Pradesh	2,959	3,883	5,931	12,773
19	Uttarakhand	0	0	316	316
	Total	24,731	64,001	93,631	182,363

Source: Ministry of New and Renewable Energy, GoI.

Towards Net Zero Emissions

The West is placing the responsibility for climate change on the Global South, demanding that developing countries drastically reduce their carbon emissions despite the positive correlation between CO_2 emissions and economic growth.

This ignores the fact that Western countries have much higher per capita carbon emissions and are responsible for the majority of historical carbon emissions. Moreover, in negotiations, the West prioritizes its interests and adopts a soft approach towards the needs of poorer countries.

Despite being the fourth largest carbon emitter, India has taken the bold step of pledging to reduce its carbon footprint by achieving net-zero emissions by 2070. This commitment was made during the COP 26 Summit in Glasgow, where India recognized the urgent need to address climate change. Notably, India's per capita emissions remain considerably lower than those of other major economies, such as the USA and Russia.

In contrast, China aims to become carbon neutral by 2060, while the USA and the EU have pledged to achieve net-zero emissions by 2050. The developed countries expected a tighter net zero deadline from India. Despite facing criticism from developed nations for its delayed net-zero commitments, India has been striving to strike a balance between the needs of its vast population of 1.4 billion people and the pressing environmental concerns. By prioritizing the well-being of its citizens and the planet, India is taking a significant step towards a sustainable future.

India has also committed to reducing the emissions intensity of GDP by more than 45 per cent by 2030, compared to the 2005 levels. This is significantly higher than the Paris targets by 33-35 per cent. India also aims to increase the share of non-fossil-based electricity generation capacity up to 50 per cent by 2030.

The objectives set by India to reduce emissions and increase the share of non-fossil-based electricity generation are certainly ambitious. However, there is reason to be optimistic as the transition towards clean energy in India is already in motion. In fact, India has surpassed its initial commitment made at COP 21 in Paris by currently generating 40 per cent of its power capacity from non-fossil sources, nearly nine years ahead of schedule. This is a remarkable feat, and the contribution of solar and wind power to India's overall energy mix has grown substantially in recent years, underscoring the country's significant strides towards achieving a sustainable and low-carbon future.

As of 31 December 2022, the country has successfully installed a remarkable 167.75 GW renewable energy capacity. This impressive figure comprises several renewable energy sources, including 63.30 GW of solar power, 46.85 GW of large hydropower, 41.93 GW of wind power, 10.73 GW of biopower, 4.94 GW of small hydropower, and 6.78 GW of nuclear power. Additionally, the country has several renewable energy projects in progress, with a combined capacity of 78.75 GW, and 32.60 GW of capacity currently in the bidding process.

Table 2: Details of generation from renewable energy (RE) sources during the last five years, i.e., 2017-18 to 2022-23 (upto December 2022) (in million units)

S. No.	*Source*	*2017-18*	*2018-19*	*2019-20*	*2020-21*	*2021-22*	*2022-23 (Upto Dec 2022)*
1.	Solar Power	25,871.07	39,268.19	50,131.09	60,402.26	73,483.94	72,924.49
2.	Wind Power	52,666.09	62,036.38	64,646.38	60,149.95	68,640.07	59,532.36
3.	Small Hydro Power	7,691.58	8,702.75	9,451.24	10,258.41	10,463.55	9,392.75
4.	Bio-Power	15,610.75	16,751.77	14,108.31	16,436.89	18,324.74	11,203.12
5.	Large Hydropower	126,122.69	134,893.61	155,769.12	150,299.52	151,627.33	137,903.61
	Total	**227,962.18**	**261,652.7**	**294,106.14**	**297,547.03**	**322,539.63**	**290,956.33**

Source: Central Electricity Authority

There has been a significant rise in installed solar capacity ever since Narendra Modi became the prime minister. Rajasthan has the highest solar power capacity among all Indian states, with a total of 16,340.75 MW. Gujarat follows Rajasthan with 8,500.74 MW and Karnataka with 7,885.56 MW. Incidentally, India's solar power generation rose by 38 per cent YoY to 95.15 BU in 2022.

Graph 1: Total Installed Solar Capacity in India

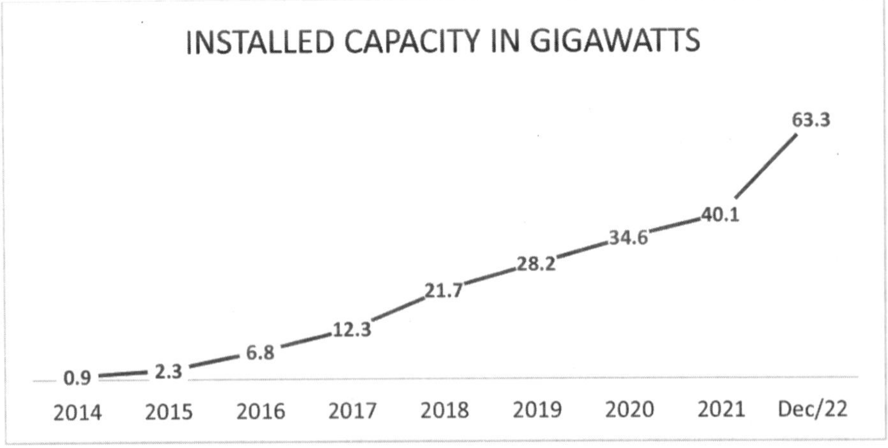

Source: Ministry of New and Renewable Energy.

India's goal of expanding the proportion of non-fossil fuel-based energy generation will necessitate the domestic solar PV module industry to fulfil the rising demand for solar PV modules. In line with this objective, GoI has introduced the production linked incentive (PLI) scheme for the National Programme on high-efficiency solar PV modules. This scheme aims to establish domestic manufacturing capabilities on a gigawatt (GW) scale for high-efficiency solar PV modules and solar PV cells, with an outlay of Rs. 24,000 crore. The implementation of this scheme is expected to catalyze the growth of the domestic solar industry, promote job creation, and support India's transition towards clean energy.

Besides, India is rapidly introducing cleaner fuel and subsidizing electric vehicles to contribute towards a reduction in carbon emissions. The Union Government has introduced Phase II of the faster adoption and manufacturing of (hybrid &) electric vehicles in India (FAME India) scheme with a significant budgetary support of Rs. 10,000 crore. Starting from 1 April 2019, this five-year program aims to promote the electrification of public and shared transportation, with a primary focus on providing demand incentives for 7,090 e-buses, 5 lakh e-3 wheelers, 55,000 e-4 wheeler passenger cars, and 10 lakh e-2 wheelers. As part of this initiative, buyers of electric vehicles can avail of incentives in the form of reduced purchase price upfront. This scheme has the potential to revolutionize the transportation sector in India by promoting the use of clean and sustainable vehicles. As of July 2022, over 13 lakh electric vehicles are plying on Indian roads. This number will significantly rise in the upcoming years.

Furthermore, on 6 February 2023, a program was initiated to promote the usage of biofuels to reduce emissions and mitigate dependence on foreign exchange-depleting imports. This program involved the introduction of petrol blended with 20 per cent ethanol, which was made available at selected petrol pumps in 11 states and union territories. This endeavour reflects the government's commitment to promoting the usage of eco-friendly fuels and reducing the country's carbon footprint

India will not stop here. The government has recently presented its long-term low emission development strategy to the United Nations Framework Convention on Climate Change (UNFCCC) during the 27th conference of parties (COP27). The salient features of this strategy include the following:

- Emphasis on the rational use of national resources while ensuring energy security and a fair, smooth, sustainable, and inclusive transition from fossil fuels. The National Hydrogen Mission, launched in 2021, aims to establish India as a green hydrogen hub, with a rapid increase in green hydrogen production, electrolyser manufacturing capacity, and a three-fold rise in nuclear capacity by 2032, as well as overall development of the power sector. In fact, the finance minister in union budget 2023 unveiled a bold initiative to foster green hydrogen production in the country. The mission spans over seven years and has a total outlay of Rs. 19,700 crore ($2.3 billion), with a first-year allocation of Rs. 297 crore. This is the first time the government has earmarked funds to bolster the production of green hydrogen, marking a significant step towards a cleaner and more sustainable future.

- India's transport sector will promote low-carbon development through increased biofuel use, especially ethanol blending, in petrol, electric vehicle penetration, and green hydrogen fuel adoption, with ambitious goals to maximize electric vehicle use, achieve a 20 per cent ethanol blending target by 2025, and shift to public transport for passenger and freight.
- India will drive sustainable and climate-resilient urban development through smart city initiatives, integrated city planning, green building codes, and innovative waste management, with focus on mainstreaming adaptation and enhancing energy and resource efficiency while urbanization continues to grow.
- India's industrial sector, which is expected to continue its strong growth in the perspective of "Aatmanirbhar Bharat" and "Make in India," will enhance energy efficiency through the perform, achieve and trade (PAT) scheme, the National Hydrogen Mission, high levels of electrification, material efficiency, and recycling, as well as exploring options for hard-to-abate sectors such as steel, cement, and aluminium.
- India has a good track record of increasing forest and tree cover alongside high economic growth, with its forest and tree cover absorbing 15 per cent of CO_2 emissions in 2016. India aims to fulfil its NDC commitment of additional carbon sequestration of 2.5 to 3 billion tonnes by 2030.
- However, the transition to low-carbon development will entail significant costs, including developing new technologies, infrastructure, and other transaction costs, estimated to be in trillions of dollars by

2050. Developed countries must provide climate finance in the form of grants and concessional loans to enhance the scale, scope, and speed of the transition, predominantly from public sources, in line with UNFCCC principles.

Conclusion

India's transition to green energy is an important and fascinating journey that reflects the country's commitment to sustainable development. The move towards renewable energy is not solely motivated by electoral considerations but rather reflects a coordinated approach by the Indian government to encourage private sector investment in green energy.

The removal of regulatory hurdles for businesses to venture into green energy is a crucial factor in this transition. With the potential for renewable energy sources such as solar, wind, and biogas to generate a significant number of green jobs, India's private sector has a clear financial incentive to invest in green energy. The potential business opportunities in the green energy sector have been likened to those in a gold mine or oilfield.

The importance of green growth has been recognized at the highest levels of the Indian government. Finance Minister Nirmala Sitharaman recently listed it as one of the four opportunities that could be transformative for India leading up to 2047, the country's 100th year of Independence. The 2023 Budget provided a substantial amount of funding, ₹ 35,000 crore, for priority capital investments towards a net-zero transition and energy security by the Petroleum and Natural Gasinistry.

The support for various sectors like green hydrogen, bio-manure, off-grid solar, and storage indicates that India is leaving no stone unturned in its efforts to ensure a sustainable future. This transition to green energy is beneficial for the environment and has significant economic benefits, including job creation and financial growth. Therefore, India's ongoing transition towards renewable energy presents an exciting opportunity for further research and academic analysis.

REFERENCES

Achen, C. H. and Bartels, L. M. (2016). *Democracy for Realists: Why Elections Do Not Produce Responsive Government.* Princeton and Oxford: Princeton University Press.

Al-Saidi, M. and Lahham, N. (2019). Solar energy farming as a development innovation for vulnerable water basins. *Development in Practice,* 29(5), 619-634.

Amirapu, A.; Clots-Figuras, I.;and Rud, J. P. (2023, 13 February). *Promarket.* Retrieved March 2023, from Climate Change Is Shifting Voter Behaviour in Low-Income Countries: https://bit.ly/3Y4hKeI

Bolsen, T.; Ferraro, P. J.; and Miranda, J. J. (2014). Are Voters More Likely to Contribute to Other Public Goods? Evidence from a Large-Scale Randomized Policy Experiment. *American Journal of Political Science,* 58(1), 17–30.

Matinga, M. and Clancy, J. (2020). Gender, Firewood and Health: The Potential of Ethnography to Inform Policy and Practice. In J. Clancy, G. Özerol, N. Mohlakoana, M. Feenstra, and L. S. Cueva, *Engendering the Energy Transition,* (pp. 33-58). Cham, Switzerland: Palgrave Macmillan.

Miles, M. R. (2015). How Fair Governance Encourages Voter Participation. *Political Research Quarterly,* 68(2), 363-376.

Naeher, L. P.; Smith, K. R.; Leaderer, B. P.; Neufeld, L.; and Mage, D. T. (2001). Carbon monoxide as a tracer for assessing exposures to particulate matter in wood and gas cookstove households of highland Guatemala. *Environmental Science & Technology,* 35, 575-581.

Nickerson, K. and Arceneaux, D. W. (2009). Who Is Mobilized to Vote? A Re-Analysis of 11 Field Experiments. *American Journal of Political Science,* 53(1), 1-16.

Parikh, J. (2011). Hardships and health impacts on women due to traditional cooking fuels: A case study of Himachal Pradesh, India. *Energy Policy,* 39(12), 7587-7594.

Planning Commission. (2006, August). *Asia Pacific Centre.* Retrieved 2023 March, from Integrated Energy Policy: Report of the Expert Committee: Integrated Energy Policy: Report of the Expert Committee.

Silwal, A. R. and McKay, A. (2015). The Impact of Cooking with Firewood on Respiratory Health: Evidence from Indonesia. *The Journal of Development Studies,* 51(12), 1619-1633.

Sinha, A. (2022, 19 March 19). *Indian Express.* Retrieved March 2023, from 'Ujjwala Effect': Study estimates over 1.5 lakh lives saved in a year, 13% reduction in air pollution deaths: https://bit.ly/3J4KL5z

12

INITIATIVES FOR ACCESS TO CLEAN AND AFFORDABLE ELECTRICITY FOR ALL

Reji Kumar Pillai

During the last century, electricity has transformed the face of the earth beyond our imagination and changed the way people live and work. The history of electrification in the twentieth century had two major milestones—one by V.I. Lenin in the USSR and the other by F.D. Roosevelt in the USA. Lenin's famous equation 'Soviets (cooperative villages) + Electricity = Socialism'[1] underscored the importance of electricity in socio-economic development and launched a massive electrification drive in Russia in 1920. About 90 per cent of Russian villages were electrified before Russia went into the Second World War. Although Thomas Edison and Nicolas Tesla invented the key equipment of power systems and built electric grids in the USA, electrification in America was confined only to urban areas even in the 1930s. The investor-owned electric utilities in the USA did not invest in extending the electric grid to rural areas where business volumes were low and the cost of grid expansion very high. When the USSR was 90 per cent electrified, the USA had electricity in less than one-fourth of the country. Considering that the erstwhile USSR had an area of 22.4 million sq km versus the USA's 9.5 million sq km, the USA was way behind Russia in countrywide electrification. This prompted President Franklin D. Roosevelt to issue a presidential order for rural electrification in 1935, which was later made the Rural Electrification Act 1936 of USA that initiated countrywide electrification and extended the coverage of the electricity network to about 5 million rural farms during the period from 1935 to 1955. The electrification of both the super powers had the personal imprints of their most powerful leaders. Similarly, in the electrification of India, Prime Minister Narendra Modi's vision and initiatives are ground breaking and exemplary as listed below.

- Gujarat Jota Gram Yolanda launched in 2003
- Vision for renewable energy development in the early days in Gujarat
- 175 GW renewable energy plan for India
- Launch of International Solar Alliance (ISA)
- Vision for One Sun, One World, One Grid (OSOWOG)
- SAUBHAGYA and completion of rural electrification in India

Narendra Modi's personal interventions in each of the above initiatives are summarized in this chapter.

Gujarat Jyoti Gram Yojana (GJY)

Rural electrification was made a top priority by the Government of India (GoI) in the late 1960s with the key objective of supplying electricity to irrigation pump sets (IP sets) to support the green revolution. To help states in the electrification drive, the Rural Electrification Corporation Limited (REC) was setup in 1969. The definition of an electrified village was limited to the extension of the grid to a village and giving one electricity connection. So, with just one electric bulb in a village, it could qualify as an electrified village. This criterion continued till the early 2000s. As a result, thousands of villages remained electrified only on paper and millions of people continued to live in darkness. In 2002, the GoI revised the definition of rural electrification and made it mandatory to provide electricity connections to all public institutions and a minimum of 10 per cent of households in a village (including the nearby hamlets) to be qualified as an electrified village. When this change in the definition was made, there were more than 100,000 villages, which were yet to be electrified.

A new programme was launched nationwide to complete electrification of all villages as per the new guidelines. In 2002, when Modi became the Chief Minister of Gujarat, there were about 18,000 villages in Gujarat that were not electrified. He was not satisfied with the modus operandi of rural electrification even if 10 per cent households were electrified. With his extensive travels in rural areas around the country for political work, he had had first-hand experience of long hours of daily power cuts in villages. Modi wanted to change the concept of village electrification radically. His vision was to provide round-the-clock electricity supply to all households and commercial establishments in a village and only eight hours of electricity supply to agricultural farms. He had several brainstorming sessions with engineers and bureaucrats and finally launched the GJY in 2003. In order to roster the agricultural supply to eight hours between 10 p.m. and 6 a.m. all households, shops and other commercial establishments in the village received 24x7 supply. Specially designed transformers (SDT) were deployed and feeders were segregated as agricultural and non-agricultural feeders.

In all, 180,000 villages and 10,000 hamlets surrounding villages were electrified and provided 24x7 supply by 2006 at a project cost of Rs. 1,290 crore of which Rs. 1,110 crore was granted by the Gujarat Government. The results of 24x7 uninterrupted electricity supply in villages changed the life of people beyond anyone's imagination. Impact assessment studies were conducted by independent institutions such as the Indian Institute of Management (IIM), Ahmedabad, and the Institute of Rural Management, Anand (IRMA), Gujarat, that have captured the amazing results of GJY's success.

24×7 power supply brought modern medical equipment to villages. Earlier, they had to go to nearby towns even for a simple x-ray. Medical stores and health centres in villages could store vaccines and other medicines in freezers, which was not possible earlier. With reliable power supply, modern medical facilities came to the villages.

24×7 power availability promoted cottage industries like chilli powder-making in villages; and average household income went up by 30 per cent as people could work after sunset and in the early morning hours with light from electric bulbs.

Access to power 24×7 made it possible to use electrical appliances like mixer/grinder, saving a lot of effort and time of rural women. The time they could save in kitchen activities could be utilized for more income-generating activities and entertainment.

Supply of power 24×7 enabled villagers to setup local dairy and in-house milk testing. Dairying is a big business in Gujarat.

Availability of power 24×7 helped villagers avail easy repair and maintenance of their machinery and vehicles through facilities of welding, lathes, etc., within villages; and communication facilities like STD/ PCO helped the villagers in emergencies and promoted small multipurpose shops. For each of these needs, people had to travel to nearby towns in the past.

Reliable power supply also empowered the villagers with mobile communication thereby making their life easy and more manageable. It made it possible for villagers to have the facilities of copier machines for their important documents and promoted entertainment and information through the medium of television.

Villagers could now run flour mills in villages, which resulted in huge time saving for them.

The key benefits of GJY are summarized below.

- With electricity at home, the working hours of people have increased, which has contributed to a rise in household income by more than 10 per cent per annum. About 53 per cent families could work during night time.
- Improved electricity load management on the grid resulted in No-Load-Shedding in the state.
- Students could use computers for education.
- Three-phase power supply available to villages 24×7 motivated people to invest in machinery for a variety of applications, which in turn created employment opportunities in the villages—a host of cottage and home industries sprouted in all the villages.
- Power availability has given rise to local dairy units in rural areas and also increased momentum in industrial activities such as diamond polishing, toiletries, agro-processing, etc.
- Provision of better health services and infrastructure facilities—people invested in medical shops, investigation centres, x-ray labs, clinics, etc.
- Migration from villages to towns has reduced by 33 per cent as overall quality of life improved in villages.
- Housewives were able to use electrical appliances at home for food preparation and other activities. Time spent on performing household chores was reduced by 26 per cent, which they could spend for learning new skills and other income-generating activities or entertainment.
- Increase in time spent by rural women lessened in—

- education by 90 per cent
- entertainment by 88 per cent
- social activities by 43 per cent
- income generating activities by 18 per cent.

- Entertainment was made available through TV and VCR; and they got access to local, national, and international news and entertainment channels. Significant increase in awareness was noticed amongst village people on health, nutrition and family planning issues, and government programmes.
- Improved quality power supply to the farms resulted in reduced failure rate of irrigation pumpsets of farmers, saving maintenance costs and time considerably.
- Drop-out of girl children from school has reduced by 80 per cent as they used to be pulled out of school to fetch drinking water from faraway places. With 24x7 power availability, people invested in tube-wells in villages, which provided drinking water in the village itself.
- School absenteeism reduced by 13 per cent and average duration of study at home for girls and boys went up by 92 per cent and 81 per cent, respectively.
- Use of kerosene as a main fuel reduced to 1.2 per cent, which was 5.2 per cent before JGY.
- Significant increase in value of the assets possessed and income growth of households and small businesses.
- Huge reduction in breakdown of electrical equipment as power quality improved in villages.
- Broad-based impact across all socio-economic categories.

The most impactful change was the 80 per cent reduction in drop-out of girl students in schools. This was mainly due to the availability of drinking water in villages. Girls used to be pulled out of school to fetch drinking water from faraway places in the past as thousands of villages had water shortages. After 24x7 electricity supply, people invested in pump sets in villages that provided adequate water to all households.

Vision for Renewable Energy Development in the Early Days in Gujarat

Narendra Modi was fascinated with new technologies and was convinced that solar energy will change the world. He setup the Gujarat Energy Research and Management Institute (GERMI) in Gandhinagar, which has now grown to become an eminent institution of international repute.[2]

Under GERMI, an experimental solar photo-voltaic (PV) plant of 1 MW capacity was set up in Gandhinagar. This centre has piloted different PV technologies—500 kW polycrystalline, 250 kW mono crystalline and 250 kW PV on dual-axis tracker. This also had an online monitoring system to track the generation of each PV panel. These systems were completed way back in January 2011 when one mega-watt of solar system cost over 2 million dollars. This was a living laboratory, which proved to be a torch bearer for solar energy development in the country. Modi has personally taken visitors from India and overseas to this pilot plant. The experience from this demonstration plant had given him the confidence to take bigger steps.

The next important initiative was installing solar panels on the irrigation canals and the development of a 1,000 MW solar park at Patan. As a pilot project, solar PV panels were installed on one kilometre stretch of the Narmada canal in March 2012. This project surprised the entire solar community around the world and showed the importance of keeping the lower side of the panels cool—the power generation from the panels installed on the canal was higher by 15 per cent owing to the cooler bottom of the panels. Evaporation from the canal also reduced as the water in the canal was covered by the panels. For a long time, the canal project was Modi's pet project and he wanted to install solar panels over thousands of kilometres of canals in the state. However, this still remains a dream project.

Gujarat Solar Park-1 (also called Charanka solar park) was developed near Charanka village in Patan district of Gujarat, and is spread over an area of 2,000 hectares (4,900 acres). This was developed to house about 1,000 MW solar PV plants. About 600 MW were completed prior to the deadline of 28 January 2012 to receive the special tariff of Rs. 15 (about US$ 0.29) per kWh for the first 12 years and Rs. 5 (about US$ 0.10) per kWh from year 13 to 25.[3] It also became the world's third largest PV power station then.

175 GW Renewable Energy Plan for India

India made a voluntary declaration at COP15 in 2009 at Copenhagen that the emission intensity would be reduced by 33 per cent by 2030 from 2004 levels. In order to achieve that target, renewable energy production was to be enhanced drastically. A new programme called JNNSM was launched in 2010 with a target of 20 gigawatt (GW) of grid connected solar power by 2020.

The Central Electricity Regulatory Commission (CERC) was mandated to fix the tariff for solar power in the country. It came up with a rate of Rs. 17 per kilowatt-hour (kWh) of electricity, which was over four times the cost of power from new thermal plants those days. States were invited to develop solar farms and allocate land to investors to build solar power plants from which the respective state electricity distribution companies would buy power at the rate of Rs. 17 per kWh for 25 years. In the first phase in 2011, 1,000 MW of solar plants were allotted to states. While most states shied away or signed up for smaller capacities, the Gujarat Government agreed to develop 900 MW. The development of South Asia's largest solar farm at Patan was by the personal effort of Narendra Modi. In 2012, the Ministry of New and Renewable Energy (MNRE) engaged NTPC to adopt the reverse auction route directly with power plant developers to allot solar farms in different states. The CERC benchmark rate of Rs. 17 per kWh was kept as the basis and bidders were asked to quote the lowest they could. The rates immediately fell to Rs. 11-12 per kWh. In the following year, prices fell to below Rs. 10 per kWh.

In 2014, Prime Minister Narendra Modi visited the USA where he noticed that its renewable energy target for 2020 was doubled by President Obama. On his return, Modi wanted to make a ten-fold increase in India's JNNSM target of 20 GW solar power by 2020, which bureaucrats and engineers maintained was impossible owing to a variety of techno-economic reasons. Finally, Modi prevailed and set a revised RE target of 175 GW by 2022, which comprises 100 GW of solar and 60 GW of wind. A new event, RE INVEST was launched in January 2015, which attracted investors and project developers from around the globe to invest in the renewable energy sector in India. As the allotment of projects under the enhanced targets commenced, the price of solar and wind energy started falling steeply. By 2017-18, the price of solar and wind energy came down to below Rs. 3.00 per kWh. This could be achieved owing to faster scaling up of solar farms and wind farms in the country. The credit for this revolution goes to Narendra Modi as he was the first person in India who dared to buy solar power at the rate of Rs. 17 per kWh for 900 MW of capacity; and changed the JNSSM target of 20 GW solar power by 2020 to 100 GW by 2022. These are undoubtedly bold and visionary steps that contributed to the evolution of an enabling ecosystem for domestic production and installation of solar and wind power in the country. Soon, Indian entities will be world leaders in renewable energy development. Presently, the Government of India has set a new target of 500 GW of renewable energy by 2030, which has taken the world by surprise.

Launch of International Solar Alliance (ISA)

At the twenty-first Conference of the Parties (COP) in Paris in 2015, Narendra Modi mooted the idea of an ISA, which was launched jointly with the then President of France, Francoise Hollande, on 30 November 2015. The United Nations (UN) adopted ISA as a UN agency headquartered in India. As of December 2022, there are 110 countries that have signed the ISA framework agreement as members while the governments of 90 countries have ratified the framework agreement. The ISA envisages the aggregation of the demands of member-countries and issuance of tenders for large volumes of different plants and equipment, which could bring prices down faster. ISA would also engage in technology development and technology transfer.[4]

Vision for One Sun, One World, One Grid

At the second RE INVEST event in 2018, which was held in conjunction with the first assembly of ISA in New Delhi in October 2018, Narendra Modi called the idea of 'One Sun, One World, One Grid' (OSOWOG) a very unique and powerful vision. Although China had initiated the concept of global energy interconnection (GEI) in 2012 and embarked on preliminary work, it remained a Chinese initiative with a hidden agenda, while Modi's idea of OSOWOG is more focused on global cooperation by interconnecting regional grids to take advantage of cheap solar energy as the sun is always shining in some part of the world. ISA has taken the lead of conducting a feasibility study on OSOWOG, which is presently in progress.

On 2 November 2021 at COP 26 in Glasgow, he ISA, India presidency of the ISA and the UK COP presidency unveiled plans for the first international network of global interconnected solar power grids, known as the Green Grids Initiative—One Sun, One World, One Grid (GGI-OSOWOG). The announcement was accompanied by the One Sun declaration, which stated that, 'Realizing the vision of One Sun, One World, One Grid through interconnected green grids can be transformational, enabling all of us to meet the targets of the Paris Agreement to prevent dangerous climate change, to accelerate the clean energy transition, and to achieve Sustainable Development Goals. These efforts can stimulate green investments and create millions of good jobs. By sharing the sun's energy, we can help to build a more peaceful and prosperous world.'

The declaration has been endorsed by 80 ISA member-countries. The project, being spearheaded by the governments of India and the UK in partnership with the ISA and the World Bank group, aims to harness solar energy wherever the sun is shining, ensuring that generated electricity flows to areas that need it the most. The GGI-OSOWOG will bring together a global coalition of national governments, international financial and technical organizations, legislators, power system operators, and knowledge leaders to accelerate the construction of the new infrastructure needed for a world powered by clean energy. In doing so, the project aims to reduce reliance on non-renewable energy such as coal by enabling them to purchase affordable solar power from other countries.

The basic idea of this OSOWOG and green grids is Narendra Modi's vision and he continues to drive this global agenda.

SAUBHAGYA and Completion of Village and Household Electrification in India

After Narendra Modi became the prime minister, he restructured the rural electrification programme and named it Deen Dayal Upadhyaya Gram Jyoti Yojana (DDUGJY). This programme promoted feeder segregation (similar to what was done in Gujarat under GJY) in areas where the power supply situation was poor. While this programme progressed well and completed the electrification of all 619,000 villages in 2018, the criteria of an electrified village remained as electrification was done to only 10 per cent of households and public institutions in a village. Narendra Modi was not satisfied with this scenario of electrification and he wanted 100 per cent electrification of households before 2019. Accordingly, the Pradhan Mantri Sahaj Bijli Har Ghar Yojana (SAUBHAGYA) was launched on 25 September 2017 for household electrification at government cost. SAUBHAGYA had a total funding of Rs. 16,320 crore of which Rs. 12,320 was gross budgetary support. This programme created a world record of electrifying over 26 million households in 18 months! Under SAUBHAGYA all 'below poverty line' (BPL) households (as per 2011 socio-economic census data) were given free electrification, while those above BPL were charged Rs. 500, which they could pay in ten instalments along with their electricity bills to the utilities. Electricity connections to un-electrified houses included service line cables, energy meter, single point wiring, LED lamps and associated accessories in line with standard specifications. In remote areas where the grid could not be extended, SAUBHAGYA provided solar PV packs of 200-300 watts with battery storage and maximum of 5 LED lamps, a DC fan, and a DC power plug along with provision for maintenance for five years. Under this programme, 26.28 million households were electrified including the creation of last-mile connectivity by March 2019. This completed the electrification of all 'willing' households in the country, a major milestone in the socio-economic development of India and the full credit for this again goes to Narendra Modi.

In conclusion, it is reiterated that in the realm of clean energy and clean energy access to rural masses and to lift them out of poverty, nobody has worked with focus and consistency over decades as Prime Minister Narendra Modi.

ENDNOTES

1. V.I. Lenin—Collected Works, vol. 33. Lenin made this famous statement at the 1920 annual convention of the Communist Party.
2. www.germi.org
3. The national solar policy had fixed tariffs of Rs. 17/kWh for solar PV in 2010.
4. More on ISA at www.isolaralliance.org

13

Climate Change and Energy Transition

Dinkar Srivastava

Climate change is an existential problem. The gravity of the situation has been underlined by a number of extreme weather events in recent years around the globe. This included the Texas blizzard in January-February 2021, the slowing down of winds in the North Sea in September 2021, and massive floods in Pakistan in 2022. North India witnessed extreme heat last year. No country or society can escape the adverse effect of global warming. Countering this phenomenon requires a series of mitigation and adaptation efforts. Mitigation involves limiting temperature increase by reducing carbon emissions. This has a bearing on energy choices. Fossil fuels have to be progressively replaced by clean energy. Most countries have adopted the goal of achieving net zero emissions (NZE) by 2050. China which has the highest annual emissions has agreed to do so by 2060. Prime Minister Modi announced at the Glasgow Conference that India will achieve this target by 2070.

Most Western narratives focus on environmental issues. There is an equally dire problem of poverty eradication. The development dimension cannot be ignored in any discussion of climate change. As emission standards become increasingly stringent, the carbon space available for future development is progressively reduced. This will impact the prospects of economic growth needed to achieve minimum standards of living for people of developing countries. India embarked on the path of industrialization only after independence and needs time to complete infrastructure development. Unless there is equitable burden sharing, billions of people the world over will remain mired in poverty. The developed countries and China have not only exhausted 80 per cent of the carbon budget, they are also eating into the meagre carbon budget remaining at a disproportionate pace. There is no convergence of emission trajectories.

Energy transition is a mammoth task. Fossil fuels at present provide 79 per cent of global energy consumption. Phasing them out will take time. The coal age has lasted more than two centuries. It still provides a substantial part of electricity generation. The oil age started a century ago with the discovery of internal combustion engines. It still provides the bulk of transport. Compressing this to less than half a century for achieving net zero transition by 2050 or 2070 will not be easy. De-coupling growth from energy consumption has no historical precedent. Service economies of the future will also require energy. Cloud computing needs server banks which consume vast amounts of electricity.

The sixth Assessment Report (AR6) of the International Panel for Climate Change released recently stated that human activities have led to global warming, with global surface temperature reaching 1.1°C above the 1850-1900 level by 2020. The report added that 'widespread and rapid changes in the atmosphere, ocean, cryosphere, and biosphere have occurred'. This has led to 'widespread adverse impacts and related losses and damages to nature and people.' The report mentioned 'the best estimate of reaching 1.5°C in the near term' as a possible scenario.[1] The goal at the Glasgow conference was to slow global warming so that this temperature threshold is reached only in 2100.

The 1.5°C threshold above the pre-industrial level has become the new norm since the Glasgow conference. This was only an aspirational goal at the Paris conference where the agreement was to limit the temperature increase to 2°C. The UN Secretary-General summed up the dire situation well: 'Humanity is on thin ice—and that ice is melting fast.' He mentioned that 'the rate of temperature rise in the last half-century is the highest in 2,000 years' and the 'concentrations of carbon dioxide are at their highest in at least two million years'. He added that the 'climate time-bomb is ticking.'[2]

The adaptation efforts referred to include measures to adapt to climate change. For instance, this includes afforestation and the introduction of climate-resilient agriculture. Prime Minister Modi has stressed the need to grow millets, which requires less water and is cheaper than wheat. Adaptation may not be enough where climate change has already wrought irreversible damage. In such cases, compensation for loss and damage is required. The 27th Conference of Parties at Cairo endorsed this principle last year. However, working out a mechanism to implement the agreement will take time. This will run into the problem of resources, where developed countries have failed to make good their previous commitments to provide assistance for adaptation measures. None of these tasks will be easy.

The Journey So Far: Historical Responsibility

Developed countries bear most of the responsibility for global emissions since 1751. According to an estimate by One World in Data, the USA has emitted 399 billion tons of CO_2 or 25 per cent of gross cumulative emissions. The 28 countries of the EU account for 353 billion tons of CO_2 or 22 per cent of global cumulative emissions. Though Chinese industrialization started late, its annual emissions already account for 200 billion tons of CO_2 or 12.7 per cent of global cumulative emissions. India bears no historical responsibility for global warming. Its cumulative emissions since 1751 are only 48 billion tons.[3]

Though India has accepted the goal of Net Zero Emissions by 2070 it has not accepted 'peaking'. India needs more time to complete its infrastructure development and industrialization. A longer transition time may not necessarily be a sufficient safeguard for maintaining India's development trajectory in case the available carbon budget gets exhausted earlier. As per current estimates by the UN, this will indeed be the case. In such a case, there will be increasing pressure from the USA and EU to cap emissions. These two economies are the largest markets for Indian exports, and where we enjoy a trade surplus. India needs to step up its pace of development while transitioning to clean energy sources.

Rise of China

Emission levels are an index of industrialization. Till the late 19th century, China was behind India on both counts. India's emission in 1858, a year after the first War of Independence was 395,000 tons. Forty years later, Chinese emissions stood at a mere 95,264 tons showing how weak the country's industry was. Both countries had been left behind by industrialization. UK's emission in 1750 was 9.35 million tons. The US's emissions in 1800 were a mere 252,816 tons in 1800.[4]

Chinese emission levels have gone up sharply since then with the country's rapid industrialization. China's share in global cumulative emissions since 1899 is 13.8 per cent. India's share in global cumulative emissions since 1858 is a mere 3.21 per cent.[5] Today, China's annual emission is the highest in the world, which is roughly double the level of the USA which is the second highest emitter. Out of global emissions of 37.12 billion metric tons in 2021, China alone accounted for 11.4 billion metric tons or 30 per cent. The Indian share was 2.7 billion metric tons or 7.27 per cent. The relative share of the Chinese in global emissions will increase by 2030 since US and EU emissions are going down. China has accepted peaking by 2030 but has not indicated a downward trajectory. China ramped up construction of new coal power plants before the Glasgow conference when it began work on 50 gig watts worth of coal power.

Climate Negotiations in Perspective

The Earth Conference in Rio established some of the core principles of climate negotiations in 1992. This included the recognition of the historical responsibility of developed countries for causing global warming through their cumulative emissions. This became the basis of the principles of equity and 'common but differentiated responsibilities and respective capabilities (CBDR&RC)' of developed and developing countries. These principles have formed the core substance of climate treaties negotiated under the UNFCCC.[6] These negotiations have been conducted at the inter-governmental level through the Conference of Parties (COP). The term alludes to inter-governmental negotiations between the countries which are party to the UNFCC.

Since the cumulative greenhouse gas emissions of the developed countries have caused global warming, they have the historical responsibility for climate action. They were required to take mitigation action to reduce their GHG emissions. In the interest of equity, developing countries with low per capita current emissions and with low cumulative emissions were exempt from mitigation commitments. The developed countries also have to provide climate finance, and technology transfer. These principles have been progressively diluted in the course of climate negotiations. The Rio Declaration (1992) was followed by the Kyoto Protocol (1997), the Paris Agreement (2015), the

Glasgow Summit outcome (2021), and COP 27 at Cairo in 2022. The principle of CBDR&RC has been progressively diluted by developed countries.

Kyoto Protocol

The Kyoto Protocol included legally binding targets for emission reduction for developed countries and advanced economies-in-transition (EIT). It came into effect in 2005. During the first commitment period between 2008 and 2012, developed countries and economies in transition were required to achieve 5.2 per cent emission reduction on an average, relative to their 1990 level. The EU-15, at the time, committed to reducing emissions by 8 per cent relative to 1990 levels. The developing countries were not required to have mandatory mitigation targets. Though the actual emission reduction targets were low, the Protocol was a step forward. It embodied the principle of 'common but differentiated responsibilities and respective capabilities (CBDR&RC)'. Developing countries did not have any responsibility for mitigation action, but could participate in the clean development mechanism. This allowed developed countries to offset their mitigation commitments by financing green projects in developing countries.

The USA signed the Kyoto Protocol but did not ratify it. The Clinton Administration did not even submit the Kyoto Protocol to the US Senate. This meant that the world's largest economy, and the largest emitter at the time, remained outside the mandatory emission reductions under the Protocol. Between 2008 and 2012, the emissions of 36 developed countries that effectively participated in the Kyoto Protocol (excluding the USA and Canada) were 24.2 per cent relative to the 1990 level. [7] During this period, emission levels in the 15 EU member-states fell by an average of 12.2 per cent against 1990 levels. This was partly due to the financial crisis of 2007-08, which resulted in a reduction in emissions and facilitated meeting the overall commitments under the Protocol.

Under the second commitment period of the Kyoto Protocol (2013-2020), and the Doha Amendment to the Kyoto Protocol, the average emission reduction target was set at an 18 per cent reduction by 2020 relative to 1990 levels. However, the Doha Amendment did not came into force till 2020. The actual emission reduction was only 14.8 per cent by 2019 relative to the base year.[8] Countries like Canada, Japan, Russia, and New Zealand did not participate in this period.

The objection of the USA and developed countries to the Kyoto Protocol was that this did not entail obligations for major developing economies like China and India to reduce their emissions. This was a departure from the principle of the historical responsibility of developed countries accepted by them earlier. Even though China had caught up with developed countries in terms of emissions, India has remained far behind both in terms of current and cumulative emissions. Developed countries also cite overall national emission figures, ignoring their much higher per capita emissions. The shift from mandatory to voluntary commitments began at the Copenhagen conference. Countries like the USA and Canada pledged 17 per cent economy-wide mitigation targets relative to 2005 levels. The process culminated in the Paris Agreement of 2015. Underlying the shift was President Obama's domestic compulsion. Though Democrats had won the Senate, he did not have the two-thirds majority required for obtaining Senate approval.

Paris Accord

The voluntary nature of commitments undertaken under the Paris Accord solved the Obama Administration's internal problem of seeking Senate approval for a legally binding treaty. The Accord also fudged the difference between the obligations of developed and developing countries and diluted the principle of special but differential responsibilities and respective capabilities. Though the commitments may be voluntary, the emission reduction targets will apply henceforth to both developed and developing countries. The countries agreed to submit their own nationally-determined contributions to the UNFCCC, with the goal of preventing global warming above 2 degrees Celsius while striving to keep it below 1.5 degrees Celsius. While the agreement mentioned both the temperature thresholds, the text made it clear that the agreed goal was preventing global warming above 2 degrees. The 1.5-degree threshold was a desired goal to strive for.

Glasgow Conference

The Glasgow conference of 2021 (COP 26) reaffirmed the Paris Accord goal to 'hold the increase in the global average temperature to well below 2 degrees C above pre-industrial levels and to pursue efforts to limit the temperature increase to 1.5 degrees above pre-industrial levels.' However, it went beyond stating both the temperature thresholds. The text added in the next paragraph (16):

> 'Recognizes that the impacts of climate change will be much lower at the temperature increase of 1.5 degrees C compared with 2 degrees C, and *resolves* to pursue efforts to limit the temperature increase to 1.5 degrees C.'[9] (Emphasis mine)

Thus the balance has clearly shifted to the lower temperature threshold. This is also reflected in the following paragraph (17) of the document which states:

> '*Also recognizes* that limiting global warming to 1.5 degrees C requires rapid, deep and sustained reductions in global greenhouse emissions, including reducing global carbon dioxide emissions by 45 per cent by 2030 relative to the 2010 level and to net zero around mid-century, as well as deep reductions in other greenhouse gases.'[10]

This is 'recognition', not an agreed commitment. Nevertheless, the shift in emphasis to the lower temperature threshold means more stringent emission standards. This also means a smaller carbon budget available to developing countries for future growth. India has to complete its infrastructure. This will require a considerable amount of steel and cement. Energy efficiency can minimize the resource requirement, but cannot eliminate it.

The second major outcome of the Glasgow conference was the endorsement of the concept of net zero emissions. This is a relative concept. It implies that the country concerned reduces emissions to a level where they are balanced by its carbon absorption capacity or sink by a chosen deadline. The concept gained wide currency in the West quickly. It reduces climate change, a global problem, to implementation at the national level. The commitment is voluntary, and countries have been given the flexibility to choose the deadline for achieving net zero emissions. However, there is a fundamental shift involved from the principles agreed upon earlier. Both developed and developing countries have to undertake mitigation commitments.

The third major outcome of the Glasgow conference was pressure to 'phase out' coal. This singled out fossil fuel while leaving out gas which is used for power generation and heating by the rich world. The resistance by developing countries somewhat watered down the formulation and replaced it with the 'phasing down' of coal but the differential approach to coal and gas—both are fossil fuels—remained. India got the blame for diluting the Glasgow text, though the formulation of 'phasing-down' of coal had been agreed upon by the USA and China days earlier in a bilateral deal on the margins of the conference. The phrase originated in the Chinese 15th five-year plan. Coal accounts for 71 per cent of power generation in India. It cannot, therefore, be 'phased down' quickly. Energy transition in India as elsewhere has to be a gradual process. It is also extremely costly.

The Glasgow conference also asked for phasing out of inefficient fossil fuel subsidies. This was partially qualified by reference to 'providing targeted support to the poorest and the most vulnerable in line with national circumstances.' This meets India's concerns. As the Indian Minister for Environment, Shri Bhupendra Yadav, explained: "Developing countries have still to deal with their development agendas and poverty eradication. Towards this end, subsidies provide much-needed social security and support."[11] The minister added, "We are giving subsidies for use of LPG to low-income households. This subsidy has been a great help in eliminating biomass burning for cooking, and has improved the health of women and in reducing indoor air pollution."[12]

An exclusive focus on phasing down coal reflects a one-sided narrative. Gas, which is also a fossil fuel, remains a major part of the energy basket of developed countries. Natural gas accounts for 40 per cent of the UK's energy production and 35.5per cent of electricity generation.[13] Fossil fuels, including gas, coal, and lignite are nearly 33per cent of Germany's energy production[14] and 40 per cent of electricity generation.[15]

According to the US Energy Information Administration, fossil fuel accounts for 79per cent of the US's energy basket[16] and 60per cent of electricity generation.[17]

At the Paris conference, the developed countries had made a commitment to provide $ 100 billion dollars per annum of financial assistance to developing countries. The developed countries are yet to fulfil the earlier commitment. The Glasgow outcome document noted 'with deep regret that the goal of developed country parties to mobilize jointly USD 100 billion per year by 2070 in the context of meaningful mitigation actions and transparency on implementation has not yet been met.'[18] The pledge to provide USD 100 billion was made when the agreed target was to limit the global temperature increase to within 2°C of the pre-industrial level. With the accent toward 1.5°C temperature threshold, emission standards have become tighter, and consequently, more resources are needed.

Sharm-el-Sheikh (COP 27)

The Sharm-el-Sheikh conference (COP 27) was held against the background of the ongoing Ukraine war which has resulted in shifting the focus from climate change to energy security. The conference highlighted the 'loss and damage' issue. The relevant paragraph from the Implementation plan stated: 'Welcomes the consideration, for the first time, of matters relating to funding arrangements responding to loss and damage associated with the adverse effects of climate change, including a focus on addressing loss and damage...'[19] Though this acknowledges the problem, there is still no binding agreement, much less a target date or figure for funding arrangement without which the provision will have little meaning.

There was no progress on the key issue of finance. The Implementation plan mentioned 'USD 4 trillion per year needs to be invested in renewable energy up until 2030 to be able to reach net zero emissions by 2050.'[20] It added 'a global transformation to a low-carbon economy is expected to require investment of at least USD 4–6 trillion per year,' but there was no commitment on the part of developed countries to scale up financing. The huge gap between the vast resources required, and what is available is clear from the following paragraph:

> 'Expresses serious concern that the goal of developed country parties to mobilize jointly USD 100 billion per year by 2020 in the context of meaningful mitigation action and transparency on implementation has not yet been met and urges developed country parties to meet the goal'.[21]

The exhortation that multilateral development banks (MDBs) provide the funding only serves to dilute the responsibility of the developed countries to provide funding. The MDBs themselves depend upon the governments of the rich countries to provide capital. If these countries have failed so far to provide 100 billion US dollars per annum, they are unlikely to channel USD 4-6 trillion per year through the MDBs. Raising money from the market would be costly and may well be out of the reach of the developing countries. The problem is compounded because the countries most vulnerable are also often most heavily indebted. For instance, Pakistan estimated that it has suffered loss and damage of USD 30 billion in recent floods. At the same time, the country is facing a dire economic crisis.

Energy Transition

The energy transition to net zero emissions stage requires moving to low carbon fuel. The choice essentially is between renewables and nuclear. India's hydropower potential is limited. According to a recent UN study on "Life cycle assessment of electricity generation options', nuclear power has the lowest emission as compared to other sources:

	Nuclear	*Solar PV*	*Wind*	*Gas*	*Coal*
Emission Levels ($g\ CO_2$ eq/kWh)	5.1–6.4	8.0–83	7.8 and 16	403-513	751-1095

Source: UNECE report on life cycle assessment of electricity generation options, file:///C:/Users/Owner/Downloads/UNECE,%20Lifecycle%20Assessment.pdf

Energy transition also has to take into account costs of different options. China and India depend upon coal for a large share of their power generation. Gas has a relatively larger share in the energy profile of developed countries. Though this is also a fossil fuel, its emission is less as compared to coal. India has a large renewable portfolio. It currently accounts for approximately 100 GW (50.77 GW of solar and 40.12 GW of wind) in addition to 51.36 GW of hydro-power. The PM has announced at the Glasgow conference that non-fossil fuels will be ramped up steeply to 500 GW by 2030. This will be 50 per cent of the total installed capacity by that year. Nuclear power is currently 6.78 GW. This will be increased to 22.48 GW by 2030. This is a rather modest share. In terms of generation, this is around 3 per cent of total generation. The share of nuclear in the generation-mix is much higher for most other major economies. It is 20 per cent both in case of the USA and the EU. China plans to commission 150 new nuclear reactors over the next 15 years boosting its share in generation to 10 per cent.

Cost

The falling tariff of solar and wind power have created an impression that renewable power is cheap, and offers the promise of lowering emissions by replacing fossil fuels and bringing down costs at the same time. This is, however, based on a major misconception. Renewable is an 'intermittent' source of power. Bill Gates in his book *How to Avert a Climate Disaster* has described this as 'the curse of intermittency'. By its very nature, solar is available at best during the day time. Wind energy is available only in two coastal states in India—Tamil Nadu and Gujarat, that too, only for four months a year. When the sun is not shining, and the wind is not blowing, the grid has to be supplied power from an alternative source. This is called 'balancing' power. In developing countries like India and China, this is provided by coal. In the rich world, balancing power is provided by gas.

The cost of balancing power is not reflected in the tariff structure in India. The 'Forum of Regulators' which included power sector regulators from all the states in India estimated in 2017 that this was an additional Rs.1.47 to Rs.1.57 per unit for Gujarat and Tamil Nadu over and above the normal tariff. They revised it upwards to Rs. 2.12 per unit of electricity in 2021. Added to a minimum tariff of around Rs. 2 per unit, this makes solar power more expensive than either thermal power (average tariff Rs. 3.25 per unit) or nuclear power (average tariff Rs. 3.43 per unit). Apart from the cost of battery storage, there is no grid scale storage solution available till now.

The higher cost of renewables as compared to fossil fuels or nuclear power is true not only of India, but other countries in the world. It is no coincidence that Germany with highest renewable penetration (46 %) in the world has also the highest power tariff. An extreme weather event will have a major impact on the electricity tariff. The cases of Germany and the UK would be illustrative. In both cases, wind power accounts for nearly one-fifth of total power generation. In September 2021, North Sea winds slowed down. This resulted in a sharp increase in power tariff in Europe. This led to a scramble for gas to compensate for loss of wind power. While this increased the price of gas on one hand, it also led to a steep hike in power tariff. In the case of the UK, the power tariff went up five-fold; in the case of Germany, it doubled. Germany was relatively less affected because it could draw power from the regional grid. The UK being an island-nation could not do so. India's situation is akin to that of the UK even though we are a subcontinent. All our neighbours are energy deficit with the exception of Bhutan. Bhutan's hydro-power exports are not enough to meet the requirement of even one province in India.

The Vivekananda International Foundation task force on India's energy transition in a carbon-constrained world has come up with some interesting findings. The study took up five different scenarios ranging from renewable high (R95N05) to nuclear high (R05N95). There were three other intermediate scenarios with different ratios of coal with carbon capture and storage (CCS).[22] The two most important finds are:

(i) India's per capita electricity consumption has to be ramped up to

20,559 kWh (R95N05) to 16,313 kWh (R05N95) per capita by 2070 to achieve net zero emissions.

(ii) The cost of energy transition to net zero emissions by 2070 would be the least in case of nuclear-dominated scenario (R05N95) at $ 11.2 trillion, while the cost in case of a renewable dominated scenario (R95N05) would be 28 per cent more at $ 15.5 trillion.

'The study has shown that there is a happy convergence between energy security and clean environment'. Reaching net zero emissions requires not only decarbonizing the power sector, but also bringing other sectors—transport, industry, and housing under electrification based on clean energy. This will inevitably increase demand for electricity which has no relationship with the previous trends of electricity consumption. The second key finding is that a nuclear dominated scenario is the most cost-effective option and a renewable-dominated option, the most costly. This takes into account the systems costs, which include both 'balancing' and transmission costs.

Hydrogen Economy

Unlike carbon, burning of hydrogen produces water. This could make hydrogen the preferred energy source in a carbon-constrained world. Hydrogen could also be an energy storage solution. Renewable energy could be used to produce hydrogen in the day time when solar power is available. This could be used at night when solar power is not available. The hydrogen could thus provide 'balancing' power for the renewables and help resolve the problem of intermittency of solar or wind power. Hydrogen is also being considered as fuel for hard-to-abate sectors like steel and cement.

There are, however, considerable challenges before hydrogen economy could become a reality. Hydrogen is highly combustible. Hydrogen molecules are too small, and hence leakage will be a problem, but the most critical factor is cost. Green hydrogen is 2-3 times more expensive than grey hydrogen or hydrogen produced from natural gas. Most countries are therefore considering a spectrum of choices which includes both blue (low carbon) to green hydrogen. The 10-point action plan announced by the former UK prime minister, for instance, mentions low carbon hydrogen rather than green hydrogen. The USA is considering both blue and green hydrogen options. On the other hand, India's hydrogen policy only mentions green hydrogen which is a very costly alternative. At this stage of technology development, we need to keep all the options open.

There is also the issue of how green hydrogen is to be produced. Production through the renewable route requires the use of solar or wind power to produce green hydrogen through electrolysis of water. This increases demand for electricity, which makes it costly. The USA, UK, France, Japan, and South Korea are exploring hydrogen production using nuclear energy for splitting water molecules through thermo-chemical reactions. This requires development of high temperature gas reactors (HTGRs). The USA and UK governments are providing funds for R&D for this purpose. China has already made considerable progress. The renewable route will also increase the demand for land, which is discussed in the next section. Land constraint has to be factored into the choice of energy form.

Land

Land use is the most politically sensitive issue, especially in developing countries. Renewables are the most land-intensive source of electricity generation; nuclear power is the densest source of energy. Bill Gates in his book *How to Avert a Climate Disaster* has pointed out that nuclear power can provide 500-1,000 watts per square metre as against 5-20 watts per square metre for solar and a mere 1-2 watts per square metre for wind power.[23] In other words, for the same energy output, solar would need 100 times more space, while wind power will need 500 times more (Source: Gates, B. (2021). *How to Avoid a Climate Disaster* (p. 58) [London]: Allen Lane). A recent report by the French Government company RTE has reached the same conclusion.[24]

A study by Prof. Sukhatme has brought out that India has a total of 200,000 square km of surplus land. There is enough land available for the target of 500 GW of non-fossil fuels announced by the government by 2030. However, most of the land for the new ultra-mega power projects will have to be found in remote areas like Kutch and the North-east. This will have a bearing on transmission costs which will increase steeply.

As the country moves towards net zero emissions (NZE) by 2070, the installed capacity will have to go up steeply. India's total installed capacity is around 400 GW currently. This will have to increase to around 1,000 GW by 2030 assuming that around 50 per cent of capacity (or 500 GW) will be from non-fossil fuels.

According to a report by the VIF Task Force on *India's Energy Transition in a Carbon-Constrained World*, India will need a 14,680 GW of solar if we rely mostly on renewable energy (R95N05) to attain net zero emissions (NZE) by 2070. This will require a total land area of 412,033 square km. This is double the total land area currently available.

The land requirement will be more manageable—183,565 square km in case we rely mostly on nuclear power (R05N95) to attain NZE.[25] This estimate is based on 10 per cent of demand met through hydrogen. In case the share of hydrogen in the total demand is increased to 25 per cent, the land requirement will go up to 1,313,500 square km.[26] This is about seven times the total surplus land available now. The actual problem will be much worse since the surplus land currently available—200,000 square km—will shrink as the population increases and India's industrialisation progresses over the next fifty years.

Future

Energy transition to net zero emissions is going to be extremely costly. The cost for India alone ranges from $ 11.2 trillion to $ 15.5 trillion over 50 years to 2070. The pledge of developed countries to provide $ 100 billion per annum *globally* pales into insignificance in comparison. Even this paltry sum has not been realized. The Western attempt is to shift responsibility from governments to multilateral development banks (MDBs) and private financial flows. The former are subject to funding being provided by governments, which have given a wholly inadequate response so far. The latter will be subject to commercial returns, which will be difficult to afford for developing countries.

We have to be prepared for painful choices. The policy of writing-off electricity dues for electoral considerations will further cripple DISCOMs to make timely payments to generators. Given the scale of resources needed, an early decision is needed. Renewable energy is best suited for distributed generation, preferably in agriculture. The country should make the fullest use of available renewable energy sources, particularly solar power. The target of 50 per cent installed capacity based on non-fossil fuels by 2030 must be met but the steep increase in generation capacity required to achieve net zero emissions by 2070 must take into account the land-constraint. There is a need for a prudential policy and all technology options have to be explored. Almost all major economies—the USA, UK, France, and China—are the exploring use of nuclear power coupled with thermos-chemical processes to produce hydrogen. This requires a review of the hydrogen policy announced so far. Nuclear power is in the government sector under the Atomic Energy Act. Therefore, government support will be critical for ramping up nuclear power to maintain India's development trajectory. This also requires providing nuclear power incentives given to renewables as both are emission-free energy sources. The Act needs to be amended to bring in more players to reduce pressure on the government to provide resources.

ENDNOTES

1. https://report.ipcc.ch/ar6syr/pdf/IPCC_AR6_SYR_SPM.pdf
2. https://www.un.org/sg/en/content/sg/statement/2023-03-20/secretary-generals-video-message-for-press-conference-launch-the-synthesis-report-of-the-intergovernmental-panel-climate-change
3. Our World in Data.
4. Our World in Data.
5. Our World in Data.
6. Under the UNFCCC, countries were divided in two main groups viz. developed countries and Economies-in-Transition (for whom emission reductions targets were mandatory) and developing countries (for whom emission reduction targets were not mandatory).
7. VIF Task Force on India's Energy Transition in a Carbon-Constrained World, citing Shishlov, R. Morel and Valentin Bellassen. Compliance of the Parties to the Kyoto Protocol in the first commitment period; *Climate Policy* Taylor & Francis, 2016, 16 (6), pp.768-782.
8. VIF Task Force Report on India's Energy Transition in a Carbon-Constrained World citing Prasad, Sumit: Spandan Pandey, and Shikha Bhasin. 2021. Unpacking Pre-2020 Climate Commitments. New Delhi: CEEW and Shakti Foundation.
9. United Nations, Glasgow Climate Pact, https://unfccc.int/sites/default/files/resource/cop26_auv_2f_cover_decision.pdf
10. United Nations, Glasgow Climate Pact, https://unfccc.int/sites/default/files/resource/cop26_auv_2f_cover_decision.pdf
11. *Indian Express*, Countries adopt Glasgow climate pact after India, China force amendment on coal reference, 15 November 2021, https://indianexpress.com/article/world/climate-change/glasgow-climate-pact-coal-subsidy-cop26-conference-7621670/
12. *Indian Express*, Countries adopt Glasgow climate pact after India, China force amendment on coal reference, 15 November 2021, https://indianexpress.com/article/world/climate-change/glasgow-climate-pact-coal-subsidy-cop26-conference-7621670/
13. VIF Task Force Report on India's Energy Transition in a Carbon-Constrained World citing Department for Business, Energy and Industrial Strategy, Govt. of UK. (2021). *Digest for UK Energy Statistics, Annual Data for UK, 2020.* https://assets.publishing.service.gov.uk/government/uploads/system/uploads/attachment_data/file/1007132/DUKES_2021_Chapters_1_to_7.pdf
14. VIF Task Force Report on India's Energy Transition in a Carbon-Constrained World citing Data extrapolated from: EIA, 2019. *Germany Country Profile* https://www.eia.gov/international/overview/country/DEU

15. VIF Task Force Report on India's Energy Transition in a Carbon-Constrained World citing De Statis, Statische Bandesamt. (2021). *Gross Electricity Production in Germany.* https://www.destatis.de/EN/Themes/Economic-Sectors-Enterprises/Energy/Production/Tables/gross-electricity-production.html
16. VIF Task Force Report on India's Energy Transition in a Carbon-Constrained World citing US EIA. (2021). *US Energy Facts Explained* https://www.eia.gov/energyexplained/us-energy-facts/data-and-statistics.php
17. VIF Task Force Report on India's Energy Transition in a Carbon-Constrained World citing US Energy Information Administration. (2021). *Electricity in the United States.* https://www.eia.gov/energyexplained/electricity/electricity-in-the-us.php
18. United Nations, Glasgow Climate Pact, https://unfccc.int/sites/default/files/resource/cop26_auv_2f_cover_decision.pdf
19. Paragraph 24, Sharm el-Sheikh Implementation Plan, https://unfccc.int/sites/default/files/resource/cop27_auv_2_cover%20decision.pdf
20. Paragraph 30, Sharm el-Sheikh Implementation Plan, https://unfccc.int/sites/default/files/resource/cop27_auv_2_cover%20decision.pdf
21. Paragraph 33, Sharm el-Sheikh Implementation Plan, https://unfccc.int/sites/default/files/resource/cop27_auv_2_cover%20decision.pdf
22. R = Renewable, CCS Coal with Carbon Capture and Storage and N= Nuclear. The five scenarios are R95N05, R60N10CCS30, R50N20CCS30, R40N35CCS25, and R05N95.
23. Gates, B. (2021).*How to Avoid a Climate Disaster* (p. 58) [London]: Allen Lane.
24. VIF Task Force Report on India's Energy Transition in a Carbon-Constrained World, p. 30.
25. Ibid.
26. Ibid.

14

Greening India's Electricity Grid: Policies Behind Progress

Lydia Powell

Introduction

In 2010, the Government of India set a target of installing 20 gigawatts (GW) of solar power capacity by 2022 under the Jawaharlal Nehru National Solar Mission (JNNSM) with the brand name "Solar India". The Ministry of New & Renewable Energy (MNRE) also set a target of installing 60 GW of wind power generation capacity by 2022. In October 2022, the installed capacity of solar energy was 61 GW, more than three times the target set by JNNSM. Wind energy capacity of about 41 GW in 2022 missed the target but overall installed capacity of renewable energy (RE) was over 119 GW, the second largest after installed capacity of coal-based power generation, accounting for about 29 per cent of total installed capacity for power generation.

The share of RE in India's primary energy basket was less than 1 per cent in 2010 and in 2022 the share had increased to about 3 per cent. RE accounts for over 12 per cent of power generation in India that makes India the eighth largest RE power generator in the world. The increase in the share of RE from less than 1 per cent to about 3 per cent in India's primary energy basket in roughly 10 years would not have materialised but for progressive policies that aimed to meet commitments to the Paris Agreement (PA) and put India's electricity grid on the path towards decarbonisation.

Growth of Renewable Energy

In 2014, the new government that came to power increased the target for RE power generation capacity to 175 GW with solar contributing 100 GW, wind 60 GW, biomass 10 GW, and small hydropower (SHP) 5 GW by 2022. Experienced observers of the Indian energy industry were sceptical over the fivefold increase in the target for RE installed capacity. The then minister for power's response to a question posed in the Upper House of the Indian Parliament in 2015 that India would need an investment of over ₹ 6 trillion ($ 89.88 billion) to achieve the proposed capacity of 100 GW target by 2022 for solar energy at ₹ 60 million per megawatt (MW) and that the central government's budget allocation for solar energy in the financial year 2015-16 was just over ₹ 331 million, a meagre 0.45 per cent of the required investment did not offer comfort to sceptics. However, in 2022, RE installed capacity crossed the mark of over 100 GW which is a significant achievement that few believed would materialise.

The installed capacity of thermal (largely coal-based) power generation capacity took 60 years to cross the mark of 100 GW. Though policies played an important role in promoting RE, structural differences between thermal and RE-based projects that contributed to the exponential growth in RE capacity addition cannot be ignored. RE projects in general and solar projects in particular have short gestation periods compared to thermal power projects. The modular nature of solar projects makes them easy to assemble and carry lower risks unlike thermal projects that involve complex engineering with higher risks. But coal-based power generators have longer life spans and generate several times more despatchable power than solar projects of comparable capacity. Solar power generation often requires additional investment in storage of electricity to compensate for intermittency in power generation.

Solar power projects in India that were dependent on imported solar modules also benefitted from the exponential increase in capacity for manufacturing solar panels in China. Economies of scale in solar panel manufacturing in China along with advances in the science and manufacturing technologies behind solar power generation brought down costs by over 97 per cent between 1980 and 2012. This facilitated a decrease in solar power tariff in reverse auctions from over ₹ 17/kilowatt hour (kWh) in 2010 to less than ₹ 2/kWh in 2020, a fall of over 85 per cent in ten years. The competitiveness of solar power became one of the driving forces behind the growth in installed capacity.

Policy Progress: India as Consumer of Renewable Energy

Legislation for Low Carbon Electricity

Key electricity sector reforms implemented in the last two decades that were critically important for the growth in RE installed capacity began when the Electricity Regulatory Commissions Act 1998 (ERCA, 1998) was enacted. Under the ERCA 1998, the central electricity regulatory commission (CERC) and state electricity regulatory commissions (SERC) were set up. With ERCA 1998, electricity tariff was set by SERCs under the guidance of CERCs rather than by state governments. ERCA 1998 was followed by the enactment the Electricity Act, 2003 (EA, 2003), a landmark in electricity sector reforms and a pivot around which progressive policies for increase in RE generation capacity could be anchored. EA 2003 replaced the legal framework for the sector hitherto governed by the Electricity Supply Act 1948 and ERCA 1998. One of the most important provisions of EA 2003 that had implications for investment in RE was the de-licensing of generation. Once generation was de-licensed, the private sector entered the power generation segment of the value chain and doubled overall power generation capacity in just a decade. The role of the private sector in installation of power generation capacity strengthened in the RE sector.

The enabling provisions of EA 2003 called for measures to provide connection to the grid and for distribution licensees to purchase a percentage of the total consumption of electricity from RE sources. These provisions enabled SERCs to mandate renewable purchase obligations (RPOs) on state distribution companies (discoms). RPOs were complimented with RE certificates (RECs), a tradable market-based instrument in 2010-11. RECs facilitated compliance with RPO mandates and served as a channel for alternative valuation for low carbon electricity generation.

India's electricity policies since the 2000s have reflected the challenge of climate change and the need to decarbonise the energy sector. The National Electricity Policy 2005 emphasised the need for specific power purchase agreements and tariff mechanisms to promote RE. The National Tariff Policy 2006 introduced preferential feed-in-tariff to promote RE. In 2008, India launched the National Action Plan on Climate Change (NAPCC) in which solar energy was to occupy the centre stage in the shift away from fossil fuels. JNNSM, launched in 2010, added momentum to the solar energy sector.

In the late 1990s and 2000s wind energy, in both the manufacture of wind turbines and in wind energy generation, was the biggest beneficiary of favourable policies, especially at the state level. These included but not limited to 100 per cent accelerated depreciation on capital investment in equipment in the first year of installation, five years' income-tax exemption on income from sale of power generated by wind energy, mandatory purchase of electricity by discoms, attractive feed-in-tariff for wind-based power generation, and industry status to wind equipment manufacturers.

Since the 2010s, installed capacity of solar photovoltaic (PV) overtook that of wind energy partly because of policy focus shifting to solar and also because of the decline in solar PV project costs. In 2001, the capital cost of wind projects in India was estimated at about ₹ 30 million/MW compared to ₹ 300 million/MW for solar projects. By 2020, the capital cost of solar projects had fallen to about ₹ 55 million/MW while the capital cost of wind increased to about ₹ 60 million/MW. The modular nature of solar projects added to the attractiveness of solar compared to wind projects. Between 2014 and 2022, wind energy capacity addition has grown at a CAGR of about five per cent while solar grew at a rate of over 50 per cent.

The "must-run" status accorded to solar and wind projects in line with EA 2003 by the Indian Electricity Grid Code 2010 (EGC, 2010), a technical directive to maintain grid stability, added to the attractiveness of investing in RE-based power generation. The "must-run" status, accelerated depreciation, waiver of interstate transmission charges, RPOs that were enforced by SERCs and long-term power purchase agreements of up to 25 years added to the attractiveness of the market for RE-based power with predictable, relatively stable, and long-term returns. India's ambitious targets for RE capacity addition also attracted low-cost finance from multilateral development banks that substantially improved competitiveness of RE projects.

The combination of structural factors such as the modular nature that lowers initial investment and simplifies assembly of solar projects at the production end and the guaranteed, stable long-term market at the demand end made the RE sector very attractive for private investment. Since 2014, the private sector has accounted for over 90 per cent of investment in the RE sector. This is a trend that differs significantly from the period before enactment of EA 2003 when most of the installed capacity in thermal power generation was publicly owned.

Other policies that facilitated the growth of RE installed capacity are notification of competitive bidding guidelines for procurement of solar and wind power under EA 2003; priority lending status for RE projects; ten year tax holiday; waiver of interstate transmission system (ISTS) charges and losses for sale of power from solar and wind power projects commissioned up to 2023; notification of long-term RPO growth trajectory, uniformly applicable to all states and union territories; green energy corridor (GEC) for installing transmission lines and sub-stations and procurement of electricity from 2,500-megawatt (MW) ISTS grid connected wind power projects with up to 20 per cent blending with solar PV power through a transparent process of bidding.

Subsidies for Clean Energy

Apart from implementing enabling policies for private investment, the government is also executing programmes underwritten by generous subsidy support for off-grid RE power generation. One of the most important off-grid programmes is the Pradhan Mantri Kisan Urja Suraksha evam Utthaan Mahabhiyan (PM-KUSUM) scheme that aims to add off-grid solar and other RE capacity of 30.8 GW by 2022. The target includes installation of 2 million standalone solar pumps and solarisation of 1.5 million grid connected pumps

In addition, the government also supports implementation of off-grid solar PV applications like solar street lights, solar study lamps, and solar power packs. To facilitate accelerated deployment of solar roof top systems, the government has offered financial incentives to households and distribution companies with a target of 40 GW installed capacity by 2022. To facilitate large-scale grid connected solar power projects, a scheme for "development of solar parks and ultra-mega solar power projects" is in place with a target capacity of 40 GW by 2022. The government offers land, power evacuation facilities, road connectivity, and other amenities along with all statutory clearances. The government is also supporting 12 GW grid-connected solar PV power projects by public sector companies with viability gap funding (VGF) support on condition that they use domestically produced solar PV components. There is also a programme in place to support waste and biomass-based co-generation in sugar mills and other industries.

India as Producer of Renewable Energy Technologies

In 2020, India announced a large-scale incentive programme to promote domestic manufacture of solar modules and storage batteries to reduce imports. In 2022, a production linked incentive (PLI) programme for manufacture of high efficiency solar modules was launched with initial support of ₹ 45 billion that was later supplemented with an additional outlay of ₹ 195 billion. India has also introduced safeguard duties and customs duty on the import of solar panels and modules to discourage imports.

At present, India has 15 GW production capacity for solar modules, but they have no upstream capacity to manufacture polysilicon or wafers. The PLI programme aims to incentivise setting up of 29 GW of fully integrated plants (from polysilicon to ingots, wafers, solar cells, panels, modules), 8 GW plants integrated from wafers to modules, and 18 GW plants integrated over cells and modules. The largest share of the incentives of ₹ 120 billion is allocated for fully integrated plants that will produce polysilicon, convert them into wafers followed by cells and modules. ₹ .45 billion of PLI is offered to manufacture of wafers, cells and modules and ₹ 30 billion for manufacture of cells and modules. The PLI disbursed is designed to increase with increase in technical efficiency of modules and with increase in domestic value addition. The minimum efficiency of cells has increased by 1 per cent between the first and second tranches of auctions to select manufacturers.

The PLI programme for solar PV manufacturing is not only expected to build domestic capacity in high efficiency solar module manufacturing but also bring in advanced technology, ensure better quality control and competitiveness, promote domestic manufacture of balance of materials like ethylene vinyl acetate, solar glass and back-sheet, attract additional investment of ₹ 940 million and generate 195,000 direct and 780,000 indirect domestic employment.

The push to increase domestic solar PV manufacturing capacity is not new. In 2010, when JNNSM was initiated, there were 15 firms manufacturing solar cells, 20 firms manufacturing solar modules and more than 50 firms assembling solar modules. JNNSM sought to transform India into a solar energy hub with leadership in low-cost, high quality solar manufacturing, including balance of system components. Proactive implementation of the special incentive package (SIPs) policy, to promote PV manufacturing plants, including domestic manufacture of silicon material, was seen to be essential.

Towards this goal, the JNNSM proposed soft loans for expansion of existing solar assembly facilities in small and medium enterprise facilities and for technology upgradation and working capital through IREDA (Indian Renewable Energy Development Agency). Provision for transfer of technology was to be built into government and private procurement from foreign sources. Simultaneously, the national manufacturing policy of 2011 (Department of Industrial Policy and Promotion [DIPP] 2011) identified solar energy as among industries of strategic importance where national capabilities were to be developed to make the country a major force in the sector. JNNSM imposed domestic content requirement (DCR) on project developers to protect the domestic manufacturing sector. It envisaged the achievement of grid parity of solar electricity through long-term and predictable policy, large-scale deployment and aggressive research and development (R&D). However, the goal of domestic production of critical materials, components and other elements of the solar value chain failed to materialise, notwithstanding a range of incentives offered by the government. The private sector which was able to capitalise on the incentives for solar project development and solar power generation did not contribute to investment in manufacturing, possibly because it carried higher risks, involved high capital investment and cutting-edge technological knowledge. It is also possible that potential Indian solar manufacturers were weary of competition from China.

Challenges

The success of policies to support investment in RE does not mean they are without shortcomings. The increase in target for RE has meant a large degree of centralisation of initiatives and programmes to increase RE capacity. Centralisation of decision making has produced mixed results. On the one hand, it has dramatically improved the visibility of India's effort to decarbonise the power sector. This has attracted large overseas players and foreign investment in the RE sector. On the other hand, centralisation has oversimplified and generalised RE projects offered on auction or tender basis which has affected their technical and economic viability. While the involvement of technologically competent international players in the RE sector has introduced advanced technology, it has also driven out small players with domestic roots. Most importantly, the constant pressure to drive down the tariff of RE projects has favoured large international players with access to low-cost finance at the expense of smaller domestic players.

In addition, the overemphasis on lower tariff has meant that tariff caps set for centrally-auctioned projects are often too low to make the projects bankable or economically viable. The case of the Indian wind energy industry that has developed domestic manufacturing capabilities over the last 30 years illustrates the challenge. In the late 2000s, the success of reverse auctions in driving down solar tariffs led the wind energy sector to adopt the model. Initially, it was welcomed by the wind sector but eventually the sector began crumbling under the constant pressure to lower tariff that was not consistent with increase in the price of steel and other wind power generator components. Thousands of small and medium enterprises (SMEs) that manufacture equipment and components for the wind energy industry provide employment for millions of people directly or indirectly. These industries and jobs are now under threat as the downward pressure on tariff has pushed many of wind the SMEs to the verge of bankruptcy.

While solar is generally location-agnostic, wind favours specific locations and this has become a major problem when tariff caps are set at low levels. Under a 'one tariff fits all' approach that centralised efforts pursue, wind projects crowd around few favourable locations around the country. This has limited wind power capacity creation. Continued emphasis on low tariff pushed projects towards cheaper components that compromised the efficiency and life of wind energy systems. This is also true in the case of solar projects. It has also contributed to creation of stranded assets that drain public finances replicating the plight of some of the conventional power generation projects.

The overwhelming emphasis of policy on decreasing RE electricity tariff and increasing the share of RE in power generation has come at the cost of domestic production of RE technologies. This is most evident in the case of solar PV where production of solar ingots, cells, modules, and panels has been literally outsourced to China. This has benefitted solar installations in India that are among the most cost competitive globally but it has also exposed the Indian RE sector to significant financial and geopolitical risk. Trade and military conflict between China and the industrialised West can interrupt solar supply chains and halt the progress of projects. This would not only mean financial compromise for investors but also a threat to India's energy security. In this light, India's effort to become a producer of RE technologies is understandable. Apart from India's own large domestic market, India is also well placed to serve Western markets that are looking for alternatives to RE supply chains dominated by China. However, as a latecomer to manufacturing RE technologies in general and solar technologies in particular, India is likely to face many challenges. Many Western economies, including the USA, have announced huge subsidies to re-shore RE manufacturing. This will substantially shrink the size of the export market for Indian RE products. The belated attempt to develop domestic solar manufacturing using trade barriers and subsidies may increase solar power tariffs contradicting the goal of increasing low-cost solar deployment to decarbonise the grid. To succeed in meeting climate and energy security goals, India must find the right balance between its industrial policy, climate change action, and geo-political manoeuvring.

15

Clean Energy and Transport Renaissance

Pathikrit Payne

For India, renewable energy was always an option in the reckoning. Some steps were taken by previous regimes as well in this direction. However, what was lacking for long was a concrete, structured, and feasible roadmap for the future, which had the backing of the government with outcomes that would benefit India. In other words, India needed an India-centric clean energy, and not just a renewable energy roadmap that would take into consideration India's requirements and India's challenges, rather than one that would be an outcome of Western lobbies imposing their will on India.

Under Prime Minister Modi's leadership, India did finally find that roadmap that was indeed India-centric. The important aspect of India's journey on the clean energy path since 2015 was that the Government of India was willing to listen to ideas and concerns of industry and other stakeholders, and was more than willing to calibrate policies that would help India, rather than being rigid in its stance. As a result, it did wonders for India.

By 2022, India was already the third-largest producer of renewable energy in the world with almost 40 per cent of the installed capacity coming from sources than can be categorised as non-fossil fuel in nature. During the COP-21 Summit in Paris, India took a pioneering initiative in terms of pledging that 40 per cent of its energy requirement would be sourced from non-fossil fuel sources by 2030. However, India reached that cusp almost a decade ahead of the set deadline.

India, under Prime Minister Modi's leadership, also pledged to make India achieve the target of net zero emissions by 2070. Also, Indian Railways, in the same league, has pledged to attain the net zero emissions target by 2030.

In this context, it important to mention that renewable energy may be considered a subset of clean energy. Nuclear energy and hydrogen-based energy derivatives are clean but not considered renewable per se. On the renewable energy front, some of the other set targets that are to be achieved in the near future are as follows:

- Increasing renewables capacity to 500 GW by 2030,
- Meeting 50% of energy requirements from renewables,
- Reducing cumulative emissions by one billion tonnes by 2030, and
- Reducing emissions intensity of India's gross domestic product (GDP) by 45% by 2030.

Source: PIB

India's pioneering initiatives in the realm of truly achieving clean energy targets for a more sustainable world, can be gauged from the fact that it was Prime Minister Modi who first proposed the idea of creation of an inter-governmental alliance for promotion of solar energy. The idea encapsulated the creation of an alliance that would include all countries that lie between the Tropic of Cancer and the Tropic of Capricorn, to harness the full potential of solar energy through a collaborative approach.

The net result of this initiative pioneered by Prime Minister Modi was the creation of the International Solar Alliance (ISA). The ISA website terms this alliance as "an action-oriented, member-driven, collaborative platform for increased deployment of solar energy technologies as a means for bringing energy access, ensuring energy security, and driving energy transition in its member-countries."

Environmental Concerns Not a Monopoly of the West

A very important aspect of the formation of the International Solar Alliance as propounded by Prime Minister Modi, and its successful operationalisation with 115 member-countries having already signed the ISA Framework Agreement, is the fact that it demonstrates that the whole concept of 'concern for environment' is not a monopoly of the global North, and that the global

South, and that the developing economies led by the likes of India, are equally concerned, or perhaps even more concerned, as traditionally, most of these countries have a unique cultural ethos of conserving and nurturing nature.

India's solar pledge was vindicated through demonstrable actions that eventually witnessed a massive rise in its installed solar power generation capacity. While, a parliamentary report stated that by February 2023, India's installed capacity of renewable energy had touched the 168.96 GW figure, the share of solar in the same was an astounding 64.38 GW. Interestingly, some of the world's largest solar power projects are coming up in India.

However, India made giant strides in other segments of renewable energy generation capacity building as well. While, by February, 2023, in the realm of hydro-electricity generation, India's installed capacity stood at 51.79 GW, in the case of wind energy it was 42.02 GW, followed by 10.77 GW of installed capacity for biomass-based power generation.

The Union Power Minister had also stated in the recent past that while construction is going on for development of an additional 82.62 GW of installed capacity for renewable or green energy, another 40.89 GW of generation capacity is undergoing the tendering process for future implementation, thereby placing India well on the path of achieving its stated targets for renewable energy generation capacity building.

Harnessing the Nuclear Option- Push for Clean Energy

In the realm of nuclear energy as well, some major developments have taken place in the recent past. While the liability clauses were indeed creating some hiccups with foreign vendors who were supposed to set up nuclear power plants in India in collaboration with India's state-owned enterprises like the Nuclear Power Corporation of India Ltd. (NPCIL), the pace for adding to the installed capacity in the realm of nuclear power generation seems to have increased recently.

In April 2023, India's Atomic Energy Minister, Jitendra Singh, informed Parliament about the decision of the Government of India to construct 10 nuclear reactors across five states of India. The 10 reactors, each with a capacity to generate 700 MW of electricity, would be of the pressurised heavy water reactor category, and would be coming up in Haryana, Madhya Pradesh, Rajasthan, and Karnataka that would entail an investment of a little more than Rs. 1 lakh crore and would witness the activation of a new mechanism wherein, after the amendment of the Atomic Energy Act in 2015, the Government of India's premier nuclear power developer, namely, NPCIL, can enter into joint ventures with other PSUs as well, for developing nuclear power projects.

Given the fact that when it comes to clean energy, nothing is cleaner than electricity generated through the nuclear option, India, along with major strides in other renewable energy segments, also has set goals to expand, by 2031, the nuclear power generation capacity to 22,480 MW, up from the present installed capacity of 6,780 MW.

Herein, it would also be interesting to mention that the seven years up to 2021, after the Modi Government came to power, witnessed a considerable increase in the installed capacity of India's nuclear power generation from 4,780 MW to 6,780 MW.

However, India's real game changer so far as nuclear energy is concerned is dependent upon the operationalisation of the prototype fast breeder reactor (PFBR) and how much India can develop technical prowess in developing the technology for making the three-stage nuclear program a real success in the future. India's development of the PFBR, named BHAVINI, has reached a critical stage, and its operationalisation would create the real inflexion point for India in the realm of charting a new, clean, and literally unending energy supply matrix for the future.

Push for Hydrogen: Focus on Clean Energy Options and Not Renewables Alone

It is also equally important to mention the impetus that is being given by the Modi Government to make green hydrogen a viable energy option for the future. In January this year, the Modi Government approved an outlay of Rs. 19,744 crore for the National Green Hydrogen Mission. The focus is ideally on exploring different dimensions of clean energy options rather than on wind and solar alone, and justifiably so.

A Press Information Bureau (PIB) note states the following as intended outcomes of the mission by 2030

- Development of green hydrogen production capacity of at least 5 MMT (million metric tonne) per annum with an associated renewable energy capacity addition of about 125 GW in the country

- Over Rs. eight lakh crore in total investments
- Creation of over six lakh jobs
- Cumulative reduction in fossil fuel imports over Rs. one lakh crore• Abatement of nearly 50 MMT of annual greenhouse gas emission

Source: PIB

The Fight Against Western Lobbies

An important aspect of India's journey towards creating a viable, feasible and pragmatic energy security matrix is that even as it strived to diversify and leverage its latent potential to harness its renewable energy generation capacity, India, in spite of massive pressure from Western lobbies, did not give up on usage of coal-based thermal power plants for electricity generation, and rightfully so.

In the first place, one has to give due credit to the Prime Minister Modi-led Government of India for standing up against the pressure that has consistently been created by Western countries against the likes of India on usage of coal. Frankly speaking, given the legendary legacy of carbon footprints that the global North has been leaving behind over the last 200 years, and the enormity of coal that was used by the same global North to carry forward their own industrial renaissance in the past, and the quantum of carbon footprints that most of the global North countries still emit, on a per capita basis, they simply do not have any locus standi to lecture the global South in general, and India in particular.

For a nation, which has been tormented and plundered for centuries through colonial invasions, followed by the horrendous nightmares of partition and post-partition conflicts, it is only now that India got its act right to fulfil the aspirations of its-billion plus population. However, till the time India was just a massive market which was lucrative for the Western companies, it made sense for them to cheer for India's growth. But the moment India started emerging from its shackles and was fast evolving into a potent competitor for many, it was time for the known quarters to put different kinds of pressures on India in the name of environment and climatic issues.

India was never, and is not even now, the reason for the vast environmental degradation that has degenerated the Earth. Much of that has to do with the culture of 'use and throw' and mindless consumerism propounded and practised by the global North. However, by outsourcing production, mostly to Asia, and by using both Asia and Africa, as dumping grounds for their discarded consumer and industrial goods, the global North made sure that their own backyard remains clean. But when the outsourcing of production was eventually resulting in developing countries learning the tricks of business and innovation, and were not only eating away Western jobs, but were also turning competitive, environmental issues started emerging fast as 'non-tariff barriers' being indiscriminately used for denying market entry to companies from India and many others, as also to pressurise incumbent governments to toe the Western lines and shun-coal based thermal power generation, as coal was fast becoming the reason for cheap energy for the global South that was making industry there more competitive in industrial production.

Even as the West pushed for renewable energy for the global South, neither the technology nor the components of the same come cheap, which results in perpetual dependence on foreign supply chains once again. For many of the coal-rich developing economies, falling into the global North-triggered 'Guilt Syndrome' for using coal would result in devastating consequences with considerable rise in the cost of power in the short run, and fall in competitiveness that may have other cataclysmic socio-economic impacts in terms of job losses and factories relocating elsewhere. It is a reality that the cost of renewable energy takes time to stabilise.

Modi Government's Independent Approach

It is from this perspective that it is heartening to witness that India, in the last nine years, has charted an independent path wherein, even as it has made major strides in the domain of capacity building for clean and renewable energy generation, the Modi Government did not abandon coal-based thermal power plants. The reason is simple. If India has to take care of the aspirations of its 1.4 billion people, it needs energy, which is cost effective, reliable and not subject to global geopolitical upheavals. While renewable energy is definitely the future, for all practical purposes, coal is still the reality of the present.

Besides, it is a known fact that renewable energy, especially solar and wind based, are subject to the vagaries of nature, including availability of a clear sky and wind, both of which are beyond human control. Even when clear and sunny days, as well as wind, is available, their intensity varies. This leads to a multitude of problems so far as stability of the grid is concerned. It is precisely for this reason that transition to renewable in entirety has to be gradual and seamless, rather than abrupt and sudden, which can severely compromise the integrity of the grid.

In other words, transition from thermal to renewable has to be calibrated and not in one go, so as to make sure that it does not lead to any major social or economic disruption. The objective is invariably to create a sustainable architecture for management of the energy matrix, which would take care of both the aspirations of the billion-plus populace as well as sustain the environment. Both are equally important and one cannot be given precedence at the cost of the other. Also, it is from this perspective that the emphasis on clean energy rather than renewable energy alone, makes more sense.

Continued Push for Thermal is thus a Necessity in the Short Term

As per reports of the Ministry of Power, India added 83,920 MW of fossil fuel-based power generation capacity between 2014 and 2021, while 4.48 GW of capacity was added up to August 2022, while as of December 2022, around 25.5 GW of thermal power plants are under various stages construction.

It is important to mention that even as India may continue to expand the footprint of its fossil fuel thermal power generation capacity, its proportion as part of the total generation capacity would continue to come down.

The EV and MRTS Revolution in India

A critical aspect of sustainable energy management is the need for a push towards electric vehicles or EVs, as well as metro rail systems. In this respect too, some major strides have been made by India in the last seven to eight years. From a massive expansion of mass rapid transport systems (MRTS) to creation of a whole new ecosystem where EV manufacturers can thrive, the achievements are no less significant.

Reports indicate that the total network for metro-based mass rapid transport systems stood at 248 km in 2014, which by April 2023 has expanded to 860 km, even as work on another 1,000 km is going on currently. Expansion of MRTS has a significant impact in terms of reduction in the quantum of vehicle-based pollution, as more commuters opt for the faster, cleaner, and efficient metro rail systems.

Further, a considerable number of emerging players along with established

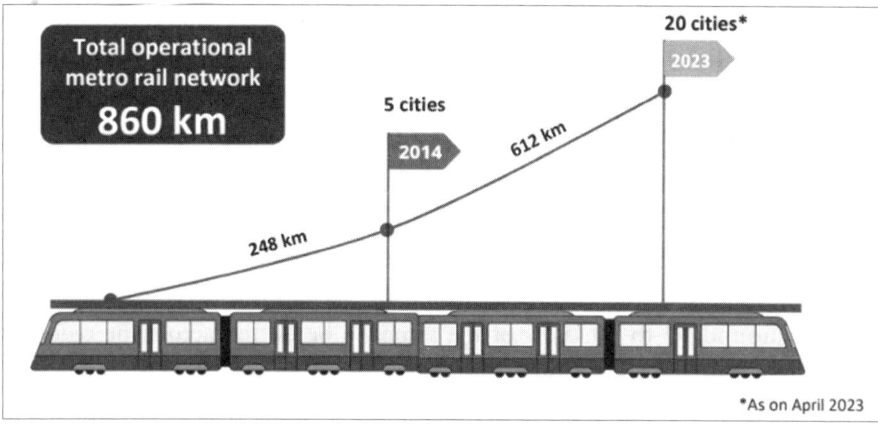

Source: PIB

players, are creating a new landscape for India's EV revolution. The same goes for India's often underrated last-mile connectivity revolution through e-rickshaws that had both a positive impact on the environment as well as in solving the last-mile connectivity challenges.

In 2022, India's total EV sales crossed the milestone of 1 million with sales of 1,054,938 units, with the sale of E-2 wheelers garnering a lion's share of an estimated 63 per cent of total sales.

Transition from Combustion to Electric Engines: Why Calibration is a Necessity

India's 2030 targets for electric vehicle sales includes a penetration level of 70 per cent for commercial cars, 30 per cent for private cars, 80 per cent for two-wheelers and three-wheelers, as well as 40 per cent of commercial bus transport.

The above-mentioned deadlines themselves evolved after a lot of recalibration and acceptance of ground realities which could not be ignored. Around 2017-18, there were reports that India would be opting for 100 per cent electric mobility by 2030. This was later brought down to more pragmatic and realistic targets keeping in mind that India's automobile industry, which in 2022 was estimated to be worth more than $ 100 billion, and which generates a significant amount of employment in the country, has been traditionally built on the combustion engine protocol. This industry not only includes the major players but also innumerable ancillary companies whose entire edifice is based on the combustion engine protocol.

Therefore, any sudden and total policy shift towards EV would have created massive disruptions and shockwaves in the sector that would have had severe downstream impacts on other sectors as well, such as on the economy as a whole as well as on society, as a result of job losses. It was thus imperative that industry be given time to recalibrate its structure and make the transition smooth.

Also, movement towards EV would entail creation of a massive infrastructure of charging stations, which by certain estimates would be no less than around 39 to 40 lakhs of the same, to be dotted across the country. This too would require time. From this perspective as well, the Modi Government's calibrated move in terms of transition to renewable energy and electric vehicle is both pragmatic and realistic.

The real accolade for the Modi Government must be the fact that it not only withstood the pressure of the Western lobbies, who would want drastic changes to be done by yesterday, without even looking into the practicality of the issues, but also for the fact that the Modi Government listened to the issues and concerns raised by the concerned stakeholders in the industry, and the sector as a whole, and synchronised the policies in a manner that it would be beneficial for the country in the long run, rather than create more problems.

The Supply Chain Challenges of Clean Energy Equipment

The COVID pandemic brought rude shocks for the world in terms of how severe supply chain disruptions such global upheavals can create for any major economy, if it has considerable dependence on another country for critical components, or end products, especially if those components are for a vital sector. As it is, from the very beginning, when the fever of renewable energy gained traction in India, there has been a trend of a sharp rise in the dependence of Indian players for Chinese components especially for solar-based renewable energy projects.

Data indicate that up to early 2020, India's renewable energy industry, especially the solar industry, had a shocking 80 per cent dependence on Chinese imports. Some other estimates put the figures as high as a whopping 95 per cent if the Chinese companies operating from countries like Vietnam and Thailand are taken into account. In the case of wind energy though, the dependence on China has traditionally not been that much skewed in favour of China, with almost 80 per cent of the wind turbines being used in India made within the country. However, in the case of wind, the import from China happens for critical components like wind turbine controllers, gear box, and special bearings, to name a few.

For any nascent industry, dependence on imports in the initial stages makes sense. However, when that industry matures and is expected to take the pivotal position in a critical sector such as the power sector, over dependence on imports may prove to be cataclysmic not just from the point of view of potential supply chain disruptions or a sudden rise in the cost of imports, or cartelisation of players, but also from the perspective of geopolitical pitfalls such dependence can create.

This is especially relevant when the country from where they are mostly sourced cannot be counted as an ally or a friend, but falls on the borderline of being termed nothing less than an adversary, or rival at the least. The issue becomes more profound when such dependence comes with the apprehensions of potential large-scale cyber-attacks on a sector as critical as power, and the kind of large-scale implications it may eventually have for the economy and nation as a whole, especially during a crisis situation.

Taking into consideration the entire gamut of challenges in hand, starting from issues related to stability of the grid in case of a sudden and total transition to renewable energy, to dependence on imports for critical components, the fact that the Modi Government made sure that thermal, for the time being, would continue to be India's prime source of power generation, even as steps are taken to consolidate India's situation in the renewable energy spectrum, is a commendable one. Once the supply chain is fairly under control, dependence on imports is reduced to manageable levels, and concerns related to grid stability are addressed, India's transition then would be more fast paced and immune from any major disruption.

Already steps are being taken to secure the supply chain and reorient production of solar panels as well as other components into India. In October 2021, as part of the production linked incentive (PLI) scheme, the Government of India announced the names of 16 companies that were eligible for the Rs. 4,500 crore incentive package for solar panel manufacturing in India. Some of the big names which made it to the final cut included the likes of Adani Infrastructures, Reliance New Energy Solar, Jindal India Solar Energy, etc. Later, the corpus was increased by another Rs. 19,500 crore.

India Set to Become a Major Hub for Clean Energy Component Manufacturing

On the positive side, going by some of the major investment proposals that have been mooted by key Indian industrial majors to create a resilient supply chain ecosystem for manufacturing of renewable energy components and equipment, it is expected that India may eventually turn out to be a major player in this segment in the next 10 to 15 years.

While the Mukesh Ambani-led Reliance Industries signed an MOU in early 2022 with the Government of Gujarat to invest $ 80 billion over the next one-and-a-half decades, which apart from setting up a 100 GW renewable energy power plant would include creation of integrated setups for manufacturing of renewable energy components such as electrolysers, solar panels and fuel cells, the Gautam Adani-led Adani Group has announced investments of over $70 billion in setting up giga factories for manufacturing hydrogen electrolysers, wind turbines and solar panels. The focus of renewable energy players is thus expanding from renewable energy generation to include manufacturing renewable energy components as well in a big way. Of course, the Modi Government's PLI is indeed playing a key role in reorienting investments towards development of the equipment manufacturing supply chain within the country.

The Lithium Reserve Discoveries: A Timely Boon for India

Add to it, India's recent discovery of a massive 5.9 million tonnes of lithium reserve in J&K followed by discoveries of lithium reserves of similar potential in Rajasthan, has opened newer dimensions for India's EV-based future mobility industry.

Lithium, the most critical component for lithium-based batteries, a panacea for the energy storage puzzle, and often termed as the 'white gold' of the present day, is no more merely a reserve of a precious mineral alone, but along with cobalt and other rare minerals that are required in making semi-conductors, fall in the category of minerals with profound geopolitical and geoeconomic potential. It is expected that in the times to come, India would be in a position to harness this reserve with requisite technology to make India a major hub for making lithium-based batteries that can change the very fortune of India's future mobility architecture and can unshackle it from the stranglehold of geopolitics of oil, to attain energy independence in its true sense.

VIEWS FROM ABROAD

16

Net Zero Pathways for India and Lessons for Other Countries

Andres Carvallo

India is one of the fastest growing major economies in the world and is also the fastest growing energy consumer. To ensure energy security and support its economic growth, the country has set ambitious targets for transitioning to a low-carbon economy. In 2015, India committed to achieving a 40 per cent reduction in its carbon intensity by 2030, and in 2020, Prime Minister Narendra Modi announced a goal of achieving net-zero emissions by 2070.

Achieving net-zero emissions by 2070 is an ambitious goal for India, and it will require significant changes to the country's energy mix. Currently, coal is the primary source of electricity in India, but to meet the target of 50 per cent renewable energy by 2030 and achieve net-zero emissions by 2070, a significant shift towards renewables will be necessary.

India's energy mix is characterized by a combination of traditional and modern sources of energy. According to the International Energy Agency (IEA), in 2020, coal was the largest source of primary energy in India, accounting for 38 per cent of the total. Oil was the second largest source, accounting for 26 per cent of the total, followed by natural gas at 8 per cent. Renewable energy sources, including hydroelectric, solar, wind, and bio-energy, accounted for 28 per cent of India's primary energy mix.

However, it is worth noting that the mix of energy sources used in India has been changing in recent years, with an increasing emphasis on renewable energy. For example, the share of renewable energy in India's primary energy mix has increased from 22 per cent in 2015 to 28 per cent in 2020. The Government of India has set ambitious targets for the expansion of renewable energy, including a goal of achieving 175 GW of renewable energy capacity by 2022.

There are several challenges that India will need to overcome to successfully transit to a low-carbon economy. One challenge is the need to modernize the country's electricity grid to accommodate variable renewable energy sources. Another challenge is the need to address the financial and technical barriers to the deployment of renewables, such as the high upfront costs of renewable energy technologies and the lack of skilled personnel to operate and maintain them.

A modern electric grid, also known as a smart grid, is an advanced electricity system that is designed to be flexible, efficient, and able to accommodate a high percentage of renewable energy.

Some of the key characteristics of a modern electric grid include:

- Advanced control systems: These systems use sensors, data analytics, and other technologies to monitor and control the flow of electricity on the grid in real-time, allowing for more efficient and reliable operation.
- Interconnections: A modern power grid is interconnected, meaning that it is connected to other grids and can exchange electricity with them. This allows the sharing of resources and helps increase the overall reliability and resilience of the grid.
- Two-way communication: A modern power grid is able to communicate with devices on the grid, such as smart meters and energy storage systems, allowing for more efficient and flexible operation.
- Integration of renewable energy: A modern power grid is able to accommodate a high percentage of renewable energy, such as solar and wind power, which are intermittent and may require advanced control systems and energy storage technologies to manage.

Overall, a modern electric grid is a dynamic and flexible system that is able to adapt to changing energy demands and sources, and is critical for supporting the transition to a low-carbon, renewable energy future.

To overcome the challenges arising from increased use of renewable energy, the government will need to implement policies and incentives that support the adoption of more renewables and compensate utilities and grid operators for modernizing the electric grid. This could include subsidies and tax credits for renewable energy projects, new business models for making the electric grid more efficient and modern, as well as regulations that encourage the use of clean energy. In addition, the government will need to invest in research and development to improve performance and reduce the costs of renewable energy technologies and distribution, monitoring and management of the use of electricity.

Another important factor in India's transition to a low-carbon economy is international cooperation. India will need to work with other countries to share best practices and technologies, as well as to coordinate efforts to reduce global greenhouse gas emissions. This could involve participating in international climate agreements and collaborating with other countries on research and development projects.

Overall, the path to net-zero emissions in India will require significant changes to the country's energy mix, as well as the implementation of policies and incentives that support the adoption of renewables. By sharing its experiences and lessons learned with other countries, India can help in accelerating the global transition to a low-carbon economy.

What has been done?

To achieve these targets, the Modi government has implemented several initiatives to increase the share of renewable energy in the country's energy mix. These include setting a target of achieving 500 GW of non-fossil fuel energy capacity by 2030, and a goal of meeting 50 per cent of the country's electricity demand with renewables by the same year. The government has also implemented policies and incentives to support the deployment of renewable energy technologies, such as subsidies, tax credits, and regulations.

The momentum of the renewable energy sector has set the stage for India to achieve its net-zero emissions goal by 2070. In the medium term, a significantly higher mix of renewables can help a large portion of India's coal stock reach its natural end of life between 2030 and 2040 and be replaced by cleaner, greener energy sources. However, the transition to a low-carbon economy is not without challenges. One major challenge is the need to modernize the country's electricity grid to accommodate variable renewable energy sources. Another challenge is the high upfront costs of renewable energy technologies and the lack of skilled personnel to operate and maintain them.

Why is energy security such an important issue for India?

Energy is a national security issue for several reasons. One is that access to reliable, affordable energy is critical for the functioning of a modern economy. A country that is dependent on foreign sources of energy may be vulnerable to supply disruptions or price fluctuations, which can have a negative impact on its economic stability and growth.

Another reason is that the production and use of certain types of energy can have negative national security implications. For example, the reliance on fossil fuels such as oil and gas can make India more vulnerable to supply disruptions and price fluctuations, which can have economic and political consequences. In addition, the extraction, transportation, and use of fossil fuels can have negative environmental impacts, which can also have national security implications.

Finally, the transition to low-carbon, renewable energy sources can have national security benefits. For example, increasing the use of renewable energy can reduce India's reliance on foreign sources of energy, which can improve its energy security. In addition, the transition to renewable energy can help in reducing greenhouse gas emissions, which can contribute to global efforts to address climate change.

Why are solar, wind, energy storage and a modern electric grid so important for India?

Solar power, wind power, and energy storage are all key technologies for reducing carbon emissions, which contribute to climate change.

Solar power is a clean, renewable source of electricity that uses energy from the sun to generate electricity. Solar panels, which are made up of photovoltaic cells, convert sunlight into electricity. This electricity can be used to power homes, businesses, and other buildings, and can also be stored in batteries for later use.

Wind power is another clean, renewable source of electricity that uses the energy of the wind to generate electricity. Wind turbines are used to capture the energy of the wind and convert it into electricity. Like solar power, wind power can be used to power homes, businesses, and other buildings, and can also be stored in batteries for later use.

Energy storage refers to the ability to store electricity for use when it is needed. This is important because solar and wind power are intermittent sources of electricity, meaning they are not always available. Energy storage systems, such as batteries, allow excess electricity to be stored and used when needed, which helps in making these renewable energy sources more reliable and efficient.

Overall, solar, wind, and energy storage technologies are key to achieving low carbon goals because they provide clean, renewable sources of electricity that can help reduce our reliance on fossil fuels, which are a major source of carbon emissions.

Modernizing the electric grid is important for achieving low carbon goals because it can help increase the integration and use of renewable energy sources, such as solar and wind power. A modernized electric grid is more flexible and is able to accommodate a higher percentage of renewable energy.

One of the main challenges of integrating renewable energy into the electric grid is that these sources are intermittent, meaning they are not always available. For example, solar power is only available during the day, and wind power is only available when the wind is blowing. A modernized electric grid can use advanced control systems and energy storage technologies to smoothen these fluctuations and better match supply and demand.

Additionally, a modernized electric grid can improve the efficiency of the overall electricity system, reducing the amount of energy that is lost during transmission and distribution. This can further help in reducing carbon emissions by reducing the amount of energy that needs to be produced from fossil fuels.

Overall, modernizing the electric grid is vital for meeting low carbon goals because it can help in increasing the use of renewable energy and improve the overall efficiency of the electricity system, both of which are important for reducing carbon emissions.

What is still Needed?

To overcome these challenges, the Modi government will need to continue implementing policies and incentives that support the adoption of renewables and the modernization of its electric grid. This could include subsidies and tax credits for renewable energy projects, new capital recovery rules for the modernization of the electric grid, as well as regulations that encourage the use of clean energy. In addition, the government will need to invest in research and development to improve performance and reduce the costs of renewable energy technologies.

International cooperation will also be critical to India's transition to a low-carbon economy. The country will need to work with other countries to share best practices and technologies, as well as to coordinate efforts to reduce global greenhouse gas emissions. This could involve participating in international climate agreements and collaborating with other countries on research and development projects.

Overall, India's efforts to transition to a low-carbon economy and achieve net-zero emissions provide valuable lessons for other countries. By sharing its experiences and lessons learned, India can help in accelerating the global transition to a low-carbon economy.

17

India's Green Energy Progress

Richard Schomberg

Energy security of supply and access at a reasonable rate is critical for economic transformation, prosperity, and well-being and is a goal that many countries are pursuing to ensure that their economies function without interruption and that their people have access to adequate, reliable, and affordable supplies of modern and clean energy. India is one of the major growing energy consumers in the world. The global COVID-19 pandemic since 2020 had severe economic fallout and jolted all countries across the globe. While many economies continue to struggle with sluggish economic growth and record-breaking inflation, India has been recognized by global institutions like the IMF and World Bank as one of the fastest growing economies of the world—"a bright spot on this otherwise dark horizon." The government's 'Aatmanirbhar Bharat Plan' turned the crisis into an opportunity and gave the much-needed impetus to economic development, that is, growth with structural change.

India is likely to become the most populous country and by 2050 will have a population in the range of 1.66 billion. The energy choices that India considers will not only have a direct bearing on its growing population but will also, in interconnected ways, affect the global energy market, carbon emissions, and the flow of technologies and capital. Energy security of supply has been a key priority of Prime Minister Narendra Modi, who has often expressed that "India would continue to do what it thinks is best in the interest of its own energy security of supply when it comes to the question of global oil trade." But Prime Minister Modi also has a clear policy articulation that India's energy development is inextricably tied to its climate goals, a sentiment that continues since the Climate Summit in Paris in 2015. Last year in Glasgow, the prime minister presented India's 'Panchamrita' or five pledges/targets:

- Achieving net-zero emissions by 2070.
- Achieving non-fossil fuel energy capacity of 500 GW by 2030.
- Meeting 50 per cent electricity demand with renewable energy by 2030.
- Reducing projected carbon emission by one billion tonnes by 2030.
- Reducing carbon intensity of India's economy by 45 per cent by 2030.

The momentum that the renewable energy pathways have set for this decade suggests that with careful planning, India can achieve its net-zero goals as envisioned by Prime Minister Modi. In the mid-term a significantly higher mix of renewable energy can help a large number of India's coal-fired power plants reach their natural end of life between 2030 and 2040 and be replaced by cleaner and greener renewable energy sources. The roadmap though has several challenges. India's pathways require its energy sector to integrate into the global energy market and at the same time align its energy policies with global practices.

The primary objective for deploying green energy is to advance economic development, improve energy security of supply, improve access to energy, and mitigate climate change. Sustainable development is possible by use of sustainable energy and by ensuring access to affordable, reliable, sustainable, and modern energy for citizens. Strong government support and the increasingly opportune economic situation have pushed India to be one of the top leaders in the world's most attractive renewable energy markets. The Modi-led government has designed policies, programs, and a liberal environment to ramp up the country in the renewable energy market at a rapid rate. A mixture of push policies and pull mechanisms, accompanied by pinpointed strategies have helped in the development of renewable energy technologies in India.

Since the wind and sun are available in abundance in India, India's focus and plan of action to achieve its targets is the following:

- To ensure that a better and affordable solar and wind technology should be easily and conveniently available to all.
- To increase the proportion of solar and wind energy in the energy mix.

- To encourage the innovation so that solar/wind and hybrid solutions can be provided for several requirements.
- To provide concessional financing and less risky finance for solar and wind power projects.
- To develop such regulatory aspects and standards that can provide a new momentum to the development and adoption of solar solutions.
- Development of consultancy support for bankable solar and wind projects.
- To create a comprehensive network of centres of excellence that can take into account local factors and situations."

The Indian wind industry has achieved remarkable growth. This growth was triggered by incentives, fiscal/non-fiscal as well as advancement in wind turbine technology so that generation can take place even in low wind velocity conditions. The initial fiscal incentive of accelerated depreciation provided by the Central Government and the provision of the banking mechanism by state governments made private investment in captive wind farms attractive in states where there was a good wind potential. These two mechanisms propelled the growth of the wind sector in the country. Wind power tariffs declined as investments scaled up. The Global Wind Energy Council estimates that the Indian wind sector is expected to add 20.2 GW of wind power capacity between 2020 and 2025. A pragmatic and viable policy framework for repowering older wind projects at high-resource sites is being put in place after stakeholder consultations. This would accelerate India's wind energy development. There is a potential of 4.5 GW for repowering old sites (GWEC, 2021).

India's plan titled 'Transmission System for Integration of over 500 GW Renewable Energy Capacity by 2030 entails connecting mega solar parks and wind power zones to the national grid. The transmission line length (ckt km) that stood at 367,851 in 2017 has increased to 448,407 in 2022. The Government has approved a plan to build transmission lines to link 20 gigawatts of reasonable energy at a cost of USD 1.61 billion over THE next five years as India moves forward towards reducing its carbon footprint by cutting carbon emissions. The plan includes construction of 8,120 circuit kilometre (ckm) of high voltage direct current transmission corridor (+800 kV and + 350 kV), 25,960 ckm of 765 kV ac lines, 15,758 ckm of 400 kV lines and 1,052 ckm of 220 kV cables. It envisages installation of battery energy storage capacity of 51.5 GW by 2030 as against the existing 27.2 GWh; the potential by 2040 is estimated at 140–200 GW. This is to provide round-the-clock power to consumers. Various initiatives have been taken to establish a conducive environment for attracting domestic as well as foreign direct investment in the sector. The public policy as well as the regulations framed by power sector regulators at central and state levels are all directed towards giving a 'big push' to the renewable energy sector, namely, renewable purchase obligation (RPO) increased from 21.18 per cent of the energy consumed in FY 2021-22 to 43.33 per cent of the energy consumed in FY 2029-30, foreign direct investment (FDI) permitted up to 100 per cent, waiver of interstate transmission of system (ISTS) charges on transmission of electricity generated from solar and wind power for projects commissioned up to 30 June 2025, etc.

The plan has identified upcoming non-fossil fuel-based generation centres. Transmission systems have been planned accordingly. This includes Fatehgarh, Bhadla and Bikaner in Rajasthan, Khavda in Gujarat, Anantapur and Kurnool RE zones in Andhra Pradesh, offshore wind potentials in Tamil Nadu and Gujarat as well as a RE park in Ladakh, among others.

Today, India is the third largest renewable power generator in the world, the fourth largest in solar and wind. It recorded the fastest growing renewable energy capacity addition in the world in 2020. India has several of the world's largest solar power plants. In order to meet its energy needs, India is also emphasizing on installing solar panels in more and more homes besides setting up large solar plants. A national portal has also been started so that people can easily install rooftop solar projects. This will help both in generating electricity at home and earning with electricity generation. Besides increasing the production of electricity, the emphasis of the government is also on saving electricity. Saving electricity means securing the future. The prime minister's scheme for upliftment of farmers (Pradhan Mantri Kisan Urja Suraksha evam Utthan Mahabhiyan, also known as 'KUSUM') is a great example of the same. Through this scheme, the Government of India is providing subsidies for installation of solar pumps by the farmers to enable them to meet their electricity requirement as well as sell surplus energy. Because of this, the food provider is also becoming the energy provider. It will also serve the purpose of rural electrification through solarisation. The UJALA Yojana (a free LED bulb scheme) has also played a major role in reducing the electricity bill of the common man of the country.

A major non-CO_2 emitting power source is nuclear power, which is the fifth-largest source of electricity in India. As of November 2020, India has 22 nuclear reactors in operation in eight nuclear power plants, with a total installed capacity of 7,380 MW. India has been making advances in the field of thorium-based fuels in order to develop a prototype for an atomic reactor using thorium and low-enriched uranium, a key part of India's nuclear programme.

India's decarbonisation journey received a boost after the announcement of the National Green Hydrogen Mission which aims to produce green hydrogen by splitting water through electrolysis. Green hydrogen has the advantage of being a clean burning molecule, which can de-carbonize sectors including iron and steel, chemicals and transportation. The mission aims to produce five million tonnes of green hydrogen annually by 2030.

The Prime Minister of India announced on the 76th Independence Day of India that India needs to become self-reliant in the energy sector with the "need to take these initiatives to the next level of energy independence"

The initiative taken by the Prime Minster of India in forming the International Solar Alliance to fulfil the mission of One Sun, One World, One Grid (OSOWOG), is extremely commendable. Let us support India in its passionate resolve and effort and hope the end result is fully successful.

18

Africa's Renewable Roadmap and Lessons from India

Abel Tella

I have had the honour of leading the Association of Power Utilities of Africa (APUA). It is an international non-profit organization created in 1970 by African electricity companies with headquarter in Abidjan Côte d'Ivoire. The APUA is a specialized institution of the African Union Commission on Infrastructure and Energy. Formerly known as UPDEA (Union of Producers, Electricity Carriers and Distributors in Africa), the name was changed in 2012 as part of the implementation of the organization's strategic action plan to rejuvenate it and make it an organization that brings value to its members.

APUA's mission is to bring together African power companies and stakeholders to make electricity more accessible, affordable, and reliable for African people. One of the flagship projects of this repositioning is the implementation, since 2016, of the activities of the project to set up the African Network of Centres of Excellence in Electricity (ANCEE). The network is composed of 10 centres of excellence across Africa.

The APUA has always played a leading role in promoting good management practices in the African electrical sector. To this end, the APUA has developed active partnership with key international organizations such as:

- The World Energy Council
- The International Hydropower Association

- The International Energy Agency
- The International Renewable Energy Agency
- The African Energy Commission
- The Global Energy Interconnection Development and Cooperation Organization
- The International Solar Alliance
- The United Nations Environment Programme
- The United Nations Economic Commission for Africa
- The Global Smart Energy Federation
- The Global Sustainable Electricity Partnership
- The World Bank
- The African Development Bank
- The European Union

These partnerships help us develop policies and programmes to deploy climate change awareness, reduce greenhouse gas emissions, and fight on an ongoing basis to reduce losses in the electrical system.

One of the activities the ANCEE organizes every year is a technical seminar with experts from APUA and power pools on a specific theme:

- The promotion, connection to grids and funding of renewable energy infrastructure
- Reducing losses in electrical systems
- Deployment of smart grids in Africa
- Combined development of energy, mines, industry, manufacturing and trade
- The assessment of energy sector reforms

Relevant proposals and recommendations from these workshops are discussed at a CEO Forum on Strategic Governance on the same theme to help decision-makers take concrete action on climate change and loss reduction.

To address the energy situation of Africa, the continent of paradoxes, let us remember that it has:

- 10 per cent of the world's hydroelectric potential
- 8 per cent of the world's oil reserves
- 7 per cent of natural gas reserves
- 17 per cent of uranium reserves
- 29 per cent of wind potential

- 15 per cent of geothermal potential
- 4 per cent of coal reserves (92 per cent of which are in South Africa)
- The world's largest solar potential, a large biomass reserve with 60 per cent of the world's uncultivated arable land

Unfortunately, this great potential is not converted into available electrical energy.

SDGs 2030

In the context of the implementation of the global 2030 Agenda for Sustainable Development, energy experts are called upon to contribute to the following two central objectives:

- Ensure access for all to reliable, sustainable and modern energy services at an affordable cost (SDG7)
- Fighting climate change and its impacts

According to the IEA, World Energy Outlook 2021 "The Net Zero Emission scenario offers a pathway to deliver electricity to all by 2030. Just under half of households gaining access to electricity do so with a grid connection, while mini grid and stand alone systems account for 30 per cent and 25 per cent of new connections, respectively. Over 90 per cent of off grid and around 70 per cent of grid solutions deployed between now and 2030 are sourced from renewables. After 2030, grids will eventually reach most customers using off grid solutions, emphasising the importance of interoperability for off grid and mini grid systems built today. Only the most remote users will not have a grid connection by 2050. Achieving full electricity access by 2030 requires annual investment of over USD 35 billion. This is a tiny fraction of global total energy investment, but well above what is being spent today: investment in electricity access in sub Saharan Africa is only around 15 per cent of what will be required (SE4ALL and CPI, 2020). Financing is a significant obstacle, since many of the projects—especially those serving rural areas and very poor communities – require public financial support via concessional and blended finance structures (IEA, 2021a) together with improvements in tendering and administrative processes, while at the same time low demand can make it hard to attract private capital. After significant progress in recent years, led by India, the COVID-19 crisis has stalled improvements in extending access; regaining momentum is vital to achieve SDG 7.1."

The differences between the trajectories induced by the NDCs (Nationally Determined Contributions representing all the actions that each country undertakes to implement to contribute towards the achievement of the objectives of the Climate Convention) and the desirable trajectories show that we are still far from the mark. Appropriate energy policies geared towards the de-carbonization of the sector and the economy is the need of the hour.

According to the IEA, Net Zero Emissions in the 2050 scenario for access and the fight against climate change, total CO_2 emissions are expected to fall by around 45 per cent by 2030 compared to 2010 levels; CO_2 emissions from the energy sector and industrial processes are therefore expected to be around 20.1 Gt.

To achieve this, large-scale actions are needed including unprecedented changes:

- Generalization of electrification (transportation) and efficient use of energy
- More than 50 per cent of passenger cars sold are electric compared to 2.5 per cent today
- Generalized energy rehabilitation of the existing building stock
- Increase in the share of renewables in the electricity mix from 27 to 60 per cent
- Increase in the rate of solar PV installation from 110 to 500GW/year
- Doubling battery manufacturing capacity every two years
- 25 per cent of industrial heat comes from electricity and low-emission fuels (Hydrogen).

However, according to the Renewables 2020 Global Status Report, Ren21, the reality of renewable energies on a global scale using IEA data base, is as follows:

1. Estimated Share of Renewables in World Energy Consumption in 2018:
    - 79.9 per cent fossil fuels
    - 2.2 per cent nuclear energy
    - 6.9 per cent traditional biomass
    - 11.0 per cent modern renewables, including
      - 2.1 per cent wind, biomass and marine energy
      - 3.6 per cent hydropower

  - 4.3 per cent solar, geothermal heat
  - 1.0 per cent biofuel for transportation

2. Estimated Share of Renewables in Final Electricity Consumption in 2019
   - 72.7 per cent non-renewable energy
   - 27.3 per cent renewable energy including
     - 15.9 per cent hydropower
     - 5.9 per cent wind power
     - 2.8 per cent solar PV
     - 2.2 per cent bio-electricity
     - 0.4 per cent geothermal, CSP and ocean electricity

In view of these data, it is important to note an increase in the share of renewable energies in the energy mixes of several countries.

Considering Africa, the reality of renewable energy, according to IRENA RE Capacity Statistics, 2020 is:

3. Estimated Share of Renewables in the African Electricity Mix in 2020:
   - 77.7 per cent non-renewable energy
   - 22.3 per cent renewable energy, including
     - 16 per cent solar
     - 4 per cent hydropower
     - 1.2 per cent windpower
     - 0.9 per cent biomass
     - 0.2 per cent geothermal

Africa has the capability to fill the gaps as the continent's energy potential is at high. Electricity demand study predicts 3,300 GW technically usable for 700 GW peak electricity demand in 2050.

Carrying out the African Energy Interconnection Project would make it possible to mobilize and organize the continental potential of clean energy. Launched in June 2021, the African Single Electricity Market (AfSEM) has been designed to bring greater energy security, sustainability, and competitiveness to AU member-states. The progressive implementation of AfSEM and its full operationalization by 2040 will make it the largest single electricity market in the world covering 55 countries and serving more than 1.3 billion people.

The implementation of AfSEM will significantly depend on a continent-wide electricity grid infrastructure that links generation resources to electricity demand centres through adequate transmission capacity. It is in this context that continental master plan power networks are being developed simultaneously as the 'blueprint' of the AfSEM central pillar for solving Africa's energy challenge.

There are significant differences in progress across countries. As the saying goes, there are 'Not one but many Africas'. The optimization of the use of available installed power is necessary. The integration of renewable energy sources will need to be done after integrated resource and investment planning in order to use the network intelligently. Sometimes it is better to mix with fossils to guarantee a basic load power.

The rise of renewable energy sources requires ensuring the dynamic stability of the networks. Storage is necessary but we also note the importance of interconnections to ensure this stability. Opportunities for this energy transition can be seen with an example like Zambia where the emergence of small entrepreneurs who power the network on a small scale/real 'prosumer' with solar panels, and jobs created by a local solar panel plant. For this reason, the satisfaction of energy needs through a harmonious development of the electricity sector is necessary because electricity is the engine of the economy.

Several African countries have set emerging economic targets for 2020, 2025, or 2030, where energy policies revolve around these issues. These policies are summed up, at the national level, by:

- Developing the means of production to fill the gaps.
- Contribute to national energy independence and the roll-out of innovations.
- Ensure universal access to energy.
- Ensure an affordable price for electricity.
- Building sustainable development of the sector taking the environment into account.

And regionally by:

- Developing electricity interconnection networks and building the regional market.
- Ensuring security of supply.
- Ensuring a competitively priced supply.
- Ensuring quality supply.
- Respecting network standards and codes.

- Ensuring sustainable and consensual development of common sources of production.
- Controlling electricity demand and reduce energy intensity.

The establishment of the Maghrebian Electricity Committee (COMELEC) (1974) and the various regional power pools: Southern African Power Pool (1985), West African Power Pool (1985, 1999), Central Africa Power Pool (2003), and East Africa Power Pool (2006), the last three of which have been with strong APUA involvement, have contributed to the strengthening and development of electricity exchange.

On the other hand, African policymakers embraced a series of reforms of their power sector with limited results. Beginning in the 1990s, development finance institutions (DFIs), especially the World Bank (WB) and the International Monetary Fund (IMF) offered countries conditional loans attached to structural adjustment requirements that encouraged economy-wide liberalization, commercialization, and restructuring. They offered financing to some governments linked to reforms in the power sector adopting the 'standard model' to respond to failures in the utilities.

The 'standard model' reform elements promoted by the DFIs recommended:

- Commercializing electricity utilities and corporatizing their management.
- Restructuring national monopoly companies to separate generation, transmission, and distribution services.
- Creating independent regulation and adopting cost-reflective electricity tariffs.
- Opening the sector to private sector participation (PSP); and
- Introducing competition in the market through large-scale procurements to reach full competition for wholesale and retail customers.

The 'standard model' reforms have targeted all segments of the power sector value-chain in Africa, and in quite different ways. However, the prescriptive form of the proposed structural adjustments in the standard model often failed to accommodate local concerns, visions, and needs. In addition, the first wave of reforms generally did not prioritize social and political goals of expanding access to electricity and clean energy sources, nor improving equity or affordability.

The power sector in Africa still largely retains the traditional integrated monopoly utility structure, although many have included independent power producers. Regulatory reform has been the first step in the reform process for most African countries.

Establishing independent regulation intends to create an equitable, rule-based playing field for electricity providers, consumers, and private operators through clear rules and mechanisms to oversee the sector and ensure cost-reflective tariffs for utilities.

Independence from government and other interests remains a challenge for many electricity regulatory bodies in Africa, hampering their ability to carry out efficient regulatory functions.

Opening capital investment flows in the African power sector is often at the forefront of reform goals. When it comes to closing gaps in electricity access and affordability, reforms are far from enough to fix the problem. Reforms have indirect effects on the performance of the power sector.

Aligning the reforms and performance indices suggests that a relationship exists between a country's adoption of reforms, its quality of governance, and the performance of its power sector, and while there are a number of outliers, which require interrogation, a defined positive trend is evident.

Managing the complex political economy of power sector governance remains a challenge for many African countries. The sector is economically central and therefore highly politicized, which creates a contested discussion around reforms.

Reform programmes are often explained as strategies to improve utility performance, attract investment, and stem financial crisis. Moreover, stakeholders invoke problems with governance, corruption, and entrenched political interests to explain the stalling or failure of reforms. Political instability has contributed to these challenges for many African power sectors.

Regarding the promotion of renewable energy and innovative technologies, the unprecedented breakthroughs in prices of solar and wind energy in the past decade have spurred African countries to take advantage of the by now well-established variable renewable generation technologies. Mini-grids and off-grid electricity supply models—especially those that harness small modular renewable generation technologies—are increasingly attractive and cost-competitive for remote communities.

Today, technological and financial innovations combine with political, economic, demographic, and environmental shifts to herald a new era for the African electricity landscape.

Disruptive technologies are opening new opportunities and provoking the need for new regulatory, policy, and economic tools to harness them. These changes can rapidly impact African power sectors.

Also, advances in smart metering, introducing and improving prepaid meters, engineering and production in Africa are a huge step forward in local technology control. However, the slow progress in the independence of regulators, and the limits on the setting of cost recovery tariffs in many cases, give a half-tone to this progress.

Policy makers need to be more attractive to the sector, especially if we are to retain and attract more private investment needed to develop the sector.

The COVID-19 pandemic in Africa, clearly brings us back to the need to consider the energy sector and electric power as the number one priority for developing any economy; this has once again been demonstrated. The first steps taken by the entire African government have been related to the utility business, so we must work for more resilient public services, and be they public or private, all utilities should build their business model with the confident support of governments and based on the interests of owners and customers.

Finally, it is hoped that policy makers, investors and all stakeholders will soon be able to understand that we cannot have real development of the energy sector in Africa if we do not combine the harmonious development of energy—electricity, mining, local processing and trade on the one hand and the use of all technologies and all energy sources with preservation of the environment on the other.

Lessons from India

Great strides have been made by the Indian government, under Prime Minister Narendra Modi, by tailoring various liberal policies and programmes for creating a conducive environment to achieve the renewable energy targets at a rapid pace.

At the United Nations Climate Conference, more commonly known as COP26, held at Glasgow, Prime Minister Modi made these five ambitious announcements that he called *panchamrut* (five nectars) to be achieved by 2030:

1) India will have 500 GB of non-fossil electricity generation capacity.
2) 50 per cent of total energy use will be from renewable sources;
3) India's net greenhouse gas emissions will be lower by 1 GT compared to projected for the year;
4) India's emission intensity (emissions per dollar worth of GDP) will be lower by 45 per cent; and
5) India will attain net zero by 2070, meaning that India net emissions will be zero.

To realise these targets, Prime Minister Modi suggested the following action points:

1) To ensure that a better and affordable solar technology should be easily and conveniently available to all.
2) To increase the proportion of solar energy in our energy mix.
3) To encourage innovation so that solar solutions can be provided for several requirements.
4) To provide concessional financing and less risky finance for solar projects.
5) To develop such regulatory aspects and standards that can provide a new momentum to the development and adoption of solar solutions.
6) Development of consultancy support for bankable solar projects.
7) To create a comprehensive network of centres of excellence that can take into account local factors and situations.

500 GW of non-fossil (solar, wind, hydro, nuclear and biomass, etc.) capacity, as targeted by India by 2030, shall approximately be 50 per cent of the total installed capacity. The CEA (Central Electricity Authority) projected a capacity of hydro, small hydro, pumped storage, nuclear and biomass for 2030 to be approximately 100 GW. Thus, approximately 400 GW of capacity has to come from solar and wind energy. This scenario does not include the transport sector. If we consider the full electrification of Indian Railways and the modest spread of electric vehicles, India can reduce the use of petroleum products in the transport sector. An enhanced solar and wind capacity of 400 GW by 2030, reduces both CO_2 and GHG (greenhouse gas) emissions by nearly one GT by 2030.

The lesson to be learnt from India is that several schemes are needed to promote renewable power in the country as can be seen from the plethora of schemes launched by the Modi government. The details of the schemes are as follows:

(a) Development of solar parks and ultra-mega solar power projects.
(b) Central public sector undertaking schemes, Phase-II (Government-producer scheme) for setting up 12,000 MW grid-connected solar photovoltaic power projects by government producers with viability gap funding support for self-use or use by government/non-government entities, either directly or through distribution companies. The object is to set up solar PV projects through government producers using domestic cells and modules in a WTO-compliant manner to facilitate national energy security and environment sustainability for government purposes.
(c) A grid connected solar rooftop programme to achieve accumulative capacity of 40,000 MW from rooftop solar (RTS) projects by the year 2022.
(d) Pradhan Mantri Kisan Urja Suraksha evam Utthaan Mahabhiyaan (PM KUSUM).
    This scheme aims to add a solar and other renewable capacity of 25,750 MW by 2022 with a total central financial support of Rs. 34,422 crore including service charges to the implementing agencies.
(e) Renewable power obligation
    To boost renewable power generation, the Electricity Act mandates that a certain percentage of the total quantum of power being supplied to an area should be renewable power.

Through these schemes, significant progress has been made in the last seven years or so in the following manner:

1) Solar capacity increased from around 2.6 GW to more than 46 GW.
2) India is now at the fourth global position for overall installed renewable energy capacity.
3) World's largest renewable energy expansion programme was at 175 GW in 2022.
4) Solar power tariff was reduced by more than 755 using the plug-and-play model.
5) 2.25 lakh solar pumps were installed between 2014 and 2019, versus a total of 11,626 upto 2014.

6) Renewable energy has a share of 26.535 per cent in the total installed generation capacity in the country.
7) The solar park scheme doubled from 20 GW to 40 GW.
8) A record low solar tariff of Rs. 1.99/unit.
9) Highest ever wind capacity addition of 5.5 GW in 2016-2017.

Now with India assuming the presidency of G-20, it is a great milestone and since India will now have a greater voice in the world, we hope that Modi's vision of a Green Earth, through the International Solar Alliance of nations, will achieve the dream of 'One Sun, One Earth, One Grid.'

ANNEXURE

Select Speeches of Prime Minister Narendra Modi on Environment and Energy

Plenary Session in CoP-21 Summit
Paris

30 November 2015

President Hollande, Excellencies,
The pain of Paris is yet to heal. So, I speak in admiration for your resilience and resolve. And, I salute the world for standing, in full strength, with France and Paris.

Over the next few days, we will decide the fate of this planet. We do so when the consequences of the industrial age powered by fossil fuel are evident, especially on the lives of the poor.

The prosperous still have a strong carbon footprint. And, the world's billions at the bottom of the development ladder are seeking space to grow.

So, the choices are not easy. But, we have awareness and technology. We need now national will and a genuine global partnership.

Democratic India must grow rapidly to meet the aspirations of 1.25 billion people, 300 million of whom are without access to energy.

We are determined to do so, guided by our ancient belief that people and planet are inseparable; that human well-being and Nature are indivisible.

So, we have set ambitious targets. By 2030, we will reduce emissions by 33 to 35% per cent of 2005 levels, and 40 per cent of our installed capacity will be from our non-fossil fuels.

We will achieve it by expanding renewable energy – for, example, by adding

175 Gigawatts of renewable generation by 2022. We will enlarge our forest cover to absorb at least 2.5 billion tonnes worth of carbon dioxide.

We are reducing dependence on fossil fuel through levies and reduction in subsidies; switching sources of fuel where possible; and, transforming cities and public transportation.

We hope advanced nations will assume ambitious targets and pursue them sincerely. It is not just a question of historical responsibility. They also have the most room to make the cuts and make the strongest impact.

And, climate justice demands that, with the little carbon space we still have, developing countries should have enough scope to grow.

This also means aggressive mitigation action by developed countries before 2020, including ratification of 2nd Commitment period of Kyoto Protocol, removing conditions and revisiting targets.

The principles of equity and common but differentiated responsibilities must remain the bedrock of our collective enterprise across all areas – mitigation, adaptation and means for implementation. Anything else would be morally wrong; and disparities.

Equity means that national commitments must be consistent with the carbon space nations occupy. We also need a strong Agreement on Adaptation and Loss and Damage.

Developed countries must fulfill their responsibility to make clean energy available, affordable and accessible to all in the developing world. This is in our collective interest.

So, we look to the developed countries to mobilize 100 billion US Dollars annually by 2020 for mitigation and adaptation in the developing countries. They must fulfill their commitment in a credible, transparent and meaningful manner.

Energy is a basic human need. So, we need an ambitious technology initiative, driven by a public purpose, not just market incentives. For this, we need to scale up Green Climate Fund that will improve access to technology and intellectual property.

We still need conventional energy. We should make it clean, not impose an end to its use. And, there should be no place for unilateral steps that become economic barriers for others.

We welcome stocktaking that is transparent, covers both support and commitments, and based on differentiation.

Ultimately, for success, moderating our lifestyle is necessary, and possible, for a low carbon future.

Excellences,

The presence of 196 countries tells us that we have a chance to unite behind a common purpose.

We will succeed if we have the wisdom and courage to craft a genuinely collective partnership that balances responsibilities and capabilities with aspirations and needs.

I am confident that we will.

Thank you.

* * *

'MISSION INNOVATION' IN COP-21, Paris

30 November 2015

President Hollande, President Obama, Excellencies, Mr. Bill Gates, Distinguished Guests,

Let me begin by saluting President Hollande and the people of France for their courage and resolve; and, to the world for coming together for Paris and France.

The outstanding arrangements reflect the character of this great Nation. The world has assembled in Paris to change the course of our planet to a sustainable path.

We must speak about goals and targets on carbon emissions and rise in global temperature. But, it is just as important to focus on the instruments that will make it natural and easy for the world to get there.

A vast section of humanity lives at the edge of poverty and in darkness after the sun sets. They need energy to light up their homes and power their future.

And, they are also the most vulnerable to the consequences of an industrial age powered by fossil fuel.

Access to energy and a better life is a universal aspiration. And, so are clean environment and healthy habitats.

As the world's majority works its way to prosperity on a planet left with very limited carbon space, we have to do many things.

We have to ensure, in the spirit of climate justice, that the life of a few does not crowd out the opportunities for the many still on the initial steps of the development ladder.

The advanced countries must leave enough room for developing countries to grow. And, we must strive for a lighter carbon footprint on our growth path. For that we must come together in a partnership to bring clean energy within the reach of all.

Innovation is vital for combating climate change and ensuring climate justice.

That is what makes this Innovation Summit very special. This unites us behind a common purpose.

We need research and innovation to make renewable energy much cheaper; more reliable; and, easier to connect to transmission grids.

We can make conventional energy cleaner. And, we can develop newer sources of renewable energy.

This is a global responsibility to our collective future. Our innovation initiative should be driven by public purpose, not just market incentives, including on intellectual property. That also means strong public commitment by suppliers to developing countries. That will make clean energy technology available, accessible and affordable for all.

This partnership will combine the responsibility of governments with the innovative capacity of the private sector. We will double our investments in research and innovation; and, deepen collaboration among ourselves. We should have an international network of 30-40 universities and labs focusing for next ten years on renewable energy. Innovation must be backed by means to make it affordable and ensure adoption.

We have a very successful models of public-private partnership with many countries present here. India is also building renewable capacity in developing countries, including small island states. The progress on clean energy technology and costs is impressive. If we raise the level of our efforts, we can transform the world. We will also lay the foundation of a new economy in new low carbon age.

We will restore the balance between ecology and economy, and between our inheritance and obligation to the future. And, live up to Gandhiji's call to care for the world we shall not see.

Thank you.

* * *

INTERNATIONAL ENERGY FORUM MINISTERIAL MEETING New Delhi

April 11, 2018

Welcome to the 16th International Energy Forum Ministerial Meeting.

I am happy to see such a large participation of Energy Ministers from producing and consuming nations, Heads of International Organisations and CEOs in this forum.

As you come together today to discuss the future of global energy, the world is seeing a great transition in energy supply and consumption.

- Consumption growth has shifted to non OECD countries: Middle East, Africa and developing Asia;
- Solar Photo-Voltaic energy has become economical compared to all other energy sources. This is changing the supply paradigm;
- Abundant availability of natural gas globally with increased percentage of LNG and natural gas is contributing to the primary energy basket;
- The US may soon become the largest producer of oil. It is predicted to meet a major portion of the additional oil demand in the next few decades;
- Coal may gradually go out of favour as a major contributor to primary energy in the OECD World and later in developing countries;
- The Transport sector will see massive changes in the next few decades with adoption of electric vehicles;
- The World is committed to the climate change agenda based on the COP-21 agreement. The energy intensity of economies will change with focus on green energy and energy efficiency;

Last month I came across an energy forecast prepared by an agency, according to which India will be the key driver of global energy demand in the next twenty-five years. India's energy consumption will grow by four point two percent a year for the next twenty-five years. This is fastest among major world economies. The report also mentions that Gas demand will triple by 2040.The number of electric vehicles will rise to three hundred and twenty million by 2030, up from three million today.

We are entering an era of energy abundance. However, one point two billion people still do not have access to electricity. Many more do not have access to clean cooking fuel. We must ensure that this situation is not exploited to the detriment of the under-privileged. People must have universal access to clean, affordable, sustainable and equitable supply of energy.

Oil and Gas are a commodity of trade but also of necessity. Whether it is for the kitchen of a common manor for an aircraft, energy is essential.

The world has for too long seen prices on a roller-coaster. We need to move to responsible pricing, which balances the interests of both the producer and consumer. We also need to move to transparent and flexible markets for both oil and gas. Only then can we serve the energy needs of humanity in an optimal manner.

Let us use this platform to build a global consensus on 'responsible pricing.' This will serve the mutual interests of both producers and consumers.

Given global un-certainties, India also needs energy security. My vision for India's energy future has 4 pillars—energy access, energy efficiency, energy sustainability and energy security.

Energy in general and hydrocarbons in particular are an important part of my vision for India's future. India needs energy which is accessible and affordable to the poor. It needs efficiency in energy use.

As a responsible global member of the comity of nations, India is committed to combating climate change, curbing emissions and ensuring a sustainable future. The launch of the International Solar Alliance is a step towards fulfilling this commitment.

We have also revamped our up-stream policies and regulations and brought transparency and competitiveness in the sector through the launch of Hydrocarbon Exploration and Licensing Policy. The bidding criteria has been changed to revenue sharing which will help reduce government intervention. Currently, a bidding round is open till the 2nd of May. I request you to participate in our endeavour towards increasing production. The Open Acreage and National Data Repository will help companies participate in fields they are interested in and help increase the exploration interest in Indian fields.

Our Government believes in an integrated approach to energy planning. And, our energy agenda in India is inclusive, market based, and climate-sensitive. This, we believe, would go a long way towards achieving three energy related components of the United Nations Sustainable Development Agenda. Namely:

Universal access to modern energy by 2030;

Urgent action to tackle climate change – in line with the Paris agreement;

Measures to improve air quality;

2500 government buildings to be fitted with super-efficient ACs for the first time in the country

The Government has decided to install super-efficient air-conditioners in 2, 500 of its buildings for the first time in the country. Launching the replacement of conventional lights with LED lights in East Delhi yesterday, Union Minister for Environment, Forest and Climate Change, Science & Technology and Earth Sciences, Dr Harsh Vardhan said that one lakh conventional air conditioners will be replaced by super-efficient ACs that will consume 30% less power and will be environment-friendly. He said that India will adhere to its commitment made in the Paris Agreement on Climate Change. Dr. Harsh Vardhan also said that all automobiles will be converted to electric vehicles, keeping in view the government's commitment to shift to electric mobility by the year 2030.

* * *

75TH UNITED NATIONS GENERAL ASSEMBLY
New York

September 26, 2020

The Prime Minister said:

It was India that initiated the 'International Day of Non-Violence' on 02 October and 'International Day of Yoga' on 21 June. Similarly, the Coalition for Disaster Resilient Infrastructure and the International Solar Alliance are realities today due to efforts of India. India has always thought about the interests of the whole humankind and not about its own vested interests. This philosophy has always been the driving force of India's policies. One can see the glimpses of this philosophy in India's Neighbourhood First Policy to our

Act East Policy, in the thought of Security and Growth for All in the Region, and in our approach towards the Indo Pacific region. India's partnerships are also guided by this very principle. Any gesture of friendship by India towards one country is not against someone else. When India strengthens its development partnership, it is not with any malafide intent of making the partner country dependent or hapless. We have never hesitated from sharing experiences of our development.

4th India Energy Forum

October 26, 2020

His Excellency Mr. Dan Brouillette, US Secretary of Energy,

His Royal Highness Prince Adbul-aziz, Minister of Energy of Saudi Arabia,

Dr. Daniel Yergin, Vice Chairman, IHS Markit,

My Colleague Shri Dharmendra Pradhan,

Captains of Global Oil and Gas Industry

Namaste!

Wonderful to see you all at the Fourth edition of India Energy Forum CERA Week. I would like to congratulate **Dr. Daniel Yergin,** for his contribution to the energy sector. I also congratulate him on his recent book "The New Map".

Friends,

The theme this year is relevant. It is "India's Energy Future in a world of Change". I can assure you, India is full of energy! India's energy future is bright and secure. Let me explain why I feel so.

Friends,

This year has been challenging for the energy sector. Energy demand fell by almost one third. There has been price instability. Investment decisions have been impacted. Leading global bodies project that there will be a contraction in global energy demand over the next few years also. But, these agencies project India to emerge as a leading energy consumer. India is set to nearly double its energy consumption over the long term.

Friends,

There are many areas in which we see this vibrancy. For example – take aviation. India is the third largest and the fastest growing aviation market in terms of domestic aviation. Indian carriers are projected to increase their fleet size from 600 to 1200 by 2024. This is a big jump!

Friends,
India believes that access to energy must be affordable and reliable. That is when socio-economic transformations can take place. We view the energy sector as one that empowers people and furthers "Ease of Living". India achieved hundred percent electrification. LPG coverage increased. These changes particularly helped our rural areas, our middle class and the women of India.

Friends,
India's Energy Plan aims to ensure energy justice. That too while fully following our global commitments for sustainable growth. This means more energy to improve the lives of Indians. But, with a smaller carbon foot-print.

Friends,
Our energy sector will be growth centric, industry friendly and environment conscious. That is why, India is among the most active nations in furthering renewable sources of energy.

Friends,
In the last 6 years, more than 36 crore or 360 million LED bulbs were distributed. The cost of LED bulbs has also reduced 10 fold. In the last 6 years, Over 1.1 crore or 11 million smart LED street-lights were installed. These have enabled an estimated energy savings of 60 billion units per year. The estimated green-house gas emission reduction with this programme is over 4.5 crore or 45 million tonnes Carbon dioxide annually. Along with all this, we also saved around Rupees 24,000 crore or Rupees 240 billion annually. It is due to such interventions that reports have said that India is the most attractive emerging market for clean energy investment.

Friends,
As I said, India will always work keeping in mind global good. We are well on track to meet the commitment we made to the global community. We had aimed to increase the renewable energy installed capacity by 175 GW by 2022. We have further extended this goal to 450 GW by 2030. India has one of the lowest carbon emissions than the rest of the industrialized world. Yet, we will continue to make efforts to fight climate change.

Friends,

India's reform journey has been on high speed for the last six years. The energy sector has seen many path-breaking reforms. Reforms in Exploration and Licensing Policy were put in place in February 2019. The focus has shifted from 'revenue' to 'production' maximisation. There is also focus on greater transparency and stream-lined procedures We plan to grow our refining capacities from about 250 to 400 Million Metric tonnes Per Annum by 2025. Increasing domestic gas production has been a key government priority. We plan to achieve 'One Nation One Gas Grid' and shift towards gas-based economy.

Friends,

For too long, the world has seen crude prices on a roller-coaster. We need to move towards responsible pricing. We have to work towards transparent and flexible markets for both oil and gas.

Friends,

To increase domestic production of natural gas. And, to bring uniformity in the market price discovery of gas, we have announced Natural Gas Marketing Reforms earlier this month. They will give greater marketing freedom in the sale of natural gas through e-bidding. India's first automated national-level gas trading platform was launched in June this year. This prescribes standard procedures to discover the market price of gas.

Friends,

We are moving forward with the vision of 'आत्मनिर्भरभारत.' A Self-reliant India will also be a Force Multiplier for the global economy. Energy security is at the core of our efforts. You would be happy to know that our work is giving positive results. During these challenging times, we have witnessed investment through the oil and gas value chain. We are seeing similar signs in others sectors too.

Friends,

We are driving strategic and comprehensive energy engagements with the key global energy players. As part of India's Neighbourhood First Policy, we are developing energy corridors with our neighbouring countries for mutual benefit.

Friends,

Rays of Sun brighten the journey of human progress. Like the seven horses driving the chariot of Sun god, India's energy map will have seven key drivers. These drivers of change are:

1. Accelerating our efforts to move towards a gas-based economy.
2. Cleaner use of fossil fuels particularly petroleum and coal
3. Greater reliance on domestic sources to drive bio-fuels.
4. Achieving the renewables target of 450 GW by 2030.
5. Increasing the contribution of electricity to de-carbonize mobility.
6. Moving into the emerging fuels including hydrogen
7. Digital innovation across all the energy systems.

There will be continuity of these robust energy policies that have been in place over the last six years.

Friends,

India Energy Forum-CERA Week is serving as an important platform between industry, government and society. I am confident that this conference will have fruitful deliberations for a better energy future. I state again—India's energy will energise the world! Thank you.

Thank you again.

* * *

G20 Summit Side Event: Safeguarding the Planet

November 22, 2020

Your Majesty and Excellencies,

Today, we are focused on saving our citizens and economies from the effects of the global pandemic. Equally important is to keep our focus on fighting climate change. Climate change must be fought not in silos but in an integrated, comprehensive and holistic way. Inspired by our traditional ethos of living in harmony with the environment, and the commitment of my Government, India has adopted low-carbon and climate-resilient development practices.

I am glad to share that India is not only meeting our Paris Agreement targets, but also exceeding them. India has taken concrete action in many areas. We have made LED lights popular. This saves 38 million tons of Carbon Dioxide emissions per year. Smoke free kitchens have been provided to over 80 million households through our Ujjwala Scheme. This is among the largest clean energy drives globally.

There are efforts to eliminate single-use plastics; Our forest cover is Expanding; The lion and tiger population is increasing; We aim to restore 26 million hectares of degraded land by 2030; And, we are encouraging a circular economy. India is making next-generation infrastructure such as metro networks, water-ways and more. In addition to convenience and efficiency, they will also contribute to a cleaner environment. We will meet our goal of 175 Giga Watts of renewable energy well before the target of 2022. Now, we are taking a big step ahead by seeking to achieve 450 Giga Watts by 2030.

Your Majesty, Excellencies,

The International Solar Alliance is among the fastest growing International Organisations, with 88 signatories. With plans to mobilise billions of dollars train thousands of stake-holders, and promote research and development in renewable energy, the ISA will contribute to reducing carbon foot-print. One more example is the Coalition for Disaster Resilient Infrastructure.

18 countries—including 9 from among the G20—and 4 international organisations have already joined the Coalition. CDRI has started work on increasing resilience of critical infrastructure. Infra damage during natural disasters is a subject that has not got the attention it deserves. The poorer nations are specially impacted by this. Therefore, this Coalition is important.

Your Majesty, Excellencies,

This is the best time for further increasing research and innovation in new and sustainable technologies. We should do so with a spirit of cooperation and collaboration. The entire world can progress faster if there is greater support of technology and finance to the developing world.

Your Majesty, Excellencies,

For humanity to prosper, every single individual must prosper. Rather than seeing labour as a factor of production alone, the focus must be on the human dignity of every worker. Such an approach would be the best guarantee for safeguarding our planet.

Thank you.

* * *

CLIMATE AMBITION SUMMIT

December 12, 2020

Excellencies,

This Summit marks the fifth anniversary of the Paris Agreement—the most ambitious step in our fight against Climate Change. Today, as we are looking to set our sights even higher, we must also not lose sight of the past. We must not only revise our ambitions, but also review our achievements against targets already set. Only then can our voices be credible for future generations.

Excellencies, I must humbly share with you, that India is not only on track to achieve its Paris Agreement targets, but to exceed them beyond expectations. We have reduced our emission intensity by 21% over 2005 levels. Our solar capacity has grown from 2.63 GigaWatts in 2014 to 36 GigaWatts in 2020. Our renewable energy capacity is the fourth largest in the world. It will reach 175 GigaWatts before 2022. And, we have an even more ambitious target now - 450 GigaWatts of renewable energy capacity by 2030. We have also succeeded in expanding our forest cover and safeguarding our biodiversity.

And, on the world stage, India has pioneered two major initiatives:

- The International Solar Alliance, and
- The Coalition for Disaster Resilient Infrastructure.

Excellencies,

In 2047, India will celebrate 100 years as a modern, independent nation. To all my fellow residents of this planet, I make a solemn pledge today. Centennial India will not only meet its own targets, but will also exceed your expectations.

Thank you.

* * *

Climate Adaptation Summit

January 25, 2021

Excellencies,

India welcomes the Climate Adaptation Summit and applauds the leadership of Prime Minister Mark Rutte towards this cause.

Climate Adaptation is more significant today than ever before. And, it is a key element of India's developmental efforts.

We have promised ourselves that:

- We will not just meet our Paris Agreement targets, but exceed them;
- We will not just arrest environmental degradation but reverse it; and,
- We will not just create new capacities but make them an agent for global good.

Our actions show our commitment.

We are targeting 450 gigawatt of renewable energy capacity by 2030.

We are promoting LED lights and saving 38 million tons of carbon-di-oxide emissions annually.

We are going to restore 26 million hectares of degraded land by 2030.

We are providing clean cooking fuel to 80 million rural households.

We are connecting 64 million households to piped water supply.

And, our initiatives have not been restricted to India alone.

The International Solar Alliance and the Coalition for Disaster Resilient Infrastructure show the power of global climate partnership. I call upon the Global Commission on Adaptation to work with CDRI to enhance infrastructure resilience globally. And, I invite all of you to the Third International Conference on Disaster Resilient Infrastructure later this year in India.

Excellencies,

India's civilizational values teach us that importance of living in harmony with nature. Our ancient scripture Yajurveda teaches us that our relationship with planet earth is that of a mother and her child. If we take care of mother earth, she will continue to nurture us. To adapt to Climate Change, our lifestyles must also adapt to this ideal. This sentiment should guide our way forward.

I thank you.

World Sustainable Development Summit

February 10, 2021

Excellency, Doctor Mohamed Irfaan Ali, President of the Cooperative Republic of Guyana,

Excellency, Honourable James Marape Prime Minister of Papua New Guinea,

Excellency, my friend, Mohamed Nasheed, Speaker of the People's Majlis Republic of Maldives

Excellency, Miss Amina J Mohammed, Deputy Secretary General, United Nations

Shri Prakash Javadekar, Minister of Environment, Forest and Climate Change, Government of India, Distinguished guests,

Namaste!

I am happy to be speaking at the World Sustainable Development Summit. This forum completes twenty years. My congratulations to TERI for sustaining this momentum. Global platforms like this are important for our present and future.

Friends,

Two things will define how the progress journey of humanity will unfold in the times to come. First is the health of our people. Second is the health of our planet. Both are inter-linked. There are already many ongoing discussions on improving people's health. We have gathered here to talk about the health of the planet. The scale of the challenge we face is widely known. But, conventional approaches cannot solve the problems we face. The need of the hour is to think out of the box invest in our youngsters and work towards sustainable development.

Friends,

The road to fighting climate change is through climate justice. At the route of climate justice is the principle of being large-hearted. Climate justice is also about thinking of the bigger and long term picture. The sad reality is-changes in the environment and natural disasters impact the poor the most. Climate justice is inspired by a vision of trusteeship—where growth comes with greater compassion to the poorest. Climate justice also means giving the developing countries enough space to grow. When each and every one of us understands our individual and collective duties, climate justice will be achieved.

Friends,

India's intent is supported by concrete action. Powered by spirited public efforts, we are on track to exceed our commitments and targets from Paris. We committed to reduce emissions intensity of GDP by 33 to 35 percent from 2005 levels. You would be happy to know that a drop of 24 percent in the emission intensity has already been achieved.

There was a commitment to achieving about 40 percent cumulative electric power installed capacity from non-fossil fuel based resources. And the share of non-fossil sources in installed capacity of electricity today has grown to 38 percent. This includes nuclear and large hydro projects. I am delighted to share that we are making steady progress on our commitment to Land Degradation Neutrality Renewable energy is picking speed in India. We are well on track to setting up four fifty giga watts of Renewable Energy generating capacity by 2030. Here, I would like to applaud our private sector and several individuals who are contributing to this. India is also increasing usage of ethanol.

Friends,

Sustainable development is incomplete without equitable access. In this direction too, India has made good progress. In March 2019, India achieved nearly hundred percent electrification. This was done through sustainable technologies and innovative models. India invested in LED bulbs long before they became the norm globally. Through the Ujala program, three 67 million LED bulbs became a part of people's lives. This reduced over 38 million tonnes carbon dioxide per year. The Jal Jeevan Mission has connected over 34 million house-holds with tap connections in just about 18 months. Through the PM Ujjwala Yojna more than 80 million house-holds below poverty line have access to clean cooking fuel. We are working to increase the share of natural gas in India's energy basket from 6 percent to 15 percent.

An estimated investment of 60 billion dollars is lined up in developing domestic gas infrastructure. Work is under way to expand city gas distribution networks. Another 100 districts would be added to the network in the next three years. Through the PM-KUSUM scheme, over 30 giga watts of solar capacity will be developed in the agriculture sector by 2022.

Friends,

Often, discussions on sustainability become too focused on green energy. But green energy is only the means. The destination we seek is a greener planet. Our culture's deep respect for forests and green cover is translating into outstanding results. According to the FAO's Global Forest Resources Assessment 2020: India is among the top 3 countries to have gained in forest areas in the last decade.

The forest cover in the country has reached almost one fourth of the geographic area. Conventional thinking may make some people think that when a country pursues development, then forest cover goes down. But, India is one of the countries showing this need not be the case.

Our mission to achieve sustainable development also includes special attention towards animal protection. Across India, people feel proud that: Over the last five to seven years, the population of lions, tigers, leopards and Gangetic river dolphin has gone up.

Friends,
This gathering brings together the best and brightest minds working on sustainable development. I would like to draw attention to two aspects: Togetherness and Innovation. Sustainable development will only be achieved by collective efforts. When every individual thinks of national good, when every nation thinks of global good, that is when sustainable development will become a reality. India has made an effort in this direction Through the International Solar Alliance.

Let us always keep our minds and nations open to best practices from all over. In the same spirit, let us always share our own best practices with others. The second is innovation. There are many start-ups working on renewable energy, environment friendly technology and more. As policy makers, we should support as many of these efforts. The energy of our youth will certainly lead to outstanding results.

Friends,
Through this forum I would also like to mention one more area which needs thought That is the enhancing our disaster management capabilities. This requires focus on human resource development and technology. As part of the Coalition for Disaster Resilient Infrastructure, we are working in this direction.

Friends,
India is ready to do whatever possible to further sustainable development.

Our human centric approach could be a force multiplier for global good. The support of research of institutions like TERI are important in these efforts.

I wish this Summit, and you all, the very best.

Thank you!

* * *

LEADERS SUMMIT ON CLIMATE CHANGE

April 22, 2021

My fellow Citizens of this Planet,

Namaskar!

I would like to thank President Biden for taking this initiative. Humanity is battling a global pandemic right now. And, this event is a timely reminder that the grave threat of Climate Change has not disappeared.

In fact, Climate Change is a lived reality for millions around the world. Their lives and livelihoods are already facing its adverse consequences.

Friends,

For humanity to combat Climate Change, concrete action is needed. We need such action at a high speed, on a large scale, and with a global scope. We, in India, are doing our part. Our ambitious renewable energy target of 450 Gigawatts by 2030 shows our commitment.

Despite our development challenges, we have taken many bold steps on clean energy, energy efficiency, afforestation and bio-diversity. That is why we are among the few countries whose NDCs are 2-degree-Celsius compatible.

We have also encouraged global initiatives like International Solar Alliance, LeadIT, and the Coalition for Disaster Resilient Infrastructure.

Friends,

As a climate-responsible developing country, India welcomes partners to create templates of sustainable development in India. These can also help other developing countries, who need affordable access to green finance and clean technologies.

That is why, President Biden and I are launching the "India-US climate and clean energy Agenda 2030 partnership". Together, we will help mobilise investments, demonstrate clean technologies, and enable green collaborations.

Friends,
Today, as we discuss global climate action, I want to leave one thought with you. India's per capita carbon footprint is 60% lower than the global average. It is because our lifestyle is still rooted in sustainable traditional practices.

So today, I want to emphasise the importance of lifestyle change in climate action. Sustainable lifestyles and a guiding philosophy of "Back to Basics" must be an important pillar of our economic strategy for the post-Covid era.

Friends,
I recall the words of the great Indian monk Swami Vivekananda. He called on us to "Arise, awake and stop not until the goal is reached". Let us make this a Decade of Action against climate change. Thank you.

* * *

Environment Day

June 5, 2021

My colleagues in the Union Cabinet Shri Nitin Gadkariji, Narendra Singh Tomarji, Prakash Javadekarji, Piyush Goyal ji, Dharmendra Pradhan ji, MP from Kheda, Gujarat, Devusinh Jesingbhai Chauhan ji, MP from Hardoi, UP, Jai Prakash Rawatji, Pune's Mayor Murlidhar Moholji, Mayor of Pimpri Chinchwad Municipal Corporation Usha ji, other dignitaries present in this program and my dear brothers and sisters,

When I was talking to our farmer friends, they were explaining in a lucid way how they are easily adopting the systems related to bio-fuel. It reflected confidence. It is natural that the agriculture sector of the country gets a huge benefit from the massive clean energy campaign that is currently underway in the country. On the occasion of World Environment Day, India has taken another major step. Today I have the privilege of releasing a detailed roadmap for the development of the ethanol sector. The ambitious E-100 pilot project for the production and distribution of ethanol across the country has also been launched in Pune. I congratulate the people of Pune and the Mayor of Pune. I wish all the very best that we are able to achieve our targets on time.

Friends,

Ethanol was rarely discussed in the country about 7-8 years ago. No one even talked about it. And even if it was, it was in a casual manner. But now ethanol has become one of the major priorities of 21st century India. The focus on ethanol is having a better impact on the environment as well as on the lives of farmers. We have resolved to meet the target of 20 percent ethanol blending in petrol by 2025. When we first thought about the target, it was decided to achieve the target by 2030. But in view of the successes in the recent past, public support, awareness among people and the realization of its importance by everybody, we have now decided to meet the target by 2025, five years before the original target.

Friends,

The courage to take such a big decision is due to the goals the country has achieved in the last 7 years, the efforts the country has made, and the success it has achieved. Till 2014, on an average, only 1.5 percent of ethanol could be blended in India which has now reached about 8.5 percent. In 2013-14, about 38 crore liters of ethanol were purchased in the country. Now it is estimated to be more than 320 crore liters, i.e., the purchase of ethanol by almost eight times. Last year alone, oil marketing companies bought ethanol worth about Rs 21,000 crore. A large part of this 21,000 crore rupees has gone to the pockets of the country's farmers. It has especially benefitted the sugarcane farmers. When 20 percent ethanol will start blending in petrol by 2025, you can imagine the huge amount of money farmers will get directly from oil companies. It will help in mitigating the challenges associated with over-production of sugar. Sometimes, there is no buyer in the world due to higher yields and the prices also crash in the country. Then there is a big challenge where to store it. Mitigating all such challenges will benefit the sugarcane farmers directly.

Friends,

The 21st century India can get energy only from the modern thinking and modern policies of the 21st century. With this thinking, the government is continuously taking policy decisions in every field. A lot of emphasis is being laid on building the necessary infrastructure for the production and purchase of ethanol in the country. So far, most of the ethanol manufacturing units were concentrated in 4-5 states where sugar production is high. Now Food

Grain Based Distilleries are being established to use the rotten grain and expand this to the whole country. Modern technology based plants are also being set up in the country to make ethanol from agricultural waste.

Friends,

India has emerged as a ray of hope in the global efforts to tackle the menace of climate change. Today, India has made its mark as a trusted partner for the welfare of mankind. The world once used to see India as a challenge to climate change because of its huge population. Today the situation has changed. Today our country is emerging as the leader of climate justice and is a big force against a formidable crisis. India is moving ahead with a lofty global vision like the founding of International Solar Alliance for realizing the vision of One Sun, One World, One Grid and the Coalition for Disaster Resilient Infrastructure initiative. India has established itself as the top 10 countries of the world in the Climate Change Performance Index.

Friends,

India is aware of the challenges that are being faced due to climate change and is also working actively. While on the one hand, we are sensitive towards energy justice in the Global South and advocate for the responsibilities of Global North, on the other hand, we are also discharging our role with utmost seriousness. India has chosen a path of energy transition in which both hard and soft components are equally important in our policies and decisions. If I talk about hard components, the world is watching very closely India's unprecedented speed to implement the big goals. Our capacity for renewable energy has increased by more than 250 percent in the last 6-7 years. India is today among the top 5 countries of the world in terms of installed renewable energy capacity. Importantly, the capacity of solar energy has increased by about 15 times in the last 6 years. Today India is building the world's largest solar and hybrid energy park in the Kutch desert of Gujarat, and has also closed 14 GW of old coal plants. The country has also taken historic steps with a soft approach. Today the common man of the country has joined the pro-environment campaign and he is leading it.

We can see how awareness has been created regarding single use plastic. People are also trying a little bit in their own way. Still more needs to be done. Look at the cleanliness of our beaches, youth are taking initiative. Or be it a campaign like Swachh Bharat, the common citizens of the country took it upon as their responsibility and have taken it forward today. Distributing more than 37 crore LED bulbs and more than 23 lakh energy efficient fans has impacted the environment protection and people have forgotten to even discuss it. But it should be a subject of a major discussion. Similarly, crores of people's dependence on wood has greatly reduced after they were provided free gas connections under the Ujjwala scheme and electricity connections under the Saubhagya scheme. Earlier, they had to spend their life in smoke by burning wood in the kitchens. Apart from reducing pollution, it has helped a lot in improving the health of our mothers and children and strengthening environmental protection. But this too is not discussed much. India has prevented the emission of millions of tons of carbon dioxide through these efforts and has made India a leader in the direction of climate change mitigation. Similarly, the country is preventing millions of tons of carbon dioxide from dissolving in the air today by setting up more than three lakh energy efficient pumps.

Friends,

India is setting an example to the world that it is not necessary to halt developmental works for protecting the environment. Both economy and ecology can go together and move forward. And this is the path India has chosen. Along with strengthening the economy, our forest cover has also increased by 15,000 square kilometers in the last few years. The number of tigers in our country has doubled and the number of leopards has also increased by about 60 percent in the last few years. Amidst all this, the Wildlife Friendly Corridor in Pench National Park is also a topic of discussion today.

Friends,

The Clean and Efficient Energy Systems, Resilient Urban Infrastructure and Planned Eco-Restoration are a very important part of the AatmaNirbhar Bharat Campaign. Be it highway-expressways with green cover, solar powered metros, focus on electric vehicles, or promotion of research on hydrogen-powered vehicles, all these are being worked out with a detailed strategy. New investment opportunities are being created in the country and lakhs of youth are also getting employment due to environment-related efforts.

Friends,

The general belief is that air pollution spreads only through industry. But the fact is that many factors like transportation, unclean fuels and diesel generators contribute to air pollution in some way or the other. Therefore, India is working with a holistic approach through the National Clean Air Plan in all these directions. The ongoing work on waterways and multimodal connectivity will not only strengthen the mission of green transport, but also improve the logistics efficiency of the country. Creation of CNG based infrastructure in hundreds of districts of the country and modern systems like FASTag are helping a lot in reducing pollution. Today, the service of metro rail in the country has increased from 5 cities to 18 cities. The suburban railway project has also helped in reducing the use of personal vehicles.

Friends,

A large part of the country's railway network has been electrified. Solar power based airports are also being built rapidly. Before 2014, only 7 airports had a solar power facility, whereas today this number has increased to more than 50. More than 80 airports have been installed with LED lights. I would like to give another example related to future preparations.

The Statue of Unity, the world's tallest monument of Sardar Vallabhbhai, has been built in Gujarat. Work is also underway to develop the beautiful Kevadiyacity as an electric vehicle city, where the Statue of Unity is located. In future, only battery based buses, two-wheelers and four-wheelers will run in Kevadiya. For this, necessary infrastructure will also be made available there.

Friends,

The water cycle is also directly related to climate change and imbalance in the water cycle also directly affects water security. The work that is being done regarding water security in the country has never been done before. The work is being done with a holistic approach from creation and conservation to use of water resources in the country. Jal Jeevan Mission is also a great medium for this. And I would like to remind you that this time a program is going on in the Jal Jeevan Mission in which I need the help of the citizens of the country. That is, save the rain water, catch the rain water.

Brothers and sisters,

In about 7 decades, piped water reached about 30 million rural households in the country, while in less than two years more than 40 million households have been provided tap water. On one hand, every household is being connected with pipes, while on the other hand, the focus is on raising the ground water level through campaigns like Atal BhujalYojana and Catch the Rain.

Friends,

Balance between development and environment is an important part of our ancient tradition, which we are also making the strength of self-reliant India. Our scriptures have always taught us the balance of the relationship of animals and nature; hostility and totality; and creature and Shiva. It is said in our country that यत्पिंडेतत्ब्रह्मांडे i.e., the body that is in the living entity is in the universe. Everything we do for ourselves directly affects our environment. Therefore, India's efforts are also increasing regarding the efficiency of its resources. In the circular economy that is being talked about today, the focus is on such products and processes, in which there is least pressure on resources. The government has identified 11 sectors which can make good use of resources by recycling them through modern technology. A lot of work has been done in the last few years on the Kachra to Kanchan (Waste to Wealth) campaign and now it is being taken forward very fast in mission mode. Be it waste from households and farms, scrap metal or lithium ion batteries, recycling is being encouraged through new technology in many such areas. Action plan related to this, which will have all aspects related to regulatory and development, will be implemented in the coming months.

Friends,

It is very important to organize our efforts to protect the climate and environment. We will be able to give a safe environment to our coming generations only when every citizen of the country makes a united effort to maintain the balance of water, air and land. It was the wish of our forefathers and they have left behind a very important message for us. What was the expectation of our ancestors from us? पृथ्वीःपूःचउर्वीभव i.e., May the whole earth, the whole environment be most advantageous for all of us and give an opportunity to our dreams. I wish all of you on World Environment Day. Take care of yourself, keep yourself healthy and keep your family members healthy. And with the expectation that there is no laxity in the Covid protocol.

Thank you very much.

* * *

UN High-Level Dialogue on Desertification, Land degradation and Drought

June 14, 2021

Excellency, President of the General Assembly,

Excellencies, Ladies and Gentlemen,

Namaste

I thank the President of the General Assembly for organising this High-Level Dialogue.

Land is the fundamental building block for supporting all lives and livelihoods. And, all of us understand that the web of life functions as an inter-connected system. Sadly, land degradation affects over two-thirds of the world today. If left unchecked, it will erode the very foundations of our societies, economies, food security, health, safety and quality of life. Therefore, we have to reduce the tremendous pressure on land and its resources. Clearly, a lot of work lies ahead of us. But we can do it. We can do it together.

Mr. President,

In India, we have always given importance to land and considered the sacred Earth as our mother. India has taken the lead to highlight land degradation issues at international forums. The Delhi Declaration of 2019 called for better access and stewardship over land, and emphasised gender-sensitive transformative projects. In India, over the last 10 years, around 3 million hectares of forest cover has been added. This has enhanced the combined forest cover to almost one-fourth of the country's total area.

We are on track to achieve our national commitment of Land degradation neutrality. We are also working towards restoring 26 million hectares of degraded land by 2030. This would contribute to India's commitment to achieve an additional carbon sink of 2.5 to 3 billion tonnes of carbon dioxide equivalent.

We believe that restoration of land can start a virtuous cycle of good soil health, increased land productivity, food security and improved livelihoods. In many parts of India, we have taken up some novel approaches. To give just one example, the Banni region in Rann of Kutch in Gujarat suffers from highly degraded land and receives very little rainfall. In that region, land restoration is done by developing grasslands, which helps in achieving land degradation neutrality. It also supports pastoral activities and livelihood by promoting animal husbandry. In the same spirit, we need to devise effective strategies for land restoration while promoting indigenous techniques.

Mr. President,
Land degradation poses a special challenge to the developing world. In the spirit of South-South cooperation, India is assisting fellow developing countries to develop land restoration strategies. A Centre of Excellence is being set up in India to promote a scientific approach towards land degradation issues.

Mr. President,
It is mankind's collective responsibility to reverse the damage to land caused by human activity. It is our sacred duty to leave a healthy planet for our future generations. For their sake and ours, I extend my best wishes for productive deliberations at this High-Level Dialogue.

Thank you.

* * *

National Statement at COP 26
Glasgow

November 1, 2021

Friends,
Today I am representing amid you, the land which gave this mantra thousands of years ago-

सम्-गच्छ-ध्वम्,
सम्-व-दद्वम्,
सम्वोमानसिजानताम्।

Today in the 21st century, this mantra has become more important, has become more relevant.

सम्-गच्छ-ध्वम्- That is, let's move together सम्-व-दद्वम्- That is, let's all interact together and सम्वोमनानसिजानताम्- That is, everyone's minds should also be one.

Friends,

When I first came to Paris for the Climate Summit, it was not my intention to add one promise to the many promises being made in the world. I came with a concern, for the whole of humanity. I came as a representative of a culture that gave the message of 'SarveBhavantuSukhinah' means that everyone should be happy.

And so, for me the event in Paris was not a summit, it was a sentiment, a commitment. And India was not making those promises to the world, but those promises, 125 crore Indians, were making to themselves.

And I am happy that a developing country like India, which is working to lift crores of people out of poverty, which is working day and night on the Ease of Living for crores of people, despite having 17 percent of the world's population today, whose responsibility in emissions has been only 5 percent, still India has left no stone unturned to show that it has fulfilled its obligation.

Today the whole world believes that India is the only big economy, which has delivered in letter and spirit on the Paris Commitment. We are making every effort with determination, working hard, and showing results.

Friends,

Today, when I have come among you, I have also brought India's track record. My words are not just words, they are cheers of bright future for the future generations. Today India is at number four in the world in installed renewable energy capacity. India's non-fossil fuel energy has increased by more than 25% in the last 7 years. And now it has reached 40 percent of our energy mix.

Friends,

Passengers numbering more than the entire population of the world, travel by Indian Railways every year. This huge railway system has set itself a target of making itself 'Net Zero' by 2030.This initiative alone will lead to a reduction of 60 million tonnes of emissions annually. Similarly, our massive LED bulb campaign is reducing emissions by 40 million tonnes annually. Today, India is working fast on many such initiatives with a strong will.

Along with this, India has also given institutional solutions to cooperate with the world at the international level. As a revolutionary step in solar power, we initiated the International Solar Alliance. We have created a coalition for disaster resilient infrastructure for climate adaptation. This is a sensitive and vital initiative to save crores of lives.

Friends,

I would like to draw your attention to one more important topic. Today the world is recognizing that lifestyle has a big role in climate change. I propose to you today a One-Word Movement.

This One-Word, in the context of climate, can become the basic foundation of One World. This is a word—LIFE...L, I, F, E, i.e. Lifestyle For Environment Today there is a need for all of us to come together, together with collective participation, to take Lifestyle For Environment (LIFE) forward as a campaign.

This can become a mass movement of Environmental Conscious Life Style. What is needed today is MindFul and Deliberate Utilization, instead of Mindless and Destructive Consumption. These movements together can set goals that can revolutionize many sectors such and diverse areas such as fishing, agriculture, wellness, Dietary Choices, Packaging, Housing, Hospatility, Tourism, Clothing, Fashion, Water management and Energy.

These are topics where each of us has to make Conscious choices everyday. These daily choices of billions of people around the world will take the fight against climate change, billions of steps forward every day.

And I consider it as a movement on every ground whether on economic grounds, on scientific grounds, on the basis of the experiences of the past century, it meets every criterion. This is the path of self-realization. This is the only way to benefit.

Friends,

In the midst of this global brainstorming on climate change, on behalf of India, I would like to present five nectar elements, Panchamrit, to deal with this challenge.

First– India will reach its non-fossil energy capacity to 500 GW by 2030.

Second– India will meet 50 percent of its energy requirements from renewable energy by 2030.

Third– India will reduce the total projected carbon emissions by one billion tonnes from now onwards till 2030.

Fourth– By 2030, India will reduce the carbon intensity of its economy by less than 45 percent.

Fifth– by the year 2070, India will achieve the target of Net Zero. These Panchamrits will be an unprecedented contribution of India to climate action.

Friends,

We all know this truth that the promises made till date regarding climate finance have proved to be hollow. While we all are raising our ambitions on climate action, the world ambitions on climate finance cannot remain the same as they were at the time of the Paris Agreement.

Today, when India has resolved to move forward with a new commitment and a new energy. So in such times, the transfer of climate finance and low cost climate technologies becomes more important. India expects developed countries to provide climate finance of $1 trillion at the earliest. Today it is necessary that as we track the progress made in climate mitigation, we should also track climate finance.

The proper justice would be that the countries which do not live up to their promises made on climate finance, must be pressured too.

Friends,

Today India is moving forward on the subject of climate with great courage and great ambition. India also understands the suffering of all other developing countries, shares them, and will continue to express their expectations.

For many developing countries, climate change is looming large over their existence. We have to take big steps today to save the world. This is the need of the hour and this will also prove the relevance of this forum. I am confident that the decisions taken in Glasgow will save the future of our future generations, giving them the gift of a secure and prosperous life.

Speaker Sir, I took more time, I apologize to you, but I consider it as my duty to raise the voice of developing countries. That's why I have emphasized on that too.

I once again thank you very much.

* * *

Accelerating Clean Technology Innovation and Deployment COP26
Glasgow

November 2, 2021

Excellencies,

Namaskar!

Today, you are all welcome at the launch of 'One Sun, One World, One Grid'. With the initiatives from the International Solar Alliance and the UK's Green Grid Initiative, my many-year-old vision of 'One Sun, One World, One Grid' got a concrete shape today. Excellencies, the industrial revolution was fuelled by fossil fuels. Many countries have prospered by the use of fossil fuels, but our earth, our environment have become poor. The race for fossil fuels also created geo-political tensions. But today technology has given us a great alternative.

Excellencies,

In the Surya Upanishad, thousands of years ago, it was said, सूर्याद्भवन्तिभूतानि. सूर्येणपालितानितु॥) (Suryaadbhavantibhutani, suryenpalitanitu) In other words, everything has originated from the Sun, the source of all energy is the Sun, and everything is sustained by the energy of the Sun. Ever since life originated on Earth, the life cycle of all living beings, and their routine, has been linked to the sunrise and sunset. As long as this natural connect has continued, our planet remained healthy. But in modern era, man in the race to overtake the cycle set by the sun, disturbed the natural balance, and caused great damage to his environment. If we are to re-establish a balanced life with nature, the path of this will be illuminated by our sun. We have to walk along with the sun again to save the future of humanity.

Excellencies,

The quantum of energy that the entire human race consumes in a year, the sun gives the same amount of energy to the earth in one hour. And this enormous energy is completely clean, sustainable. The only challenge is that solar energy is available only during the day and is also weather dependent. 'One Sun, One World, One Grid' is a solution to this challenge. Clean energy from a world-wide grid will be available everywhere at all times. This will also reduce the need for storage and increase the viability of solar projects. This creative initiative will not only reduce the carbon footprint and cost of energy, but will also open a new avenue of cooperation between different regions and countries. I am confident that the synergy of One Sun: One World: One Grid and Green-Grid Initiatives will lead to the development of a cohesive and robust global grid.

I also want to inform today that our space agency, ISRO is going to present a solar calculator application to the world. With this calculator, the solar power potential of any place in the world can be measured based on satellite data. This application will be useful in deciding the location of solar projects and will also strengthen 'One Sun, One World, One Grid'.

Excellencies

Once again, I congratulate ISA, and thank my friend Boris for his cooperation. I would also like to express my gratitude to the leaders of all other countries for their presence.

Thank you.

INDEX